Facebook Marketing

FOR

DUMMIES

2ND EDITION

Facebook Marketing

FOR

DUMMIES®

2ND EDITION

by Paul Dunay and Richard Krueger

WILEY

Wiley Publishing, Inc.

Facebook® Marketing For Dummies®, 2nd Edition

Published by
Wiley Publishing, Inc.
111 River Street
Hoboken, NJ 07030-5774
www.wiley.com

Copyright © 2011 by Wiley Publishing, Inc., Indianapolis, Indiana

Published by Wiley Publishing, Inc., Indianapolis, Indiana

Published simultaneously in Canada

For general information on our other products and services, please contact our Customer Care Department within the U.S. at 877-762-2974, outside the U.S. at 317-572-3993, or fax 317-572-4002.

For technical support, please visit www.wiley.com/techsupport.

Wiley also publishes its books in a variety of electronic formats. Some content that appears in print may not be available in electronic books.

Library of Congress Control Number: 2010943057

ISBN: 978-0-470-92324-5

Manufactured in the United States of America

10 9 8 7 6 5 4 3 2 1

WILEY

About the Authors

Paul Dunay is an award-winning marketer with more than 20 years success in generating demand and creating buzz for leading technology, consumer products, and financial and professional services organizations.

Paul is Global Managing Director of Services and Social Marketing for Avaya, a global leader in enterprise communications. His uniqude approach to integrated marketing has led to recognition as a *BtoB* magazine Top 25 B2B Marketer of the Year for 2009 and 2010 and winner of the DemandGen Award for Utilizing Marketing Automation to Fuel Corporate Growth in 2008. He is also a six-time finalist in the Marketing Excellence Awards competition of the Information Technology Services Marketing Association (ITSMA) and a 2005 and 2010 gold award winner.

Richard Krueger is founder and CEO of AboutFaceDigital, a social media marketing agency specializing in Facebook promotions. Recognized as an online marketing innovator, Mr. Krueger is also co-founder of Samepoint, LLC, a leading social media analytics company. He brings more than 20 years of experience to his roles at both companies.

Richard previously served as Chief Marketing Officer for Boonty, Inc., a worldwide digital distributor of casual games. Prior to that, he served as VP of Marketing and Business Development for Kasparov Chess Online, where he led marketing and brand licensing efforts for Garry Kasparov, the former world chess champion. Before his entrepreneurial career, Richard worked at several top-ten advertising and public relations agencies in New York City. He is a regular blogger and contributes numerous articles to advertising and PR trade journals.

Dedication

We dedicate this book to marketers everywhere who are in the middle of the biggest sea of change in marketing history. There's never been a better time to be a marketer, and tools like Facebook are rewriting the rules. In fact, we believe that Facebook will become the preferred platform for marketers to acquire new customers, interact with existing customers, and sell products and services. We hope that by providing you with straight forward, step-by-step advice, as well as sharing our real world experiences in marketing companies via Facebook, you'll become better at your craft and thereby take everyone to levels in marketing people have yet to explore.

Authors' Acknowledgments

This project couldn't have succeeded without the help and support of many people who truly helped make this book a success.

First, we want to acknowledge both of our families for allowing us to pursue our passion for Facebook marketing. We appreciate all your understanding and support throughout the time we took away from you all to write this book.

We want to thank the superb team at Wiley. Amy Fandrei, who originally reached out to us because of our blogs and held our hands through the entire process. Kim Darosett, our project editor, who kept us on track every step of the way and ensured the book conformed to *For Dummies* standards. And all the other Wiley folks behind the scenes who made the book possible.

Thanks to scores of bloggers, too many to list, who kept us informed about changes at Facebook and what they meant to businesses. Most of all, we want to thank Facebook founder Mark Zuckerberg and his team of young entrepreneurs and software developers for their vision in realizing the most popular online social network on the planet.

Publisher's Acknowledgments

We're proud of this book; please send us your comments at http://dummies.custhelp.com. For other comments, please contact our Customer Care Department within the U.S. at 877-762-2974, outside the U.S. at 317-572-3993, or fax 317-572-4002.

Some of the people who helped bring this book to market include the following:

Acquisitions and Editorial

Project Editor: Kim Darosett

Acquisitions Editor: Amy Fandrei

Copy Editor: Jen Riggs

Technical Editor: Michelle Oxman

Editorial Manager: Leah Cameron

Editorial Assistant: Amanda Graham

Sr. Editorial Assistant: Cherie Case

Cartoons: Rich Tennant (www.the5thwave.com)

Composition Services

Project Coordinator: Sheree Montgomery

Layout and Graphics: Timothy C. Detrick, Laura Westhuis

Proofreader: ConText Editorial Services, Inc.

Indexer: Dakota Indexing

Publishing and Editorial for Technology Dummies

    Richard Swadley, Vice President and Executive Group Publisher

    Andy Cummings, Vice President and Publisher

    Mary Bednarek, Executive Acquisitions Director

    Mary C. Corder, Editorial Director

Publishing for Consumer Dummies

    Diane Graves Steele, Vice President and Publisher

Composition Services

    Debbie Stailey, Director of Composition Services

Cartoons at a Glance

By Rich Tennant

The 5th Wave — By Rich Tennant

"I know it's a short profile, but I thought 'King of the Jungle' sort of said it all."

page 7

The 5th Wave — By Rich Tennant

"Jim and I do a lot of business together on Facebook. By the way, Jim, did you get the sales spreadsheet and little blue pony I sent you?"

page 57

The 5th Wave — By Rich Tennant

"I hope you're doing something online. A group like yours shouldn't just be playing street corners."

page 159

The 5th Wave — By Rich Tennant

"It's Web-based, on-demand, and customizable. Still, I think I'm going to miss our old sales incentive methods."

page 193

The 5th Wave — By Rich Tennant

Make sure to pick keywords that people will associate with our brand.

How about "sleazy," "tacky," "overpriced" ...

ONLINE ADV

page 249

Cartoon Information:
Fax: 978-546-7747
E-Mail: richtennant@the5thwave.com
World Wide Web: www.the5thwave.com

Contents at a Glance

Table of Contents

Introduction

With more than 500 million active users and 250,000 new registrants every day, Facebook has become a virtual world unto itself. Harvard dropout Mark Zuckerberg originally started Facebook as a dorm room exercise to extend the popular printed college directory of incoming freshmen online, but he has since developed it into an international organization employing more than 1,700 programmers, graphic artists, and marketing and business development executives with offices across the United States as well as in Dublin, London, Milan, Paris, Stockholm, Sydney, and Toronto.

For many, Facebook is a social experience, a place to reconnect with an old college chum or poke a new friend. But in April 2007, Zuckerberg did something so revolutionary that its aftershocks are still being felt throughout the business Web. He opened his virtual oasis to allow anyone with a little programming knowledge to build applications that take advantage of the platform's *social graph* (or network architecture). In that open software act, Facebook redefined the rules for marketers looking to gain access to social networks — and it will never be business as usual again.

About This Book

Facebook Marketing For Dummies provides you, the marketer, with in-depth analysis into the strategies, tactics, and techniques available to leverage the Facebook community and achieve your business objectives. By breaking down the Web service into its basic features — creating a Facebook Page for your business, adding and developing applications for your Page, hosting an event, creating a Facebook group, advertising, and extending the Facebook Platform to your Web site through social plug-ins — we lay out a user-friendly blueprint to marketing and promoting your organization via Facebook. Furthermore, we cite numerous real-world examples of how businesses have effectively used Facebook to further their cause, underscoring the treacherous road that marketers must navigate while traversing this capricious landscape.

Foolish Assumptions

We make a few assumptions about you as the marketer and aspiring Facebook marketing professional:

✔ You are 14 years of age or older, which is a Facebook requirement for creating your own profile.

✔ You're familiar with basic computer concepts and terms.

✔ You have a computer with high-speed Internet access.

✔ You have a basic understanding of the Internet.

✔ You have your company's permission to perform any of the techniques we discuss.

✔ You have permission to use any photos, music, or video of your company to promote it on Facebook.

Conventions Used in This Book

In this book, we stick to a few conventions to help with readability. Whenever you have to enter text, we show it in bold so it's easy to see. Monofont text denotes an e-mail address or Web site URL (for example, www.facebook.com). When you see an italicized word, look for its nearby definition as it relates to Facebook. Facebook features — such as Pages and Marketplace — are called out with capital letters. Numbered lists guide you through tasks that must be completed in order from top to bottom; bulleted lists can be read in any order you like (from top to bottom or bottom to top).

Finally, we often state our opinions throughout the book. We're avid marketers of the social network medium and hope to serve as reliable marketing tour guides to share objectively our passion for the social network world.

What You Don't Have to Read

This book has been designed to be a modular guide to Facebook marketing. Chapters don't need to be read in a linear fashion, chapter-to-chapter, but rather as a research tool to help you market your company on Facebook. You can also use the index in the back of the book to find exactly the topics that are of most interest to you. We've incorporated real-life marketing scenarios to help you get a sense of what has worked and not worked for other marketers using Facebook. Following are some other helpful guidelines to using this book:

✔ Depending on your existing knowledge of Facebook, you may want to skip around to the parts and chapters that interest you the most.

✔ If you have a good working knowledge of Facebook, you can skip the first two chapters.

✔ If you want to set up a Page for your business, go directly to Chapter 4.

> ✔ If you have a Page for your business and are interested in advertising and promoting it, go directly to Part II.
>
> ✔ And if you have a Page and want to start going viral with your marketing, go directly to Part IV.
>
> ✔ Don't read supermarket tabloids. They're certain to rot your brain.

How This Book Is Organized

We organized this book into five parts. Each part and chapter are modular, so you can jump around from topic to topic as needed. Each chapter provides practical marketing techniques and tactics that you can use to promote your business, brand, product, or organization in the Facebook community. Each chapter includes step-by-step instructions that can help you jump-start your Facebook presence.

Part I: Adding Facebook to Your Marketing Strategy

Are you ready to add Facebook to your marketing mix? Before you can answer that question, you have much to consider. Part I gives you an overview of some of the topics we discuss in detail in the book, such as how and why to build a presence on the social network, how to leverage content to build a fan base, how to put viral marketing features to work for you, and how to build a winning strategy for your business. You need to make a subtle mind shift along the way that we can only describe as being more open and transparent. Many companies struggle with this transition, but those that embrace it go on to have a new level of relationships with their customers and prospects.

Part II: Building Your Facebook Presence

All marketers — young and old — are looking to build a Facebook presence for their companies, small businesses, or clients. In this part, we show you how to secure a spot for your business on Facebook, how to design a great Page, and how to make promotions, groups, and events work for you. We also discuss how to cross-promote your page and how to measure your Page's fan engagement activity.

Part III: Engaging in Facebook Advertising

Part III helps you create a new source of revenue for your business. We tell you how to advertise on Facebook by targeting a specific audience, creating and testing your ads, and then measuring your ads' success. You discover how to optimize an ad campaign and get insights into your customers' interactions with your Facebook Page. And we show you how to create effective landing pages and techniques to drive conversions.

Part IV: Riding the Facebook Viral Wave

In Part IV, we lead you through a discussion of Facebook applications that you can add to your Page or create yourself, and that can help promote your brand. We also discuss how to encourage visitors to like your Page and other ways to leverage the Like button to build your fan base. Finally, we show you how to extend the Facebook Platform to your own Web site through social plug-ins in a way that further expands the viral marketing effect of Facebook.

Part V: The Part of Tens

The chapters in this part give some quick ideas about how to conduct yourself on Facebook in a way that best meets your business goals, and what top business applications you can use on your Facebook Page.

Appendix

The appendix focuses on the basics of getting started on Facebook with your own account. We also cover best practices when it comes to your profile picture, making the most out of your Info tab, and some tips on what not to post to maintain your online reputation. Finally, we provide some common-sense advice on how to optimize your privacy settings to keep some of your more personal information from being public. As a marketer on Facebook, one of the first things you need to know is that there's a thin line between your personal and professional personas, and understanding how to protect your privacy will help ensure that you don't compromise the latter.

Icons Used in This Book

This icon points out technical information that's interesting but not vital to your understanding of the topic being discussed.

This icon points out information that is worth committing to memory.

This icon points out information that could have a negative impact on your Facebook presence or reputation, so please read it!

This icon refers to advice that can help highlight or clarify an important point.

Where to Go from Here

If you're new to Facebook and an aspiring Facebook marketer, you may want to start at the beginning of the book and work your way through to the end. A wealth of information sprinkled with practical advice awaits you. Simply turn the page and you're on your way.

If you're already familiar with Facebook and online marketing tactics, you're in for a real treat. We provide you with the best thinking on how to market your business on Facebook based, in part, on our own trials and tribulations. You might want to start with Part II of the book, but it wouldn't hurt to take in some of the basics in Part I as a reminder and read about some of the new menus and software features — you're sure to pick up something you didn't know.

If you're already familiar with Facebook and online marketing tactics but short on time (and what marketing professional isn't short on time?), you might want to turn to a particular topic that interests you and dive right in. We wrote the book in a modular format, so you don't need to read it from front to back, although you're certain to gain valuable information from a complete read.

Regardless of how you decide to attack *Facebook Marketing For Dummies,* we're sure that you'll enjoy the journey. If you have specific questions or comments, please feel free to reach out to us via our Facebook Page at www. facebook.com/fbmarketingfordummies. We'd love to hear your personal anecdotes and suggestions for improving the future revisions of this book. And in the true spirit of sharing on which Facebook is built — we promise to respond to each of your comments.

Here's to your success on Facebook!

Part I
Adding Facebook to Your Marketing Strategy

The 5th Wave   By Rich Tennant

"I know it's a short profile, but I thought 'King of the Jungle' sort of said it all."

In this part . . .

Are you ready to market your company on Facebook? Part I talks about what to keep in mind when entering the world of Facebook marketing, such as how to add Facebook into your marketing mix, how to maximize the networking effect within Facebook, and how to develop a marketing plan that will best promote your business on Facebook.

Chapter 1

Marketing the Facebook Way

*I*f Facebook were a country, it'd be the third most-populated nation in the world. Imagine being able to get your message in front of the Facebook nation for free. That is exactly what Facebook offers savvy marketers — and a whole lot more.

Facebook is increasingly becoming an integral part of a company's marketing strategy. Whether you're a small business or large corporation, retailer, B2B (business to business) service provider, or consultant, you need to have a presence on Facebook. However, Facebook isn't just the world's largest social networking site; it's extending its presence to your Web site by offering free software — *social plug-ins* — that enable you to employ many of the same social Facebook features on your Web site. Major brands, such as CNN, TripAdvisor, and Levi Strauss & Co., were quick to leverage these features and have seen remarkable engagement (interaction) levels from their users as a result. Fortunately, you don't have to be a Fortune 500 company to take advantage of these features. Thousands of businesses — small and large — are finding ways to make these tools work for their Web sites.

As Facebook has grown in scale to a size previously unimaginable, its influence as a new marketing channel is being felt across the Web. By extending its platform to Web site owners with social plug-ins, Facebook has the potential to affect the way people market well into the future. One thing is for sure, marketers flock to the social network in huge numbers, attracted by its many possibilities. For them, Facebook represents more than just another techno-driven fad; it's nothing short of a marketing revolution.

In this chapter, we give you an overview of how you can utilize Facebook as a marketing platform for your business. We explain the importance of putting together a marketing plan and why you need to create a Facebook Page for your business. Finally, we introduce two tools to help you gauge the performance of your Page and advertising campaign.

Introducing Facebook as a Marketing Platform

Although practically everyone is familiar with Facebook, businesses are just beginning to wake up to its potential as a marketing platform. With more than 500 million members worldwide, Facebook far surpasses the potential reach of any other media provider. Think about it: Every day, Facebook attracts more than ten times the TV audience of the Super Bowl. That's a lot of eyeballs.

Facebook offers marketers a number of unique ways to interact with customers and prospects. Many, such as Facebook Pages, Groups, and Events, are free for any individual or business. In fact, the very same social features (such as News Feeds; comments; and the ability to share things like links, photos and videos, and updates) that have helped Facebook become a mass phenomenon are transforming the way companies market themselves.

Other paid opportunities — for example, Facebook Ads, which can be purchased on a cost per click (CPC) or cost per impression (CPM) basis — are increasingly popular because they enable to you to reach as narrow or wide of an audience as desired, often at a fraction of the cost of other online media outlets, such as Google AdSense. And because Facebook members voluntarily provide information about their personal interests and relationships (or *friends*), Facebook has a wealth of information about its members that advertisers can easily tap into. (We discuss Facebook advertising in detail in Chapter 10.)

The new Facebook marketing paradigm is rewriting all the rules. As marketers scramble to understand how best to leverage this powerful new communications channel, those who don't jump on board risk being left behind at the station.

Homesteading on a Facebook Page

You can hang a shingle out for your organization on a *Facebook Page*. A Page serves as a home for your business — a place to notify people about an upcoming event; provide your hours of operation and contact information; show recent news; and even display photos, videos, text, and other types of content. Pages also allow you to carry on conversations with your customers and prospects, providing a new avenue for finding out more about what they want from your business.

Facebook Pages are visible to everyone online, regardless of whether that person is a Facebook member. For this reason, search engines, such as Google and Microsoft's Bing, can find and index your Page, often improving your company's positioning in search results.

In the following sections, we give you the lowdown on what a Facebook Page is and why your business needs one. (Chapter 4 goes into the details on how to create a Page.)

Understanding the anatomy of a Page

Here's a look at some of the elements that make up a Facebook Page (see Figure 1-1):

- ✔ **Wall:** The Wall tab serves as the central component of a Page and allows you to upload content such as photos, videos, links, and notes. These actions generate updates and display as *stories* on your fans' News Feeds.

- ✔ **Like button:** When someone clicks your Facebook Page's Like button, she is expressing her approval of your Page. She becomes a *fan* of your Page, and a story appears in her News Feed, which is distributed to her friends who are then more likely to like your Page. (We discuss the Like button in detail in Chapter 14.)

- ✔ **Status update box:** This is the box with the What's On Your Mind? text. (This box is not shown in Figure 1-1.) If you want to push out a message, you can send a status update. Pages allow you, the Page administrator *(admin),* to send a limitless stream of updates (short messages up to 420 characters in length), which, in turn, appear in your fans' News Feeds.

- ✔ **Info tab:** Here is where more detailed information about your company is located including your location and Web site address.

- ✔ **Discussions:** Discussions are another feature that allows anyone to create a topic of conversation and permit follow-up comments. Members can add to any discussion by typing their comments in the appropriate box and clicking the Post Reply button.

- ✔ **Applications:** You can customize your Page with a host of applications *(apps).* Facebook offers a wide range of apps that you can use on your Page, anything from virtual business cards to RSS feeds from your favorite news services. (We discuss apps in detail in Chapter 12.)

Figure 1-1:
The anatomy of a Facebook Page, as displayed to users.

Why your business needs a Page

The Facebook Platform stands as one of the most powerful platforms for businesses since Google launched AdWords in 2001. Where else in reality — or on the Web — can you find some of the most connected and social people on the planet, all ready and willing to engage with you and your business? Better still, where can you find an ad platform that can target not only by keyword (like Google can do) but also by age, gender, location, and personal likes and interests such as favorite types of music, movies, or food?

Here's a rundown of some key benefits to creating a Facebook Page for your business:

✔ **Get more attention from search engines:** One of the best things about a Facebook Page is that the major search engines index it, so it can appear in search results for your company name within days. Both profiles and Pages are indexed and considered a strong source of relevant content in the eyes of the search engines. Much like a blog with frequent posts of fresh content, your Facebook Page will reap the benefits of increased search engine traffic when your content is updated regularly.

✔ **Tap into the social network:** Another benefit of having a Page for your business is that anyone can find your business on Facebook in ways perhaps that you never dreamed of. Sure, they can find your business by doing a search, but the real beauty of Facebook are the numerous ways that your business can be found just by being part of Facebook and updating your content regularly. Friends of fans can experience your business by seeing any updates you post from your Page when they look at their friend's News Feed. Fans can share your Page with others, thereby helping you to tap into a new audience for your business with their endorsement.

✔ **Target a global digital audience:** The Internet is global in nature, and anyone can find your business on the Web if they know what to look for. While Facebook's membership keeps growing, you have an opportunity to get your business noticed by people across the globe. Think about your ideal customer and the hobbies and activities that customer enjoys. If Web surfing and socializing sound like a fit for your audience, Facebook is the place for your business.

✔ **Attract unlimited fans and potential new clients:** Unlike a profile page, where Facebook limits the number of friends you can have to 5,000, your company's Facebook Page can have an unlimited number of fans. This is why you want to update your Page regularly with interesting content. If you want to attract thousands to your Page, consider the quality of and the frequency by which you can post content. This is the key to building your fan base.

✔ **Engage your audience:** Facebook is free for everyone, so why wouldn't you want to have more traffic, more awareness, more fans, and more business as a result? Adding a provocative topic to your Page's Discussions tab and inviting all your fans to comment actually allows your target audience to do some marketing for you because they can spread the word to their friends, who may not yet be fans of your Page. In doing so, they act as a viral (word-of-mouth) accelerator to your marketing.

✔ **Sync your company blog to your Facebook page:** Creating compelling content is a challenge in all forms of social media and social networking. You want to be sure your content flows from one form of social media to your other forms of social media. In other words, if you have a company blog, synchronize it with your Facebook Page so that when you post to your blog, the content also posts to your Facebook Page for your Facebook audience to read. (See Chapter 4 for details.)

✔ **Track fan promotions:** When you have something to send to your entire fan base, you can do it with Facebook. This is a great way of reengaging fans with your business. If you want to run a promotion or send a discount to drive them to your offline store, you can do that. But don't forget to track your efforts so you can close the loop and monitor the effectiveness of the promotion. This could be as simple as collecting the coupon code you used; having a check box on an order form to gauge where the lead came from; or asking the callers, if they are calling into your call center, where they heard about the promotion. You don't want to lose the opportunity to see how much business and return on investment (ROI) you can generate from this medium.

✔ **Facilitate fan-to-fan interaction:** Another important benefit of a Facebook Page is the ability to encourage fan-to-fan interaction. Where else can your fans engage in direct conversations with each other and your company? This capability can be exceptionally helpful for businesses that sell complex products. Your Page can work as an outpost where fans can support each other by answering questions and providing tips on how to make your product work better. Moreover, your Page can work like a year-round focus group. Use your Wall to generate valuable feedback, and don't forget to continue the conversation as you move your fans down the sales funnel through conversion.

✔ **Host a fabulous event:** Using Facebook Events is a great way of getting people together virtually or in person to support your local business, brand, or product (see Figure 1-2). Setting up events through your Facebook Page is also an economical way of getting the word out beyond your normal in-house marketing list by inviting the fans of your Page. Fans can also help you promote your Facebook event to their friends by sharing the event if it seems of value to their friends. (We discuss events in detail in Chapter 7.)

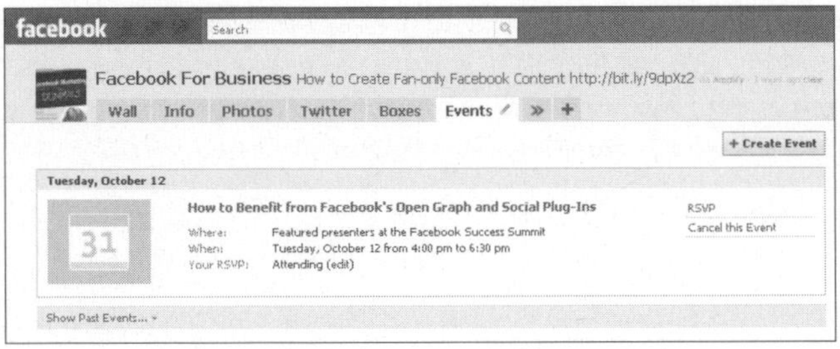

Figure 1-2:
Publicize
an event on
your Page.

How to Benefit from Facebook's Open Graph and Social Plug-Ins

✔ **Promote a worthy cause:** Take a tip from Lance Armstrong, the world-famous cyclist, who is also known for his philanthropic activities. His Facebook Page has more than 1.4 million fans. He brands himself relative to his expertise and what he's known for, being a bicyclist and the founder of LIVESTRONG. Armstrong provides up-to-date notices on his latest races and appearances, videos, and pictures of his current location and different athletic equipment that he likes.

Social media is the perfect tool to unite fans around a cause that matters to you. Be authentic, engaging, and true to your cause by updating your Page frequently with relevant information, such as links to news stories pertaining

to the subject or photos from any charity events you may have attended. This shows your fans that you're passionate about the cause and are involved on a deeper level than just through a Facebook Page.

Developing Your Facebook Marketing Strategy

Before you run blindly into the eye of the Facebook storm, you need to have a plan. Achieving success marketing your business on Facebook doesn't happen by accident; it requires a well-mapped plan and strategic approach that takes many factors into consideration, including:

- ✔ Knowing your target audience
- ✔ Identifying objectives
- ✔ Developing a content strategy
- ✔ Creating a conversation calendar; in other words, who in your organization is responsible for updates as well as what and when content will be shared
- ✔ Mapping a customer response plan, meaning how you're going to answer customer inquiries and any complaints that may come in
- ✔ Measuring results with the most salient data

Without understanding your goals and objectives from the outset, you can't possibly know whether your efforts are succeeding. We go into detail about how to create a Facebook marketing plan in Chapter 3, but in general, you want to keep these key points in mind when building your marketing plan:

- ✔ **Know your audience:** Who do you want to join your community, and why will they want to join? These are two questions that must be answered before you dive in. Where is your audience hanging out online? What do they consider as their influences? Understanding who you're marketing to is the most important factor in creating your plan, so you better get it right. Perhaps you have two or more distinct groups that make up your audience; how do you address the needs of each respective target group? This might require you to segment your fans and enlist separate plans of action to manage the individual communities.

✓ **Build relationships:** Whether your objective is to sell more widgets, make people aware of your cause, or build credibility as an expert in a particular subject matter, it all breaks down to establishing a relationship with your fans. In fact, in part thanks to Facebook, marketers must spend a lot of time thinking of how to build better relationships with their customers. Facebook allows your fans to find out more about your business, and just as importantly, it provides a two-way communication channel for you to get to know them. One of the best ways to establish a relationship is to show your fans that you're interested in what they have to say by listening and responding to their comments and concerns in a timely manner.

✓ **Make your business likeable:** Simply responding to your fans' comments isn't enough. Facebook literally flips traditional push-pull marketing on its head. Instead of simply *pushing* out information in the form of advertisements or the customer *pulling* more information from a company by initiating contact with them, Facebook allows its members to actually champion an organization, a celebrity, or virtually any business on the site. From there they can proclaim their affirmation to all their friends via a Page's Like button. This presents both a tremendous opportunity and an incredible challenge for Facebook marketers: how to encourage your target audience to *like* your Page. Although making your business likeable may seem shallow and simplistic on the surface, it needs to be at the heart of any Facebook marketing plan.

✓ **Focus on quality, not quantity:** Chances are good that 10 percent of your fan base will be responsible for 90 percent of the activity on your Page. A good Facebook plan takes into account ways to influence the *influencers* (the most vocal contributors). Rather than trying to be all things to all fans, focus on building a smaller, more connected community at the outset. More times than not, this strategy outperforms one that focuses on quantity over quality.

✓ **Maintain your authenticity:** In developing your Facebook marketing plan, you want to reinforce certain qualities and virtues, such as your impeccable customer service record or your commitment to creating quality products. Whatever these might be, being true to what and who your organization stands for needs to shine through. Don't pretend to be something you're not. Nobody likes a phony, and it's easy to spot one within Facebook. Likewise, be transparent because in the end, there are very few secrets online.

✓ **Incentivize your fans:** This is the "what's in it for you" factor. You need to treat your Facebook fans like they're special. After all, who doesn't like to be treated, well, special. That might mean special discounts, access to limited merchandise, free French fries with every entrée, or the opportunity to download a free e-book. Your marketing plan needs to take into account what's attractive to your fans and how best to leverage that reward.

Starbucks enlisted the help of Sarah McLachlan to treat its Facebook fans to a live concert, and its fans responded *en masse* to this online event. In Figure 1-3, you see how the best content can also serve as a good incentive to engage fans.

Leveraging Content

Facebook is all about connecting and sharing. On Facebook, members connect with old and new friends, near and distant relatives, present and past coworkers, and people with similar interests or common interrelationships. However, the sharing part is what's so exciting to marketers.

Sharing is all about the content. Whether that content is videos, photos, comments, links, blog posts through your RSS feed, or likes, a whole lot of content sharing goes on inside Facebook. In fact, more than 25 billion pieces of content are shared each month among its members. The key to Facebook marketing success can be summed up in three words: content, content, content.

Here are some general points to keep in mind when sharing content on your Page:

✔ **Take into account how best to involve your audience.** The fan *engagement factor* — getting your community emotionally involved, participating, and sharing — can help expand your audience. For example, in Figure 1-4, reality TV star and professional chef Bethenny Frankel shares a recipe with her fans. Here she asks a question of her fans and offers a good suggestion, complete with information on how to prepare the meal. Her fans expressed great interest in the recipe, and some even responded with questions or comments regarding their plan to make the salad, showing an even further level of engagement on their part.

Figure 1-4:
Bethenny Frankel's Facebook Page regularly posts links to new recipes and asks fans to comment.

> **Bethenny Frankel** Here's a great lunch suggestion. What do you usually do for lunch?
>
> **Cranberry–Almond Chicken Salad | Bethenny Frankel**
> www.bethenny.com
> A low-cal lunch that still tastes great!
>
> Yesterday at 12:54pm · Comment · Like · Share · Report
>
> 👍 426 people like this.
>
> 💬 View previous comments   50 of 348
>
> Can you use hellmans light mayo instead?
> 22 hours ago · Like · 👍 1 person · Flag
>
> yummmmmmm! Will have tomorrow...
> 22 hours ago · Like · Flag
>
> Tomato sliced with oil and lemon, garlic powder, salt&pepper, fresh basil, a thin slice of sharp cheddar and 2 everything crackers. Approx 260 cals.
> 22 hours ago · Like · Flag

REMEMBER

✔ **Maintain a steady stream of updates; however, be careful to strike a delicate balance to not overwhelm your fans.** At a certain point, an overly enthusiastic update strategy could be viewed as spam and turn away your fan base, who can easily hide the flow of updates from your Page.

Updates are short messages that are sent by the Page admin and appear in your fans' News Feeds. Other pieces of content, such as links and photos, can be attached to the updates.

✔ **Create a schedule for your posting updates.** Just as a magazine follows an editorial calendar, Facebook marketers need to create a *conversation calendar*, detailing who in your organization is responsible for updates as well as what and when content will be shared. Also include room for spontaneity, personality, and current events. Some of the most successful, engaging updates a business can make may have nothing to do with business. For example, home improvement retailer Lowes regularly asks questions of its fans such as "Indoors or outdoors?" Around Halloween time, Lowes asks its fans, "Anybody in your house — big people or small — dressing up for Halloween? As what?" Not only is this a change from home improvement-related content, but it also engages fans with the store — and each other.

For more on creating and implementing a content strategy, see Chapter 5.

Who's in charge here?

Facebook requires dedicated resources and support at all levels of the company. However, someone needs to take ownership over the day-to-day responsibilities of managing an organization's Facebook community instead of these decisions being made by a group or committee. Individuals can respond much quicker in this instant feedback environment. Whether that individual is the CEO, a college intern, or an outside agency, you need a clear line of command when dealing with who's in charge of your company's Facebook presence. A key thing to remember, though, is that whoever takes the reins of your Page must have a clear understanding of your brand messaging and the tone that their updates must have. Consistency is key.

Incorporating Analytics into Your Plan

After you put together a marketing plan and decide what content you want to share, you need to focus on the *metrics,* or key performance indicators, to determine what level of success you've achieved. Your metrics are partly dictated by your goals. For example, if your goal is to acquire new customers, you may want to look at how many of your Web site's contact forms were completed by people looking for more information, and the total number of fans for your Page. Or if your goal is to focus on providing existing customers with superior customer service, you need to look at how many comments and responses were made by your customers.

Using Insights

Facebook offers new and improved tools for tracking your Page's performance — Insights. Facebook *Insights* provides plenty of analytics to understand who visits your Page; where those folks come from; and what they do while there, such as comment on a post, click a link, or watch your videos.

Facebook Insights is available to all Page admins after you have 30 fans of your Page, and it provides graphs and charts that make it easy to analyze trends in your Facebook Page's traffic. A host of tools includes the ability to visualize the data in different ways. These graphs can all be downloaded to your computer so you can show your boss how your Page performs. In Figure 1-5, the Insights Dashboard shows fan activity and the number of likes and comments in easy-to-understand graphics. (See Chapter 9 for more on Insights.)

Figure 1-5:
Facebook
Insights
provide
graphs and
metrics
that track
a Page's
performance.

Measuring ad performance with the Ads Manager

Facebook provides a full set of analytics to help you track your Facebook ad performance. You can view your ad analytics with Facebook's Ads Manager at www.facebook.com/ads/manage. Figure 1-6 shows an example of what a current campaign looks like in the Ads Manager. It shows which campaigns are active and paused, the ad budget, the number of impressions it has had, the social percentage and its average cost (based on CPC or CPM), the number of clicks and impressions, the click-through rate (CTR), and the total amount spent per campaign.

To find out how to use the Ads Manager to track the performance of your ads, check out Chapter 10.

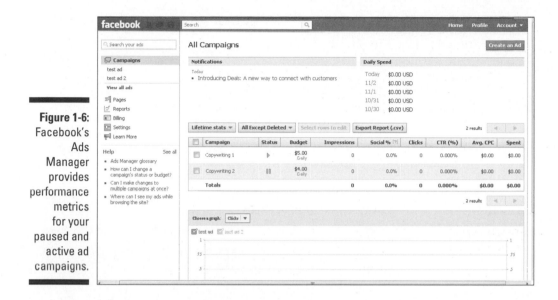

Figure 1-6:
Facebook's
Ads
Manager
provides
performance
metrics
for your
paused and
active ad
campaigns.

Adapting to Facebook Changes

One caution as you enter the world of Facebook marketing: Facebook is an ever-changing universe, and some of the features and guidelines you've grown to rely on could be in jeopardy with every new design iteration and policy change. You need to build in contingencies to account for potential shifts in technology and policies. Entire ad formats have been announced, launched, and died an early death just when you thought they'd be ideal for your next ad campaign.

Although many Facebook changes are cosmetic in nature, many refinements take place in regards to the data made available to marketers, the policies that apply to member privacy settings, and what and to whom you can advertise. Remember that marketing on Facebook is an evolutionary process, and your marketing plan will forever be a work in progress.

Staying on top of Facebook developments

It is very important to keep up to date on recently made and upcoming changes to Facebook's policies and regulations. This is especially important if you plan on running promotions using the Facebook Platform, as discussed in

Chapter 7. There are specific procedures you must adhere to so that you can run a promotion on your Page. If you don't follow Facebook's stringent guidelines, your account may be suspended or — even worse — deleted altogether.

Some good sources for the most current information on what's new and improved at Facebook is its blog located at `http://blog.facebook.com` and the Notifications section at the top of your Ads Manager (refer to Figure 1-6). While you're at it, why don't you become a fan of Facebook's own Page located at `www.facebook.com/facebook`? Not only do the good people at Facebook update their content frequently (maybe they're reading this book just like you!), but they also have numerous tabs on their Page that offer some creative ideas that you may want to incorporate into your own Page. Facebook Live is one such idea. This is the live-streaming channel out of Facebook's California headquarters featuring discussions on the latest company innovations and events as well as demos of the newest features.

Navigating unchartered waters can be difficult. Facebook is notorious for rolling out sweeping changes, often with profound implications for marketers. But if you check in regularly with Facebook's marketing Pages and glance at the blogs and news sources that report on Facebook, you'll have a good sense of the wind of change before it blows.

Addressing growing privacy concerns

Another factor that needs consideration in your marketing plan is the privacy concerns that continue to plague Facebook. These range from legislative attempts to ensure that Facebook guarantees a certain level of privacy rights on behalf of its members, to backlash from members seeking to protect their personal information. You need to understand and be able to adapt to both Facebook's privacy guidelines as well as your fans' changing expectations. This is a hotbed issue, one that will no doubt remain a thorn in Facebook's side. Marketers need to address these concerns while adopting policies that ensure their fans' rights are respected.

Chapter 2

Focusing on Facebook Features

· ·

· ·

*F*acebook is all about making connections. Whether reuniting with old high school chums or meeting new people with similar interests, Facebook provides a framework that makes it easy to discover, reach out, and share with others. Smart marketers are discovering ways to attract and grow their network of Facebook clients, or *fans* in the Facebook universe, to achieve their objectives.

To market your business to Facebook members, you need to be part of the Facebook community. Facebook offers plenty of opportunities for organizations to get exposure, many for free. But before you can create a Facebook Page, start your own group, run an ad campaign, build an application, or organize an event, you need to be a Facebook member.

You must have a personal Facebook account to create a Page for your business and serve as the *administrator* — or *admin* — of that Page. If you have an existing Facebook account, you can create a Page for your business, create a group or event, and interact with other users. If you're not a member, you need to register on Facebook. In doing so, you create a personal profile that allows others to find and friend you. (See the appendix at the back of this book for details on setting up a Facebook account.)

An admin is the pilot of the aircraft called a Facebook Page. This person controls everything, and we mean *everything,* associated with the Page, including things like what content gets posted and who gets to post it. Do you want to be the only one who can upload photos and videos? There's a setting for that. How about what fans see when they first land on your Page? The admin holds that key as well.

In this chapter, you discover how to tap into Facebook's networking potential, attract fans, and influence communities. We discuss the basics of viral marketing and key features that drive viral campaigns within Facebook, such as sharing and the News Feed.

Networking in Facebook

If you imagine a map representing all your relationships and then expand it to include the external relationships of those contacts, you get an idea of the concept behind a social network like Facebook. When a user connects with folks through the Facebook confirmation process, it's as though the user is inviting them into his circle. Figure 2-1 shows a graphic representation of a Facebook member's circle of friends.

Whether you represent yourself, a business, a nonprofit organization, a polka band, or a political cause, in Facebook, just like in the real world, your ability to form strong relationships and influence your fans determines your ultimate success or failure in achieving your objectives (that is, getting what you want).

Engaging with your fans

Facebook wasn't the first online social network, but it has arguably done the best job in providing its members with a safe, social environment in which their actions (for example, posting a photo album), if they so choose, can be automatically broadcasted as news stories to those friends who want to read them.

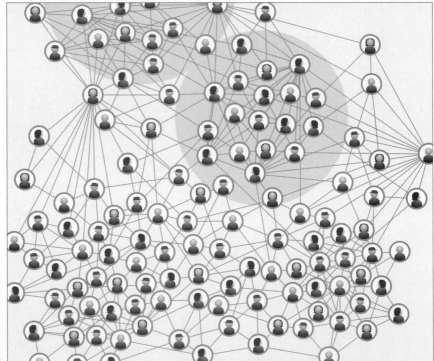

Figure 2-1:
Intersecting circles of profile pitures that represent Facebook members' interrelationships.

Businesses are now realizing the value of being part of Facebook to engage their fan base. The network's ability to broadcast actions as news stories has helped fuel the growth of Facebook and made it an ideal environment for *viral,* or word-of-mouth, marketing.

Embracing openness

Although no man is an island, Facebook makes it harder and harder to live in anonymity. That's why Facebook members need to have implicit, trusted, symbiotic relationships with the people in their circle of friends. Remember, in Facebook, your personal and professional lives often cross over. Bosses and employees can be friends. Your Facebook friends' actions might very well end up on your Facebook Wall, and similarly, your actions could end up on their Walls. This trade-off between privacy and openness is difficult to balance for most new members, not to mention marketers looking to leverage social media while protecting their online reputation. A good rule of thumb is to always ask yourself this before posting any content: Would I want my grandmother to see this?

To some extent, Facebook requires a new mindset based on the concept of openness. Facebook marketers need to embrace openness while understanding the inevitable challenges and pitfalls that go along with it. For example, if your Facebook friend posts and tags a picture of you in a compromising situation, it could impact your personal brand. You can untag the picture and ask that person to take down the post, but once information is out there in cyberspace, cyberspace doesn't like to give it back.

So, everyone needs to consider the ramifications of Facebook actions and interactions. Unlike traditional mass media (such as print, radio, and television), Facebook is a two-way medium, lending itself to a new kind of relationship between consumer and marketer — a relationship based on trust, openness, and transparency.

There is a major generational shift in the amount of information people disclose via online social networks. The younger generation (teens and college students) has much less fear and trepidation of broadcasting their lives, warts and all, via Facebook, YouTube, Twitter, blogs, and other social media, whereas those who didn't grow up with the Internet are typically much more hesitant to release even the slightest bit of information. As a marketer, you need to consider this generational shift and adapt your strategy accordingly. If you're targeting a younger demographic, you probably have a richer set of targeting data available. Likewise, if you're targeting an older demographic, sharing and commenting are new experiences for this audience and might require greater patience and persistence on your part.

Because the lines blur between many people's professional and personal lives, business relationships may cross over and become part of your personal network of friends on Facebook. That doesn't mean your entire life or business needs to be an open book. So, whether you're updating your profile or posting to your business Page, some basic common-sense rules that apply while on Facebook include

- ✔ Only disclose information that you're okay making publicly available.
- ✔ Don't be nasty or offensive because you never know who will read your post.
- ✔ Don't reveal personal details, such as thoughts on politics, religion, and so on, that you might regret later.
- ✔ Never publish your personal contact information.

Sharing through Your Facebook Page

Sharing is the new currency in social media marketing. There's a tangible value in creating content that people actively share. When a piece of content is shared in this way, it "goes viral" and is considered the Holy Grail for Facebook marketers. Imagine posting a humorous video on your Facebook Page that links to your company's Web site. Your fans notice the video, watch it, click the Like button, share the video with their friends, and so on, and so on. When content, such as a video or blog post, goes viral, it extends well beyond your immediate circle of contacts. This boost in audience brings greater brand awareness for your company and, ultimately, more sales potential. Because there is no additional cost for your content to be seen by a wider audience, viral marketing offers a potentially huge return on your investment. (We discuss how to create a Facebook Page in Chapter 4.)

You can find many examples of viral hits on Facebook — from causes like the breast cancer awareness What Color Is Your Bra? campaign (see Figure 2-2), which moved millions of women to publish their bra color via their Facebook status update; to blender manufacturer Blendtec's *Will It Blend?* video series that's been viewed on Facebook and YouTube by more than 2 million people resulting in a sales increase of 400%. Many organizations have realized huge traffic and buzz thanks to the simple gesture of users sharing something of interest with their friends.

You can share all sorts of content via your company's Facebook Page, in much the same way that individuals can share content via their profile page on Facebook. The What's On Your Mind? box (which we refer to as the status update box) at the top center of your Facebook Page serves as the central publishing hub from which to share your content (see Figure 2-3).

Figure 2-2:
The What Color is Your Bra? campaign for breast cancer awareness affected millions of status updates, achieving its goal of bringing awareness to a cause.

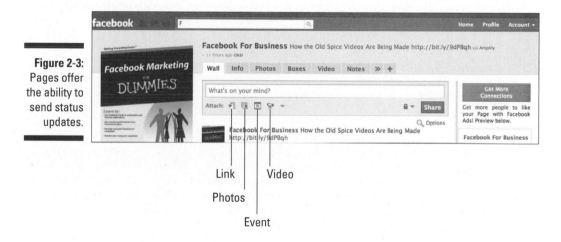

Figure 2-3:
Pages offer the ability to send status updates.

Link
Photos
Event
Video

Only an official Page admin can publish to your organization's Facebook Page. But any Facebook user can comment via the Comment link, located under each update on the Wall of your Page. If you discover a comment that's inappropriate or offensive, you can delete the comment. To do so, hover your mouse to the right of the comment until an X appears. Simply click the X button and confirm that you want to delete the comment (see Figure 2-4).

Figure 2-4:
You can
delete an
unacceptable
comment on
your Page.

Click to delete comment

Your Facebook Page can have more than one admin; in fact, there's no limit to the number of admins a Page can have. A word of caution, though. Be sure to add only trusted admins who know your brand and the image you want to present to your fans. While it may be tempting to anoint a number of people as admins, too many hands in the proverbial pot could be a recipe for disaster. See Chapter 4 to find out how to add additional admins to your Page.

To get a sense of Facebook's viral potential, you need to understand its most basic parts: the status update box and News Feed distribution system, which we describe in the following sections.

Status updates

The status update box (also known as the What's On Your Mind? box or Publisher) is where you share content, such as text, photos, videos, notes, music, and so on with your Facebook fans. (Refer to Figure 2-3.) The question What's On Your Mind? appears inside the status update box, and you can address the question directly by sharing text messages up to 420 characters, which then appear in your fans' News Feeds.

To update your status and post your message, follow these steps:

1. **Click in the status update box at the top of your screen.**

2. **Type the text that you want to share (and/or attach a photo, video, or Web link; or schedule an event).**

   See Chapter 6 for details on how to attach a photo, video, or Web link; or how to set up an event.

3. Click the Share button.

Your status update appears at the top of your Page's Wall.

You (and any other Page admins) can engage your fans by posting messages about new content, promotions, upcoming events, and more through status messages. The messages appear as stories on a fan's Wall.

Facebook also gives you the option to send longer messages called Updates. Users can access Updates by clicking the Messages icon in the top left of any Facebook page (as shown in Figure 2-5) and then clicking the See All Messages link at the bottom of the menu that comes up. The Updates section appears under the Messages heading and includes the number of unread updates, if any, as shown in Figure 2-5.

Sending an Update to all of your fans is different from posting a status message, and it doesn't show up on your Wall or in their News Feed. It's an important feature, though, because it allows you to type more than 420 characters and to target a specific demographic of your fans, if you wish. You can also record a video or attach a link. To send an Update for your Page, do the following:

1. Click the Edit Your Page link on the left side of your Page under your profile picture.

2. Click the Marketing link in the menu on the left.

3. Click the Send an Update link.

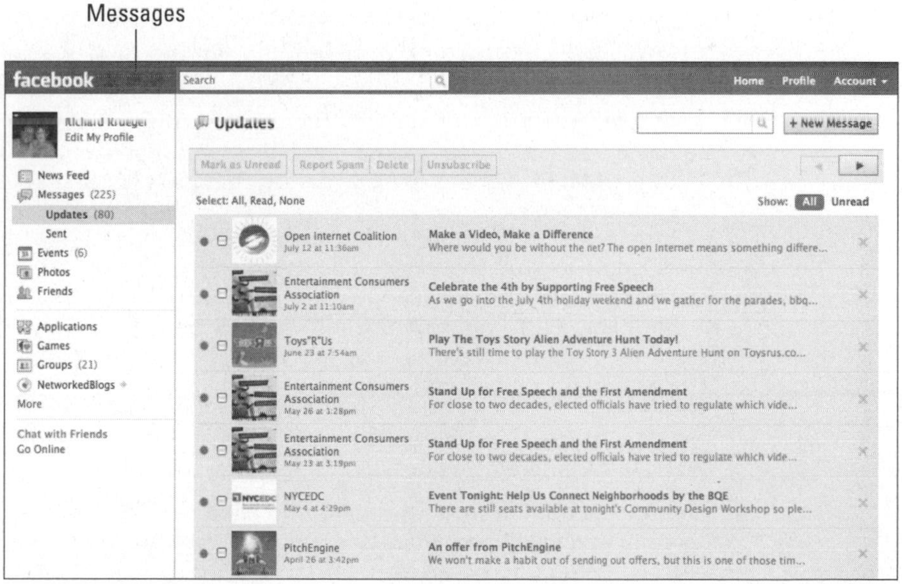

Messages

Figure 2-5: Users can check for status updates from your Page on their Inbox's Updates page.

The target audience for this update is set to all fans by default, but you can narrow the target by clicking the Target This Update check box where you're given additional options, such as the specific country, gender, and age of the recipients. This is useful if you're only offering a special deal at your store, for example, and you don't want to fill up the Updates box of your fans from a different country.

For your Page, you have to be extra careful when you share messages, photos, links, videos, and so on with others. If your fans find your updates boring and irrelevant, they'll hide you from appearing in their News Feeds. An inappropriate update could result in a drop in fans. Keep in mind the following basic do's and don'ts when posting updates on behalf of your business to keep your fans engaged.

Status updates do's

When updating your status, keep your content fresh. Do the following:

- **Make an effort to post updates on a regular and ongoing basis.**

- **Post relevant statements and questions to your fan base to encourage participation.**

- **Be upfront with your posts.** This speaks to your company's willingness to be open and transparent with fans.

- **Include links to drive traffic to appropriate information and resources.**

- **For links that are overly long, use a URL-shortening service, such as TinyURL.com or bit.ly, to condense the length of a URL.** bit.ly (`http://bit.ly`) can even provide stats on how many people actually click through to the page, giving you additional metrics for gauging their effectiveness. However, you must initially register and sign into your bit.ly account to be able to track visitors.

- **Include a direct call to action.** If you want your fans to click a link to read your blog post, say so. If you want them to engage and comment, ask them to share.

Status updates don'ts

Never make the following mistakes, which can make your Page feel like a distraction to fans:

- **Don't make updates that are irrelevant to your audience.** Your fans are looking for you to provide content within your given sphere of expertise, so stay within your business matter.

- **Don't send a lot of updates in a condensed period of time.** This turns off your fan base and dilutes any newsworthy updates.

✔ **Don't be too personal.** Your Page's sole purpose is to promote your business, not to update fans on your personal life. Commenting about topics like politics and your world view at large is likely to turn off some percentage of your fan base who are in the opposing camp.

✔ **Don't use a hard-sell approach in your updates.** Overly aggressive marketing may result in fan revolt.

News Feed

Facebook uses the News Feed to deliver news and information as they relate to a user and that user's friends' activities, as shown in Figure 2-6.

News Feeds offer tremendous opportunities for you to leverage content to drive more news stories for your organization. News stories also include links back to the original posts. So by delivering a steady stream of stories to fans, as well as friends of fans, you can use News Feeds to gain greater exposure and drive traffic to your Facebook Page.

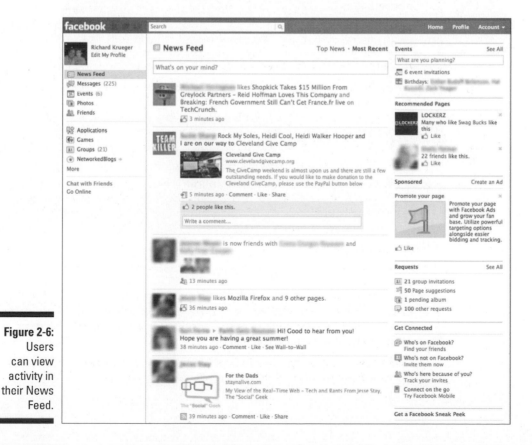

Figure 2-6:
Users can view activity in their News Feed.

This is another reason why you should devise a very solid content strategy, as we discuss in detail in Chapter 5. The last thing you want to do is publish a large number of status updates and other content such as links and videos that aren't capturing the attention of your audience. This will no doubt lead to your fans hiding your updates, which is the kiss of death for a Facebook Page. The good news is you can keep an eye on these metrics by using Facebook Insights, a built-in analytics program that we cover in Chapter 9.

Building Your Friend Network

People are social by nature. Humans have a herd mentality; they seek solace in the company of others. They're drawn to the familiar — those with similar interests and backgrounds. Facebook recognizes this basic human need to connect with others and provides a set of tools to help members find and share with their friends, acquaintances, relatives, and those with similar affiliations.

Facebook doesn't allow you to use your business Page to reach out and friend other members; friend requests can be sent only from your personal account. But often on Facebook, your personal and professional lives collide. Building out your personal friend network can have a resonating effect on your professional persona. By encouraging your friends to become fans of your Page, your updates will be published on their News Feeds and will increase your Page's exposure to all of *their* friends. All good Facebook marketers know that their friends can be valuable viral enablers within Facebook.

Finding friends

You can find friends and contacts by using several search and import capabilities within Facebook. To start, follow these steps:

1. **Go to your Home page by clicking the Home link on the top navigation bar.**

2. **Click the Friends link on the right side of the page.**

   The Friends page appears, as shown in Figure 2-7.

3. **If you want to import contacts from your e-mail client, click the Find Friends link and enter your e-mail address and password. Click Agree to give Facebook access to your contacts and then decide which contacts you want to add as friends.**

   You can import contacts from providers like Yahoo!, Windows Live Mail, Gmail, and so on.

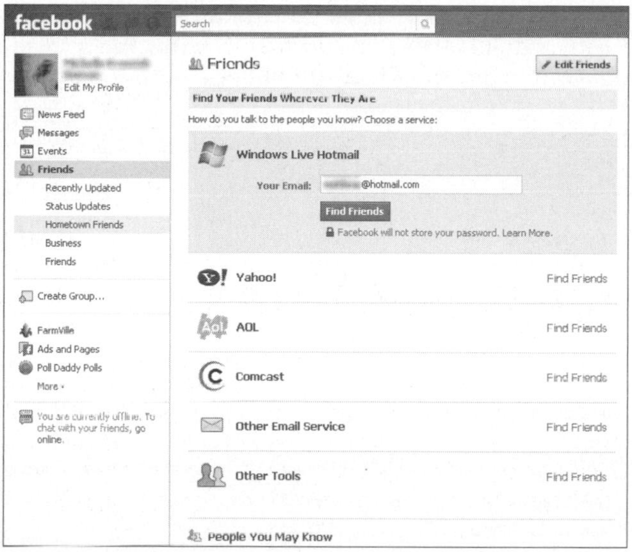

Figure 2-7:
Facebook
provides
tools to
help you
discover
contacts
and grow
your friend
base.

4. **Click the Other Tools link at the bottom to find former high school classmates, current or past college classmates, or current or past coworkers. Click the appropriate link for the group you're interested in and then browse the list on the search results page.**

   These tools are useful for tracking down old friends, family members, and associates. There's also a default search box for searching via name or e-mail address at the top of the screen or by navigating to www. facebook.com/search.php (see Figure 2-8).

   On the search results page, you can filter the results based on a number of different options. For example, for a classmate, add the class year(s) that you attended or graduated from a particular school, or leave the year fields blank to return the widest possible matches. By experimenting with narrowing and widening the results, you can discover many close contacts, familiar names, and old friends long forgotten.

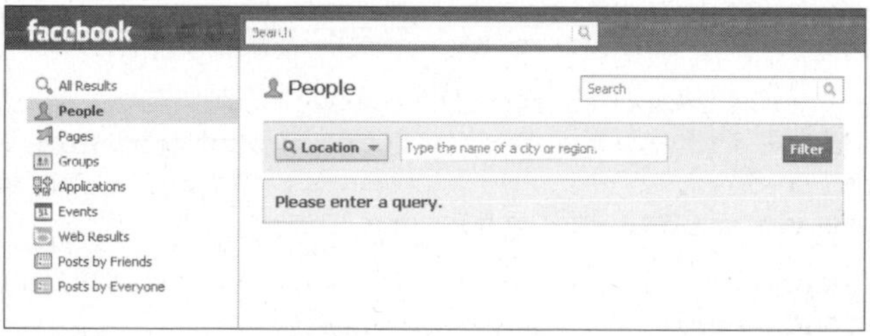

Figure 2-8:
Looking
for friends
using
Facebook's
Search
feature.

5. **After you identify a Facebook member that you are interested in recon-
necting with, extend a friend request by clicking the Add as Friend link
to the right of that person's name within the search results.**

If you find someone who would be a good contact, it's worth the time
to write a personal note; that way, the person has a point of reference
when she receives your friend request.

You can also send a friend request from within someone's profile page.
Simply visit that person's profile page and then click the Add as Friend
button. (*Note:* Because you're not already friends, you have access only to
profiles of members with a common network, depending on their privacy settings.) By clicking this button, you send a friend request to this person and
then receive notification if the request is accepted. Additionally, you can also
click the Send *Name* a Message or Poke *Name* links without being a friend. If
you *poke* someone, she receives notification that she's being poked by you
the next time she logs in to Facebook. This is a gentle way to let someone
know that you're thinking of her.

By viewing a person's friends, you can get a good sense of his network, which
might then lead you to discover additional friends. This social graph is how
people tap into friends of friends in an effort to expand their own network. If
you visit a friend's profile page, Facebook even shows you names and profile
pictures of friends in common. After all, a social network can be thought of as
circles that intersect at certain points. Or, six degrees of you!

If you receive a friend request from someone, you don't have to accept it. If
you don't know the person or don't have any friends in common, a good rule
of thumb is not to accept the request unless your goal is to expand your network no matter what. You can find all outstanding friend requests on your
Home page. If you want to accept the request, simply click the Confirm button.
If you don't want to accept the request, click the Ignore button.

Creating Friends lists

After you have a healthy number of friends, Facebook lets you organize your
gaggle into lists, or groups. For example, you can create a work list that consists
of coworkers or business contacts. Lists allow you to quickly view friends by
type and then send messages to an entire list. Facebook allows up to 100 lists
with up to 1,500 friends per list.

Using lists can be a powerful feature for someone doing business on Facebook.
By segmenting your friends, you can separate work contacts from personal
connections and better tailor your content for each audience. You can also
save time by setting privacy permissions based on lists. For example, you
can block one list from viewing your summer photo album while sharing that
album with another list.

To create a list, follow these steps:

1. **Click the Friends tab in the left navigation pane on your home page.**

   The Friends page appears.

2. **Click the Edit Friends button at the top right of the page.**

3. **On the page that appears, choose All Friends from the drop-down list and then click the Create a List button.**

   The Create New List dialog box appears.

4. **Enter a name for the list in the Enter a Name box.**

   For example, enter **Work Friends**, as shown in Figure 2-9.

Figure 2-9:
Organizing friends into lists allows you to send a message to an entire list.

5. **Select friends by clicking their profile pictures.**

   To find the friends to include in your new list, you can either browse your friends list or enter a person's name in the search field at the top right of the dialog box.

6. **Click the Create List button.**

   A page appears where you can edit the new list's name, or add and remove friends from that list.

You can send a message to a list from within your personal Inbox. To do so, follow these steps:

1. **Click the Messages tab in the left navigation pane on the News Feed page.**

   The Messages page appears.

2. **Click the New Message button.**

3. **In the To field of the New Message dialog box, enter the name of the list to which you want to send a message.**

   When you select the desired list, it expands to show all members of the list; the title of your list is never visible to other members of Facebook. So, if you put a bunch of geeks in a list and name it **Geeks**, they'll never know you classified them as such. Another advantage is that you can create separate privacy settings for each list. (We discuss privacy settings in the appendix at the back of this book.)

4. **Enter a subject and message, and specify any attachments you want to include, such as links or videos, and then click Send.**

Chapter 3

Developing a Facebook Marketing Plan

*O*ne of the great things about Facebook is that it gives you access to a very large and growing audience at relatively low or even no cost. All that's needed is some sweat equity on your part. But that doesn't mean you shouldn't have a strategy for what you want to achieve for your business.

Whether you're a small business, an artist, or a celebrity, or you sell a well-known (or soon to be well-known) product or service, you need to think about your audience — who they are, how they want to be spoken to, and what they want. This chapter helps you decide what message you want them to receive and the Facebook tactics that will get them to interact with that message.

Understanding What to Include in Your Marketing Plan

Traditional marketing methods like print or TV ads — advertising or "shouting at" your customers to get them to buy something — doesn't work in a social network like Facebook. In fact, the shouting might even work against you. Social networks represent a shift in the way that people use the Internet. Rather than just search for information, Facebook members can search for and interact with like-minded people who have similar interests.

With Facebook and other social networks, your business can take advantage of *viral marketing* — a technique of promoting brand awareness by word of mouth. For example, when a Facebook user becomes a fan of your company's Page, confirms attendance at your Facebook event, or installs your application on his profile, these social actions are automatically turned into stories that appear on the member's Wall. In essence, the user passes along your marketing message to other Facebook members, expanding word-of-mouth awareness of your business.

Before you can take full advantage of the viral marketing power of Facebook, you need to put together a Facebook *marketing plan,* which is a structured way to align your strategies with your objectives. Here are the general steps for creating your plan:

1. Develop your value proposition.

2. Understand your audience.

3. Define your marketing goals.

4. Develop a content strategy.

5. Monitor and measure your Page activities.

6. Integrate your online and offline campaigns.

The rest of this chapter explains each of these steps in more detail. By putting these steps into practice, you can begin to put your marketing strategy in place by the end of this chapter.

Developing Your Value Proposition: Why Customers Should Buy Your Offering

When developing a formal marketing plan, the first thing you need to consider is your organization's *value proposition,* or *Unique Selling Proposition* (*USP*). The USP describes how your company is different than the competition and why people should do business with you. You may have a different value proposition for each audience segment you target, or for each product or service you offer. Your marketing plan should detail the ways in which you plan on communicating these values to your target audience.

To understand your value proposition, answer the following questions:

✔ **How are you different from your competitors?** By knowing your competition and what separates your offering from theirs, you can begin to develop your *product differential,* a key ingredient that goes into your value proposition. So what makes your product or service different from — and better than — your competitors? The answer to this question is what sets you apart from them. Do you offer a longer free trial of your product than your competitors? Do you have the capability to tailor your service to meet your customer's exact needs? Whatever that difference is, exploit it.

✔ **What value do you provide to your stakeholders?** *Stakeholders* are your customers, shareholders, employees, partners, and anyone else impacted by your company. Understanding the value you provide is key in developing your messaging and communications strategy. By having a clear picture of what you want to accomplish with your marketing plan, you open a world of opportunities for your business. The key is communicating this to your stakeholders. When your employees know your brand messaging, they can pass that information on to your customers in the form of knowledge and better service. When your stakeholders know you have a clear plan of action, they'll be more comfortable with the direction that you are taking the company, which leads to greater support for your ideas and plans in the future.

✔ **What are your big-picture goals?** Some goals are more obvious than others. They could include increasing company sales or driving more traffic to your Web site, both of which can be done when you clearly define and communicate your value proposition. Some are not as obvious, such as improving your company's reputation or creating a more friendly face for the brand. Whatever your company's goals are, make sure all your Facebook marketing activities align with these goals.

Understanding Your Audience

Whatever your business goals, always assemble the best information that you can about your audience. The better you understand the culture and viewpoint of your audience — what they like and don't like, where they spend their time, and what information sources they rely on — the more effectively you can capture their attention and deliver your message. Understanding the lives of your customers and prospects is key when communicating your business or product to them.

Finding out what makes your fans tick

Facebook provides some powerful insights into your fans. In fact, identifying and then reaching a specific audience has never been this exact and cost-effective. The Facebook Insights tool helps you find out more about who visits your Facebook Page, including a demographic and interest breakdown of your fans. And the Facebook ad targeting capabilities makes it relatively easy to get your message to the right target audience within Facebook.

Understanding your fans' psychographic profiles is an important element in knowing who they are. *Psychographic* variables (such as music a user loves, politicians he endorses, or causes he supports) are any qualities relating to a user's personality, values, attitudes, interests, or lifestyles. These variables are in contrast with *demographic* variables (such as age and gender) and *behavioral* variables (such as usage rate or loyalty) and can help you better understand your customer segments.

Gathering this information can be fairly easy if you know where to look and how to go about doing it. For example, ask your customers to fill out satisfaction surveys or a quick questionnaire through your e-newsletter or Web site. Another option is to search Facebook for some companies similar to yours and read through the comments posted by *their* fans to see what makes them return to that Page — or not.

Psychographics is exceptionally relevant in any discussion of social networks because your target audience is more likely to interact with you along the lines of their interests, their values, and their lifestyle. Examples of this can be seen in Facebook apps similar to *iLike,* which integrates users' favorite music and makes recommendations on their profile. Another example is Tom's of Maine, a company that produces all-natural personal care products like toothpaste and soap. Tom's of Maine takes advantage of the fact that many people are concerned with making positive changes to their communities and the environment, and are going green. In fact, its site has an entire tab devoted to the idea that "Good Matters" and that creating positive change starts with each individual.

Understanding what motivates your fans

After you understand your target customers, you need to understand what motivates them. Customers want to feel as though they're being treated special on Facebook. They want to know that their business is important to you and that their concerns are being heard. But most of all, they want something in return for their attention and loyalty. Facebook members love free stuff, special discounts, and promotions.

It's not surprising that Facebook members are looking for real value in the form of informative and engaging content from marketers on Facebook. Unlike

Google, in which users are further down the intent-to-purchase road by the very nature of their search, Facebook users aren't necessarily looking for specific products and services to purchase. That's why marketers need to grab their attention through special offers.

Special incentive offers can be found throughout Facebook in the form of ads and on Facebook Pages. In Figure 3-1, NortonLive Services, a company owned by Symantec, offers a 10 percent discount just for becoming a fan of its Facebook Page. Cleverly, new specials are posted regularly on the Page with the actual offer grayed out just enough to allow people to see it, without providing the ability to take advantage of the discount. To redeem the offer, the user must like the Page and become a fan.

Although pricing discounts serve as good incentives for some, savvy marketers want to provide value in different ways that reinforce their proposition value. For example, the Hallmark Channel allowed its fans to create multimedia tributes to their moms around Mother's Day and then tied those tributes into its premiere of *Meet My Mom,* an original Hallmark movie. Through a dedicated Meet My Mom tab on Hallmark's Facebook Page, as shown in Figure 3-2, users uploaded testimonials to their mothers for all to see and comment. The promotion was advertised on the Hallmark Channel and via its Web site and Facebook Page. Within its first week of running the promotion, the company added 5,000 new fans, bringing its total number of fans to just over 65,000.

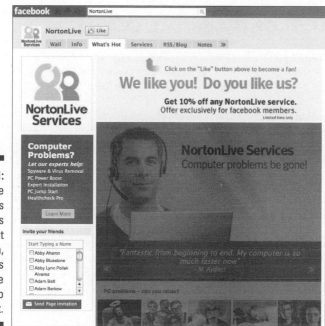

Figure 3-1: NortonLive Services offers fans a discount promotion, but requires they like the Page to redeem it.

Figure 3-2:
The Hallmark Channel provided tools to allow fans to create multimedia tributes to their moms to honor them around Mother's Day.

Honor your mom for Mother's Day by uploading a video tribute at Facebook.com/HallmarkChannel beginning March 17. Your contributions will go live starting April 19!

STARRING
Lori Loughlin
Johnny Messner
Stefanie Powers

A HALLMARK CHANNEL ORIGINAL MOVIE

MEET MY MOM

Hallmark Channel salutes the troops when "Meet My Mom" premieres Saturday, May 8 (9pm/8c)

Hallmark CHANNEL

Defining Your Marketing Goals

After you have a better understanding of the makeup of your Facebook audience and some knowledge of the demographics and psychographics of your audience, you need to define a few goals for your Facebook marketing strategy.

Your Facebook marketing plan needs to include at least these four objectives:

✔ Building your brand's awareness

✔ Driving sales

✔ Forming a community of people who share your values

✔ Listening to feedback about your brand

We discuss each objective in more depth in the following sections. But keep in mind that these objectives aren't mutually exclusive but rather can be used in combination. You can start with one method and advance your strategy in other areas while you go along.

Building your brand's awareness

The concept of branding can be traced back in history to the early Romans. But the story that always stuck with us was the concept of farmers branding their cattle with branding irons so they could be recognized by the farmer. Branding was a way of distinguishing their product from other products that looked very similar.

These days things are very similar. A *brand* is how you define your business in a way that differentiates you from your competition; it's a key element in defining your marketing goals. With a Facebook Page, you can build awareness of your brand with all your current and prospective customers.

A Facebook Page serves as the home for your business on Facebook, and it should be created with your company's brand — and image — in mind. It's a place to notify people of an upcoming event; provide hours of operation and contact information; show recent news; and even display photos, videos, text, and other types of content. A Facebook Page also allows for two-way interaction between you and your customers, providing them a place to post messages, and it's a great feedback loop for you to find out more about your customers' needs.

After you've created your Page (as described in Chapter 4), here are a few ways to let people know about it and start building awareness for your brand:

- ✔ **Reach out to existing customers, friends, and contacts outside Facebook through your normal marketing channels.** Let these folks know your business has a Page on Facebook. For example, you can send them an e-mail blast or include the address for your Page in a printed newsletter or flyer. Something as simple as "Join us on Facebook!" does the trick.

- ✔ **For those customers and friends with Facebook profiles, utilize the Suggest to Friends link and the Share button located on the left side of your Page.** There's no doubt that the people you interact with on Facebook would love to know that your business has a Page. Don't be shy about spreading the word. After all, Facebook makes it easy for you, so put those links to good use.

You can also use the Share button to send an e-mail to folks who may not be on Facebook so that they can view your Page. Just click the Send as a Message Instead link at the bottom of the message box, enter an e-mail address and message, and then click the Send Message button (see Figure 3-3.)

Figure 3-3:
Using the
Share
button to
send an
e-mail
about your
Page.

Driving sales

Whether you're a local, a national, or an international business, Facebook can help you drive the sales of your products and services. As another potential sales channel, you can leverage the social network in a number of ways to achieve your sales objectives:

- ✔ **Communicate special offerings and discounts and provide an easy path to purchase with a simple link to your company Web site.** Some larger retailers bring the entire shopping cart experience to Facebook. For example, 1-800-Flowers.com launched a flower store within their Facebook Page on the Shop tab, as shown in Figure 3-4. This tab provides a secure-transaction environment for Facebook members to make a credit card purchase and send a dozen roses to a friend in the real world.

- ✔ **Target your audience with a Facebook ad campaign.** In addition to creating a free Facebook Page, many marketers are also discovering the potential in Facebook as a cost-effective advertising medium. You can test and launch targeted ad campaigns that employ traditional direct marketing techniques, such as ads with engaging copy and pictures that capture a reader's attention. The most successful offer is an incentive that appeals to your audience. (We discuss advertising in more detail in Chapter 10.)

- ✔ **Create a Facebook event to generate buzz about a product.** For example, you can hold a new product launch party or a wine tasting for potential new customers. And you can throw a Facebook-only event for fans and allow them to network as well. (See Chapter 7 for a discussion of Facebook Events.)

Forming a community with a Facebook Group

One of the best uses of a social network is to build a *community* — that is, a group of people who share the same interests and passion for a cause. No matter what your marketing goals are, forming a community takes some effort. We generally think it's arrogant for marketers to feel they can build a community that people will flock to — the proverbial "build it, and they will come" model. However, with a Facebook group in addition to a Page for your business, that very model is possible.

A *Facebook group* is a page that is based around shared interests or goals. With a group, you can create a community focused on an existing cause that matches your business goals and give your group members the tools to communicate with each other on Facebook. Or another reason to create a group is if you have an interest or hobby outside of your business that you want to share with others. For example, if you own a hardware store but have a passion for building furniture, you can start a group for the purpose of uniting people who share your love of woodworking. A group would be a great place for you — and other group members — to share tips and tricks for practicing your craft.

You could also build a Facebook group around a cause related to your brand. For example, Lee National Denim Day supports breast cancer awareness and the search for a cure — a good cause, and who doesn't like to wear denim? The Lee National Denim Day cause informs the Facebook community about wearing jeans to support breast cancer awareness, as shown in Figure 3-5. By calling attention to a cause Lee is passionate about, it shows its customers that it's not all business all the time and to show that Lee takes the time to support a charitable cause.

Figure 3-5: Lee National Denim Day to support breast cancer awareness.

Spirited discussions are prominent in Facebook Groups, so plan for someone in your company — a product expert or someone on the communications team — to lead regular discussion threads weekly, bimonthly, or even monthly. Keep in mind, though, that you probably want people coming back to the group more often than monthly, but less often than weekly. For example, weekly updates from your group might be too much for your fans to handle, but because of the nature of the Web — there are loads of information from multiple sources like News Feeds bombarding people daily — remind them to come back to your site more often than monthly just to keep your group fresh in their minds.

For a more in-depth discussion of groups, check out Chapter 7.

Listening to feedback

You can listen to feedback from Facebook members in a number of ways:

✔ **Monitor discussions in your group.** As discussed in the preceding section, a Facebook group lets you create a community and have discussions with your group members. But a noteworthy byproduct of forming a Facebook group is the ability to get feedback from the members. For example, the next time you think about launching a new product or service, consider having the members of your group (in addition to fans of your Page) weigh in on it before it goes to market. And don't worry about a delay getting the product to market; it only takes a few days to get feedback from members. Of course, you have to build up your member base before you can tap into it.

Facebook doesn't publish group discussions to Internet search engines. Therefore, they aren't *indexed,* which is how a search engine finds its information. This may change, but currently, you can't monitor Facebook Groups via the Internet because they exist behind a password-protected community.

✔ **Search for discussions about your brand.** Facebook is fertile ground for open, honest, peer-to-peer discussions about your business. Just plug in any search terms related to your business into the Facebook search box and see what comes up. You might be surprised to find other fan pages devoted to your brand.

✔ **Review fan postings on your Wall.** Your fans will post comments, questions, and even suggestions to your Page's Wall. Make sure you closely monitor those as well and respond appropriately and in a timely manner.

Developing Your Content Strategy

Keep in mind that content drives engagement. How can you tailor your content to appeal to your fans? What assets do you already have (such as videos, tips, customer testimonials, and so on) that will enhance your brand while delivering real value to your fans? In essence, you need a content strategy and plan to make Facebook and social media work for your business.

When developing your content strategy, look at your different channels of communication — your Web site, Facebook Page, Twitter presence, e-newsletter, and so on — and then decide which content is right for each channel. For example, you may realize that your Twitter followers want a different stream of updates than your Facebook fans, and your Web site visitors would be better served with more product-focused content. Because you want different types of engagement across all your channels, the content you publish needs to address each audience's needs and concerns.

Here are some ways to develop your content strategy on Facebook:

✔ **Post to engage fans:** Although some content you post will be purely informative in nature, such as broadcasting a particular price promotion to your fans, *engagement posts* are designed to garner feedback and participation from your fans. The key is to engage your fans and solicit responses from them so that you can benefit from the viral effect: Every time a fan comments on your Facebook Page, a story publishes to her News Feed, which will just end up on her *friend's* News Feed.

So tactically, these stories provide links back to the original post and often generate additional traffic to the content. In this way, your fans invite others along for the ride. But there's also another reason to foster fan participation: to build an engaged community, one comment at a time.

✔ **Provide discounts and special offers:** As we touch on earlier in this chapter, Facebook marketers are discovering great success through extending discounts, special offers, and giveaways to attract Facebook fans. Ads that generate the greatest responses on Facebook offer something of perceived value for very little effort on the member's part. Often, these offers are based on a prerequisite, such as the completion of a form or that they like the Page.

When developing a promotion, keep in mind that the offer must interest your target audience. Sometimes, the offer doesn't even have to be tangible, but merely the chance to have a shot at glory. In Figure 3-6, Klondike appeals to its fans' competitive nature, offering them a chance to beat their friends' scores in the *Bar Slinger* video game. The Page even shows their high scores.

✔ **Deliver content in a format accessible to your audience:** When developing your content strategy, it's important to consider the range of media at your disposal. Facebook allows you to publish content in a number of formats (including photos and videos), making this content accessible directly through Facebook with a click of the mouse. Why not take advantage of the convenience of having everything in one easy-to-access location?

Likewise, if your fans enter into a dialogue on your Facebook Page's Wall, continue to use Facebook as your communications channel. Don't reach out to that individual on Twitter, LinkedIn, or some other social network unless requested to do so by the fan (otherwise, you could seem too aggressive). Maintaining a consistent approach to communicating with your Facebook fans will keep them a fan for the long term.

The culture of Facebook is formed by young, digitally fluent adults who understand when they're being talked at versus engaged in a conversation. So the key is not to interrupt them with a continuous stream of messages, but to instead use content to encourage participation. By creating a steady stream of rich content, you can engage the right audience and get them to interact with your brand. For more on fine-tuning and implementing your content strategy, check out Chapter 5.

Figure 3-6:
Klondike created games that challenge fans to beat their friends' high scores.

Monitoring and Reporting Page Activity

The last piece of the puzzle for an effective marketing plan is taking the time to monitor and measure your Page activities. Only through careful analysis can you figure out what content resonates with your audience. And, because actions within Facebook are measurable, your Page's metrics, or *key performance indicators,* can give you lots of insights into your fans interactions with your Page.

A marketing campaign is only as good as your ability to measure it. The number of people who like your Page aren't worth anything to your business if you can't peel away the layers to gain greater meaning into their actions. You need to translate those analytics into real-world lessons that you then apply to your content. If you don't see any performance changes, it might be time to rethink your content strategy.

Facebook provides some powerful analytic tools to help you discover what's really happening on your Page. Here are just a few things to keep in mind when taking stock of your Facebook Page's analytics.

Using Insight for Pages

Facebook has an internal analytics system — *Insights* — through which you can gain a greater understanding into your visitors' behavior when interacting with your Page. Facebook Insights is available for free to all Page admins and is located at www.facebook.com/insights. By understanding and analyzing trends within your user growth and audience makeup as well as content consumption and engagement, you gain valuable, well, insights, into how your fans interact with your Page. You'd be wise to pay attention to your Page's Insights.

Facebook Insights focuses on three areas of data: your fans, your interactions, and the quality of your posts, as shown in Figure 3-7. (We explore these in greater detail in Chapter 9.) Insights provides information on the demographics of your audience, tracks the growth of fans on your Page, and the number of likes and comments your content has received. By keeping tabs on some key metrics, such as the increase in the number of fans over the previous week or the number of interactions following a particular post, you can get an idea of what works and what doesn't. For example, if you notice that a number of fans have opted out of being a fan after a particular post, you might draw a correlation between the content you posted and the drop-off rate.

We suggest that you check out your Insights metrics regularly and stay on top of increases in engagement numbers and activity. Also, keep track of which posts people respond to and which ones they don't. If you don't see any performance changes, it might be time to rethink your content strategy.

The Insights Dashboard provides the ability to see an aggregate of your fans' geographic and demographic information without identifying any individual's location or demographic, as shown in Figure 3-8.

Figure 3-7:
Facebook Insights provides metrics on how your fans interact with your Page.

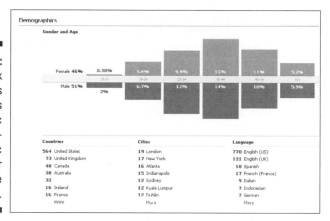

Figure 3-8:
Facebook
Insights
also offers
geographic
and demo-
graphic
data on your
audience
makeup.

Flying blindly into your Facebook marketing plan is a fool's journey. The more you know about how and what your fans react to, the easier it is to tailor your content to the audience, giving them more of what they want.

Creating benchmarks and setting goals

As we discussed, your Facebook efforts are indeed measurable. You need to have an idea of where you stand at the beginning of your efforts to compare it with where you end up at the end of a promotion, ad campaign, event, or activity. By creating *benchmarks,* or the key indicators that define your Page's activity level, you can gauge your progress. Without knowing how many fans your Page had prior to a promotion, how can you calculate the success of the campaign? For example, take note of the number of views each specific tab on your Page gets, which can be found under the Users link on your Insights page. Are there certain tabs, such as your Photos tab, that get more views than others? Make it a point to update the content on the other tabs to see whether this increases their views. If views increase, you know that your fans are looking for you to update *all* your tabs more frequently, not just your Wall.

In addition to benchmarks, set goals attached to your various Facebook marketing efforts. For example, Japanese electronics manufacturer JVC set a goal to acquire as many fans as possible over a 60-day period through a daily contest promoted via Facebook Ads. The contest required that members like its company Page before entering the contest. The promotion proved so successful that JVC saw an increase in fans from fewer than 1,000 at the outset of the contest to more than 34,000 in 30 days (see Figure 3-9).

Although anticipating the success of a campaign or particular post prior to going live with it is difficult, by forecasting the outcome, you have to consider the results at the outset of your planning. Therefore, you can better manage your coworkers, and more importantly, your boss's expectations.

Figure 3-9:
A look
at JVC's
Insights
Dashboard
showing
a major
increase in
fan engage-
ment during
a contest
promotion.

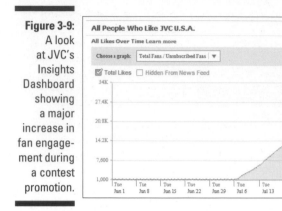

Keeping an eye on key metrics

The Facebook Page performance metrics that are important to you are, in part, determined by what your goals are. If your goal is to drive clicks to an external Web site, tracking referrals from your Facebook Page is an important indicator for you. Likewise, if your goal is to drive engagement, the number of comments associated with your content is most likely the metric you need to measure. But most of all, you need to take this data and translate it into real-world insights to make it valuable.

Here are ten key metrics to consider when tracking the performance of your Facebook presence:

- ✔ **Views:** A fundamental measurement is measuring the number of views or visitors your content receives, and your Facebook Insights page is the place to go for this information. Understanding where people spend their time on your Facebook Page gives you a good idea of what information they find valuable.

- ✔ **Comments:** The number of comments you receive for a particular post is a great way to track performance. This also helps you identify what posts resonate with your fans. Typically, the more comments a post receives, the more interested your fans are in that content. Insights provides your Page's comment activity in an easy-to-read graph.

  When measuring the number of comments, don't forget to consider the sentiment of those comments. If all the comments are negative in nature, you could have a backlash if you produce similar posts.

- ✔ **Clicks and downloads:** If you post downloadable content or a link to content on an external Web site, it should always be trackable. Several URL shorteners, such as bit.ly (`http://bit.ly`) and TinyURL.com (`http://tiny.cc`), provide third-party click-through metrics on any link you shorten through their service. This is an excellent way to track the interest in a particular link or download.

✔ **Length of visits:** The amount of time someone spends on your Facebook Page is a strong indicator of your fans' interest in your content or lack thereof. Although Facebook doesn't provide these types of metrics at this time via Insights, you can install third-party analytics on a Facebook Page to provide this data. Google Analytics (www.google.com/analytics), for example, offers a tracking service for free that can be integrated into your Page with a little technical knowledge; see Chapter 9 for details.

✔ **Shares:** If your content strikes a chord with your fans, chances are your fans will share the content they find valuable with their own network. By monitoring the number of times content you post is shared using Insights, you can get a good sense of what's of interest to them.

✔ **Inbound links:** Although linking is more common on external Web sites, Facebook Pages are linked to by bloggers, media outlets, search engines, and people who are generally interested in your Page. Searching Google using your Page URL as a search term tells you how many sites link to your Facebook Page. Typically, the more links into your Page, the better.

✔ **Unique versus repeat visitors:** Tracking *unique* (or new) and repeat visitors is a good indicator as to how valuable your content is to keep them coming back for more. Pay special attention to the increase in the number of repeat visitors over time because this lets you know whether your content strategy pays off. This is another metric that you can track with Google Analytics.

✔ **Brand mentions:** If you're doing a good job marketing your business on Facebook, chances are it'll have a spill-over effect across other social media outlets. A number of free social-media search sites track brand mentions, such as Samepoint (www.samepoint.com), social mention (http://socialmention.com), and OneRiot (www.oneriot.com). Make a point to run a search of your company name on these sites on a regular basis. Monitoring what people say outside Facebook provides numerous insights into your marketing effectiveness.

✔ **Conversions:** A *conversion* occurs when a visitor undertakes a desired action, such as completing a transaction on your Web site, filling out a registration form, subscribing to your e-newsletter, or signing up for an event. Conversions are one of the strongest metrics you can measure and track. If looked at as a ratio of total visitors to those that have converted on a particular action, the higher the percentage of people who undertake that action, the better.

One of the most important metrics not represented in this list is the good old-fashioned practice of listening to your fans. Paying attention to their comments, discussions, and communications helps you better align your content strategy with their interests. If you're not getting the kind of helpful feedback to make this analysis, just ask them. Fans love to share their thoughts and opinions with marketers, and sometimes all they need is a little prodding.

Integrating Your Online and Offline Campaigns

When you start to solidify your Facebook marketing strategy, you may question what support systems and resources you need or wonder how to integrate your social network marketing strategy with your existing marketing plans. In this section, we make some suggestions on how to support the effort without overloading you or your marketing team.

There's no reason why you can't leverage your existing offline campaigns with a social network, but be sure that you incorporate the campaigns into Facebook the right way. That is, include all elements of your campaign on Facebook. If you're throwing an event or starting a campaign, for example, mention it to your Facebook fans. Pretty much anything you currently do can be digitized and used on your Facebook Page.

Here are some ways that you can integrate your offline campaigns with your Facebook marketing activities:

- ✔ **Promote face-to-face events.** You want people to attend your event, right? Mention it on your Page and even link to any outside information you have posted, such as on your Web site. Better yet, create an event using the status update box and get a head start on your head count on those RSVPs that are going to come rolling in via your Page. (See Chapter 7 for more information on setting up events within your Facebook Page.)

- ✔ **Adapt advertising campaigns to be used for Facebook ads.** Just be sure to make the campaign more social and conversational in tone by creating short, attention-grabbing headlines and utilizing eye-catching pictures. Remember, you have a limited number of characters to use in a Facebook ad, so make every character count.

- ✔ **Sell products in the Facebook Marketplace.** Facebook Marketplace (http://apps.facebook.com/marketplace) is the classifieds section of the Facebook Platform. Here you can post help wanted or services offered ads as well as sell everything from collectibles to houses to vehicles. The best part about this is that it's a tab that can easily be added to your Facebook Page so all your fans know exactly what you're selling on the Marketplace without their having to go to the page and search.

- ✔ **Adapt promotions so that they have a social element and drive awareness of your brand.** Everyone likes free stuff, and people like to win promotions. When your fans know you're running a promotion with a cool prize, they're more likely to not only enter the promotion but also refer their friends to your Page. (See Chapter 7 for details.)

> ✔ **Compare research within Facebook to offline efforts.** Have you found that you have a better response rate to your Facebook marketing activities than, say, sending out a direct mailer? Did Insights tell you that you got more visits to your Web site because of something you posted on your Page when compared with the number of phone calls from prospective customers as a result of your mailers? Take some time to view both your online and offline marketing results to get a clear picture of what's working and what isn't. After you compile this information, you can focus more on what gets you the most results.

The following sections explain how to evaluate your media budget and take inventory of your content assets.

Deciding on a media budget

Believe it or not, the cost of the technology used for social network marketing is rather low. For example, a blog costs nothing to start, a podcast can cost up to $2,000, a wiki can cost up to $6,500 per year, and a video can cost up to $15,000. Your Facebook Page is free, but a private, branded app on Facebook can cost up to $100,000.

Unlike traditional media — print, TV, and radio — that can cost big money, social networks' upfront costs are very little. A blog or Facebook Page costs nothing to start, but the real (and potentially large) cost is creating a steady stream of rich content to fill these new media channels.

 We recommend dedicating up to 25 percent of your traditional media budget to nontraditional media. This gives you a healthy budget to experiment with for advertising, apps, and promotions, and for creating content to be successful in social networks like Facebook.

Hiring an online writer

To create a steady stream of rich content that attracts the right audience, plan to have access to some additional, perhaps dedicated, writing resource for all your social content needs.

Social writing is a unique skill because the writing needs to be conversational. Headlines need to be provocative and entice the reader into wanting to know more. Above all, body copy needs to have a colloquial tone without a trace of sales or marketing speak.

We recommend hiring a separate writer for social network marketing content unless you happen to be one. Most people tend to think they can use the same writing resource for research papers, fact sheets, brochures, Web site copy, e-mail copy, and social content. This is a dangerous practice. Having someone who truly understands the medium can help tailor existing content, and writing new content helps to ensure that you always put your best foot forward.

Part II
Building Your Facebook Presence

The 5th Wave   By Rich Tennant

"Jim and I do a lot of business together on Facebook. By the way, Jim, did you get the sales spreadsheet and little blue pony I sent you?"

In this part . . .

All marketers are looking for ways to put Facebook to work for their companies, small businesses, or clients. Part II shows you how to start a Page for your business on Facebook, create tabs that will engage your fan base, and promote your Page to get more likes. We also help you create a long-term content strategy for your business to develop more conversations and engage with potential customers.

You find out how to virally build your fan base throughout the Facebook Platform and discover the distinctions between Facebook Pages and Facebook Groups. We also discuss how to host Facebook events and promotions to leverage your social network to achieve your marketing objectives. Lastly, we show you how to measure your Page's activity within Facebook.

Chapter 4

Creating a Page for Your Business

*I*f someone offered you retail space in the heart of Times Square, rent free, would you open a business? Of course, you would. Well, that's exactly what Facebook does with Facebook Pages. As a result, more than 3 million businesses, personalities, and nonprofits have hung their shingles on the social network via Facebook Pages.

In this chapter, you find out all about what Facebook Pages are and how to use them for your business. We walk you through creating a business Page and give you tips on how to convert visitors into fans. We also help you understand the value of creating specialized tabs to serve as landing pages. Finally, we discuss the emergence of stores within Facebook Pages, which is a growing trend among e-commerce companies looking to leverage the social network's tremendous reach.

Setting Up a Home for Your Business on Facebook

Facebook Pages, also known as Fan Pages, give your business a presence on Facebook to promote your organization. Facebook Pages are the business equivalent of a Facebook member's profile. Members can *like* your Facebook Page (similar to becoming a friend to your profile), write on your Wall, find out about special promotions, upload content (photos, videos, and links), and join other members in discussions through commenting. And you can share your status updates with *fans* (members who like your page) to keep them engaged and informed.

Unlike profiles (where the number of friends is limited to 5,000), Facebook doesn't limit the number of people who can like your Page. Your business can send updates to all those members who like your Page at any time. Therefore, think of a fan as an opt-in subscriber, with Facebook providing the infrastructure for you to reach your fans via its internal e-mail and Wall features, among others.

Another key difference between Facebook Pages and profiles is that Facebook Pages are public by default. This means that anyone can search and find your Page with the Facebook search engine and with Internet search engines, such as Google and Yahoo!, thereby helping your business gain visibility and broadening your audience beyond just Facebook.

For even more search engine visibility, consider getting a customized user-name, or a *vanity URL,* on Facebook, which can include your company name in your Facebook Web address. We discuss how to create your own username in Chapter 8.

Facebook Pages found with a search engine are visible to non-Facebook mem-bers, but they require the user to join Facebook and like the Page if he wants to interact with the Page, such as make a comment or enter into a discussion.

Exploring the elements on a Page

Facebook Pages come in three categories:

- **Local Business:** Local pages are meant for businesses that would benefit from a strong local market presence. Examples are a breakfast cafe, a pizza shop, or an advertising agency.

- **Brand, Product, or Organization:** These pages are meant for larger national businesses, which could include nonprofit organizations or soft drink companies. Starbucks and Coca-Cola are good business-to-consumer examples; Avaya and Oracle are good business-to-business examples.

- **Artist, Band, or Public Figure:** These pages are good for a politician, an artist, or a musical group. President Barack Obama or the band Nine Inch Nails are examples.

Fortunately, Facebook Pages allow for a flexible layout. Some of the Page elements are universal to every Page and come loaded when you create your Page, such as the picture on your Page, the Wall tab, and the Info tab. This helps maintain a consistent look across all Facebook Pages. However, you can add new tabs (predefined or custom built) to your tab list, and many ele-ments to the left column, which you can reposition by dragging and dropping the box that outlines each element.

Depending on which business category you select when you create your Page, your tab display may vary. For example, if you choose Local⇨Cafe, you see a Reviews tab in your tab list, as shown in Figure 4-1.

Figure 4-1:
Facebook
lets you add
any of the
following
universal
tabs, and
more.

Universal Page elements include

✓ **Profile photo:** When projecting an image — figuratively and literally — your picture is one of the most important elements of your page. Be sure to choose a good, clear image that best represents your business.

✓ **Wall tab:** This is another important element for creating conversations. Here, you can leave updates about your business and fans, or friends and fans can leave comments that everyone can read.

✓ **Info tab:** This tab provides general info about your company. Fields are category-specific to your business. For example, government businesses ask for parking and hours of operation; and fashion businesses ask for Web site, company overview, and mission. You can leave these fields blank initially and fill them in later.

The fields on the Info tab can help you with the search engine optimization (SEO) of your page, so fill them in with content that contains keywords that best describe your business to optimize your position on a search engine.

You can also add a bunch of default Page tabs (as described in the section "Adding Tabs to Your Page," later in this chapter):

✓ **Photos:** Lets fans tag photos on your Page and notifies other fans via a link to view the pictures. This is a fun, key feature because tagging photos spreads the word about your Page. (See Chapter 6 for more information about uploading and tagging photos.)

✓ **Events:** Lets you organize events or gatherings with your fans; it also allows you to alert your community about any upcoming events you may be having. (See Chapter 7 to find out how to host an event.)

- ✔ **Notes:** Lets you share happenings in and around your company with your fans. You can also tag fans of your company in notes to encourage them to add a comment. (See Chapter 6 for more on notes.)

- ✔ **Video:** Provides a high-quality video platform for Pages. You can upload video files, send videos from your mobile phone, and record video messages to all your fans. Additional features include full-screen playback, tagging your fans in videos, rotating videos, and more. (Chapter 6 gives the lowdown on uploading videos.)

- ✔ **Discussions:** Lets your fans express their ideas, questions, and suggestions. Discussions let you know exactly what your fans and customers think and want from your company. Think of this section as a community section. (See Chapter 6 for more on discussions.)

Facebook Pages also allow you to add *applications* (apps) — small interactive software programs — to your Page to engage your readers with videos, notes, links, discussions, Flash content, and more. Depending on which category of Facebook Page you choose, you can see that some apps are standard and can't be removed, such as your Wall, Events, and Notes. Facebook also maintains a large library of third-party apps that you can use to make a Facebook Page your own. (See Chapter 12 for details on adding applications to your Facebook Page.)

Designing within boundaries

Before creating a Facebook Page (as described in the next section), give some thought to basic design principles. Although there are always exceptions to the rules, some best practices in Facebook Page design include

- ✔ **Keep it clean:** Too many elements on the Page can detract attention from the brand. Although some apps are productive and useful, try to keep the number to a minimum.

- ✔ **Keep it fresh:** By continuously updating your Page, you give your fans a reason to come back often, which generates social stories that attract more fans.

- ✔ **Keep on topic:** Your Facebook Page should focus on your business. Although adding Really Simple Syndication (RSS) feeds and other dynamic content is encouraged, you need to keep it relevant to the business and your fans. As much as you may love Elvis, he doesn't belong on your second-hand jewelry page.

- ✔ **Keep your fans in mind:** Design your Page with your customers in mind. Every element should be of value to them; otherwise, it doesn't belong on your Page.

- ✔ **Position your company as an authority:** Your Facebook Page signposts your business to the world. This is your chance to show what you know and let your expertise shine.

- ✔ **Inject some personality into your Page:** Even though a Facebook Page is for business, it should reflect your personality. Find and maintain your company voice throughout your communications. Have fun with it, but convey a professional, quality organization.

- ✔ **Value feedback:** Facebook, unlike radio and TV, is a two-way medium. Companies shouldn't overlook or ignore the value of feedback received via your Facebook channel. You should encourage feedback through discussion boards, polls, surveys, promotions, user-generated comments, and general fan interaction. Feedback is very valuable because so few people actually take the time to give it.

- ✔ **Foster a give-and-take relationship:** Your fans want to engage with your Page, but it's a two-way street — you must give in order to receive. Make special content available exclusively through Facebook or offer prizes in exchange for feedback — just two ways to show fans that you value their input.

- ✔ **Generating social stories is key to viral success:** Facebook uses a snazzy sophisticated algorithm to publish social stories that are relevant to like-minded users. You, or your Page administrators (admins), should always think of what social interactions you can perform — or can encourage your fans to perform — to fuel the Wall Items.

- ✔ **Follow general guidelines and limitations:** The Page layout is generally very flexible, but brand guidelines on Facebook must be strictly followed. Any links away from Facebook must open a new window. Facebook doesn't allow pop-ups or pop-unders.

Creating Your Facebook Page

Facebook makes setting up a Page easy. (Keep in mind, you need to create a personal profile first; see the appendix for details.) Just log in to your account, and with some basic information about your company, you can get started.

The person who sets up the Page also becomes the default admin of it.

To create your Page, follow these steps:

1. **Go to www.facebook.com/pages/create.php.**

2. **Select the business type that best describes your business.**

   Here are your options:

   - *Local Business* ranges from Automotive to Travel Service.

   - *Brand, Product, or Organization* ranges from Airline/Ship/Train Station to Web site.

   - *Artist, Band, or Public Figure* ranges from Actor to Writer.

For this example, the rock band X-Factor, we selected Artist, Band, or Public Figure as the category, Band as the type of business, and then named the Page X-Factor, as shown in Figure 4-2.

WARNING!

It's important to choose the correct category while creating your Page because the resulting templates that Facebook generates have different options. For example, if you choose Brand, Product, or Organization, your Page elements are different from a Local Business café. The Local Business café has a section for reviews from your patrons; the Brand, Product, or Organization does not.

3. **Type your business name in the Page Name field to secure your organization's name on Facebook.**

   When you name your Page, it's permanent, so make sure you choose a name that you want your fans and customers to associate with your business. When you get more than 25 fans, you can claim a username for your Page on Facebook, as described in Chapter 8.

4. **Select the check box below the name of the Page to accept the Facebook terms.**

   Selecting this check box certifies that you are the official representative of the business, organization, entity, or person that's the subject of the Facebook Page — and that you have the necessary rights to create and maintain the Page.

5. **Click the Create Official Page button.**

   Congratulations, you've created your Facebook Page! See the next section for details on customizing your page.

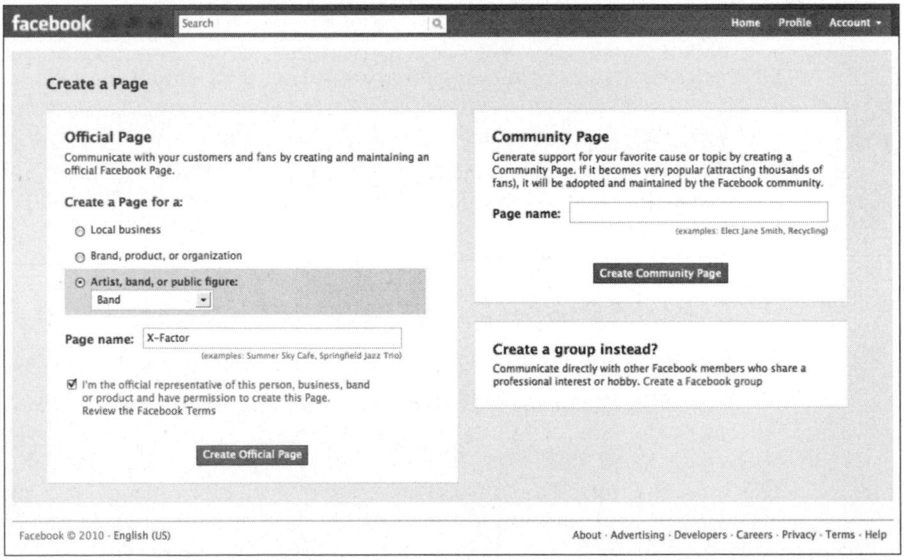

Figure 4-2: Select the category and type of Page you want to create.

Customizing Your Page

Beyond certain universal elements, Facebook Pages allow you to customize your Page to your liking. Most of the items on the page are movable, thanks to a very slick technology called AJAX. For example, to change the order of items on the Page, click the item bar and drag it to the desired location. The following sections give you the lowdown on tweaking a few of the basic elements on your Page.

Asynchronous JavaScript and XML (AJAX) is a group of interrelated Web development techniques used to create interactive Web apps that users can customize.

Uploading a profile picture

A good place to start customizing your Page is to upload your company logo or a photo of your product. This picture represents you on Facebook, so make it a good one. Or, you can add an animated GIF that has several photos of your product from various angles. If you're a services company, you can have several photos of happy people using your service.

You can upload photos in JPG, GIF, or PNG formats only. Pictures can be up to 396 pixels wide with a height three times the width. Maximum file size is 4MB.

To upload the first picture for your Page, follow these steps:

1. **Hover your mouse on the question mark in the upper-left corner of your screen.**

2. **Click the Change Picture link that appears and then choose Upload a Picture from the drop-down list, as shown in Figure 4-3.**

   The Upload Your Profile Picture dialog box appears.

3. **Browse to the picture you're looking for and click the Open button to start the upload process.**

Providing contact info with the Info tab

The Info tab contains two sections: Basic Info and Detailed Info. The individual details that appear in these sections depends on which category and business type you chose when you created your Page. For example, we chose the Artist, Band, or Public Figure category to promote our Band, X-Factor, so the Info tab looks like Figure 4-4.

Here's a general rundown of the two Info sections:

- ✔ **Basic Info:** Enter your basic contact information, such as business address and phone number, as well as hours of operation. For example, for bands, this would include band member names and type of music.

- ✔ **Detailed Info:** Enter more in-depth information here. For example, for bands, you can add your Web site, current location, general manager, booking agent, press contact, other artists you like, influences, band interests, and biography, as shown in Figure 4-5. For more business-focused categories, detailed information would include

  - *Web site:* Add your Web site's URL.

  - *Company Overview:* Add your company's boilerplate text on who you are and what you do. Or, you can add content that is more social and less "corporate" to give your Page more personality.

  - *Mission:* Add your mission statement. You don't have to enter one if you don't have one, or you can make up something provocative.

  - *Products:* Add a listing of your products or services.

Be sure to click the Save Changes button when you're finished entering information on the Info tab.

Facebook Pages are public, and these fields can help you with the search engine optimization of your Page. So, fill them with content that contains the keywords under which you wish to be found on a search engine.

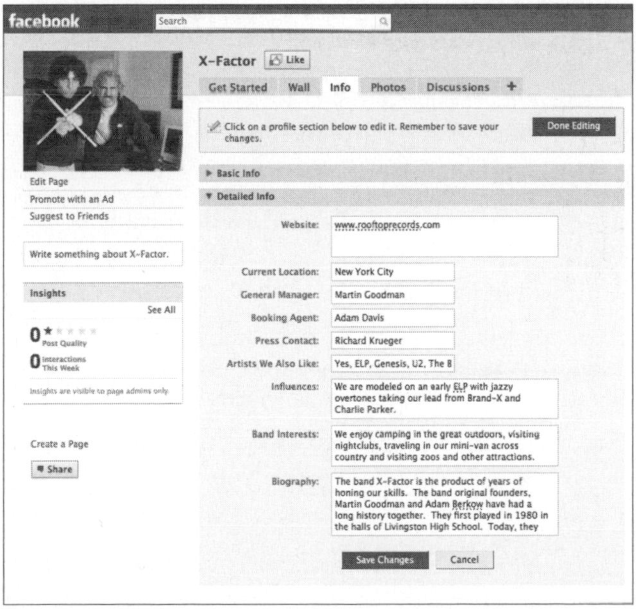

Figure 4-5: Your Info tab shows detailed info about your business, or in this example, for the band X-Factor.

Staying in touch with the Wall tab

The *Wall* on your Page (see Figure 4-6) is where fans of your brand can interact with you, such as leave a comment, thought, or idea about your company. Also, you can share what's on your mind. Think of this area as a very public message board. You can get creative and use the Wall to post jobs for your company to let people know you are hiring, announce an upcoming product launch, and gauge interest from your fans.

Figure 4-6: The Wall tab is a great place for a welcome message for your visitors.

Your Wall generates and displays *stories* for anyone who is a fan of your Page. Keep your Wall active by posting content you already have, such as links to the latest blog post from your company, by using the status update box. Or, you can add a link to a news item that covers your industry. Here's a list of the items that you can post on your Wall:

- ✔ **Content:** Type a text message up to 420 characters in length. Use this area to discuss anything of interest that is happening at your company.

- ✔ **Links:** Add any links from your corporate Web site or any news coverage you may get with your fans.

- ✔ **Photos:** Add photos of new products, launch parties, or any photos of people who work at your company. Single photos can be uploaded from your hard drive; larger groupings of photos can be made into an album.

- ✔ **Events:** Add an event from your company. You just fill out the Title, Location, and Time and then click the Share button. (See Chapter 7 for details.)

✔ **Videos:** Add a video from your company. You can record a video with a Webcam or upload it from your hard drive.

Every time you update the information section of your page, an update posts on your Wall. Also, anytime you add a discussion with the Discussions tab or write on someone else's Wall, it appears on your Wall. For more information about adding content to your Wall, see Chapter 6.

Adding other admins

Facebook gives you the option to add other administrators to your Page. To do so, just follow these steps:

1. **On your Page, select the Edit Page link, which appears below your profile photo.**

2. **Select the Manage Admins tab on the left navigation menu.**

3. **Type the name (or e-mail address) of the person you want to add as an admin to your Page.**

   The person you added can now manage the Page from her Facebook profile.

Setting Page Access

Before you go live with your Page, you might want to consider limiting the access that certain readers have to your Page and controlling what actions readers can take when interacting with your Page. To access these settings, you click the Edit Page link under the profile picture on your Page.

Facebook allows you to restrict access to your Facebook Page by country: U.S., Canada, U.K., Australia, and several others. You can also restrict access by age: Anyone (13+); People Older Than 17, 18, 19, or 21; and Alcohol-Related (which represents the legal drinking age where the user resides). Restricting by age is something you may want to consider if you're a local bar or a tobacco brand.

To access your Page permission settings:

1. **Click the Edit Page link under the profile picture on your Page.**

2. **Click the Manage Permissions tab on the left side menu, as shown in Figure 4-7.**

3. Select any of the following settings to restrict access to your Page:

- *Country Restrictions:* List the countries you want to restrict access to.

- *Age Restrictions:* Make a selection if you want to restrict access to your Page based on the user's age.

- *Wall Tab Shows:* Choose between All Posts or Page to determine what posts appear on the Wall.

- *Wall Spam Filter:* Select whether the spam tools on your Wall are visible to the Page admin, or hidden.

- *Default Landing Tab:* From the drop-down list, choose the tab a user will land on.

   The default landing tab is set to Wall, but you can change it to any tab. This is a good way to test different landing pages to see which one is most effective.

- *Posting Ability:* Check the boxes to allow anyone to post comments, photos, and videos to your Wall. Our advice is to allow as much interaction as you can with your fans, so be sure to select these check boxes. However, if you're in a heavily restricted industry, such as the pharmaceutical industry, and have a specific legal requirement to maintain control of your message, you might want to restrict your visitor's ability to contribute.

- *Delete Page:* By clicking this link, you permanently delete your Page.

4. When you're finished, click the Save Changes button.

Figure 4-7: Manage permissions to your Page.

Adding Tabs to Your Page

Facebook makes further customizing your Page through the use of tabs easy. *Tabs* are, in essence, additional pages that enhance your Facebook presence. Facebook provides some preset tabs that add additional functionality to your Page, including an Events tab, Video tab, Links tab, and Notes tab.

To add one of these tabs to your page, follow these steps:

1. **Click the plus (+) symbol at the far right end of the tab bar at the top of your Facebook Page.**

   The Add a New Tab pop-up menu appears, as shown in Figure 4-8.

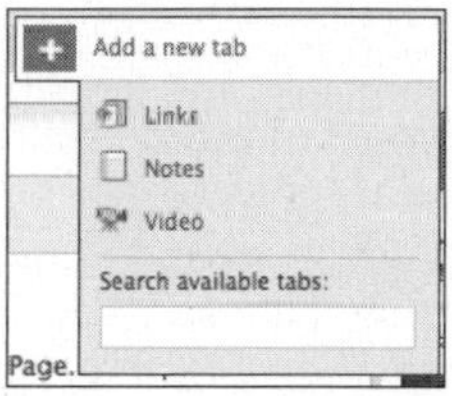

Figure 4-8: Customize your Page by adding new tabs.

2. **Click the tab you want to add.**

   If the pop-up menu doesn't show the tab you want to add, you can search for it using the Search Available Tabs field. If you don't find the app you're looking for, you can visit the Facebook Application Directory, at www.facebook.com/apps/directory.php and add the app to your Page.

   Facebook adds the new tab to the list of tabs at the top of your Page.

3. **Click the pencil icon next to the tab's label to add related content to the tab.**

In the following sections, we discuss how Facebook allows for a certain degree of customization in creating new tabs. By creating a custom landing tab on Facebook, you control the flow of information the way you want it presented to your visitors. From promotions to newsletter sign-up forms to music downloads, and even storefronts, companies are leveraging tabs in all sorts of unique ways.

Creating unique landing pages

You can control the first experience visitors have with your company's Facebook Page by directing them to your most engaging information, such as a Flash video or a well-crafted promotional offer on its own tab. Or, depending on the nature of your business, you might want visitors to go directly to your Info tab to view your basic contact info. If you're an artist, for example, you might want to send visitors directly to sample photos of your work. If you're a local landscaper, maybe you want visitors to see a video of your work. For Pop Tot Tees, we send visitors to our Wall to view our latest products and promotions.

You can take this concept a step further by running ads on Facebook that target specific tabs and have different promotional offers on each one. See Chapter 10 for details.

Smart marketers design landing tabs to convert visitors into fans, by getting them to like the Page. You can do this in a variety ways. For example, Red Bull, the popular energy drink, captures your attention immediately upon landing on its Facebook Page with a call to action to get you to "Like Our Page. Hint, Hint." (See Figure 4-9.) Sometimes humor serves to lighten the load, as everybody likes to be in on the joke.

Some of the best landing pages simply inspire their fans to share. For example, Toyota USA's Facebook Page lands on an AutoBiography tab, featuring stories of real owners, submitted by them and encouraging everyone to send in their own autobiographies. (See Figure 4-10.)

Adding a custom tab

If you visit popular Facebook Pages, such as Red Bull or Starbucks, the one thing they all have in common is a custom tab. Custom tabs help companies stand apart from other Facebook Pages. They can also serve to increase the number of likes to the Page, drive e-newsletter sign ups, and encourage a promotion. Furthermore, you can make the custom tab a landing page within your Facebook Page, so it's the first content visitors see when they land on your Page.

Facebook has announced that it will no longer support its popular *FBML* app, which allowed you to create a customized tab using HTML, the basic Web standard. All tabs already created with the program won't be affected. But any new tabs will have to support *iFrames,* another Web standard, as opposed to Facebook's proprietary FBML language.

Figure 4-9:
Red Bull does a great job of driving your attention to the Like button on the top of its landing page.

You can get a professionally designed customized tab from companies such as Buddy Media and BlitzLocal. There are also many third-party apps that allow you to create a customized tab for your Facebook Page with little or no technical knowledge. Some come at a price while others are free. Here we explore several custom tab-creation app options:

✔ **PageLever:** Offering an easy and free way to create a custom tab, Page-Lever (www.pagelever.com) allows you to upload an image to your custom tab (see Figure 4-11). Although you can't embed any links into the image, you can still design an interesting Page with a single image. A more advanced version of the app, available for $20 per year, offers the ability to add fan-only content so that when a visitor clicks the Like button, the content automatically changes. This is ideal for rewarding fans with a coupon code or special content.

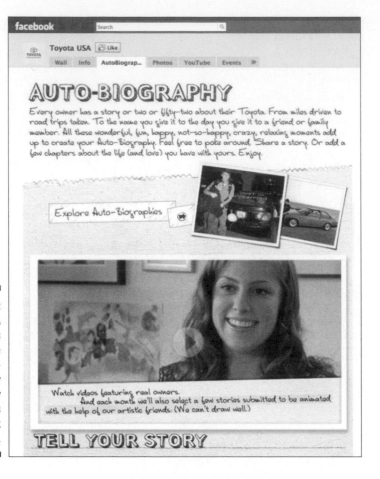

Figure 4-10:
Toyota USA invites fans to share their auto-biography when they land on its Facebook Page.

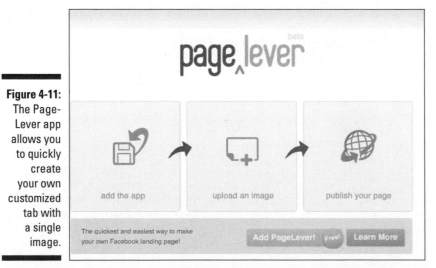

Figure 4-11:
The Page-Lever app allows you to quickly create your own customized tab with a single image.

✔ **Involver:** One of many apps for Facebook Pages, Involver's Welcome Tab app, allows you to create an attractive splash, or introduction page, to welcome your Facebook visitors (see Figure 4-12). Part of the company's Pro Apps offering, there is a $200 monthly subscription fee associated with this app, which also gives you access to any of the company's professional apps. Visit www.involver.com to purchase a pro plan.

Figure 4-12: Involver's Welcome Tab app makes a great first impression.

✔ **TabSite:** Facebook application developer TabSite specializes in customizable tab page software, allowing you to create and manage the content on your custom tab for $5 per month. The app supports single and multiple images, as well as videos and text. TabSite also offers the ability to have up to five subpages, all accessible via your custom tab (as shown in Figure 4-13).

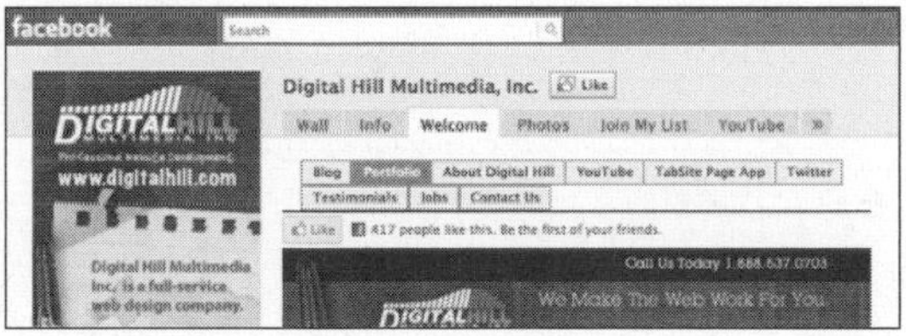

Figure 4-13: TabSite supports up to five subpages on the customized tab.

Adding tabs for promotions

Promotions are some of the most effective ways to get visitors to like your Page and share content. Many retailers use a promotions tab (or discounts, specials, and so on) to push their latest coupons and special offers. Several apps are available that can help you in setting up a promotion. Wildfire Interactive (http://wildfireapp.com) offers one of the most popular promotion apps.

But you don't just have to offer freebies or coupons to drive engagement. By allowing fans to customize something that's associated with the brand, you can also drive engagement. Kit Kat does exactly that with its Ideal Break promotion (see Figure 4-14). When visitors go to the Kit Kat Page, they can answer a few simple questions to discover their ideal break, and who to take it with.

If you launch a promotion or special offer, require the person to like your Page before they can participate or benefit from the special offer. (See Chapter 7 for details on creating a promotion.)

Figure 4-14: Kit Kat gives fans a quiz to discover their ideal break.

Integrating a Storefront

Merchants are increasingly turning to Facebook as a channel to sell their wares. Attracted to Facebook's mass reach and inexpensive, targeted ads, businesses create custom tabs to present their products. Some companies even conduct transactions directly within the social network, whereas others pass them off to their own Web site to complete the payment.

Some third-party applications are available to facilitate the shopping. Here are a few that we recommend:

✔ **CoreCommerce** (www.corecommerce.com) has an application with fees starting at less than $20 per month, based on the number of products you include in your store. Presently, this application powers about 1,200 stores.

  ✔ **Volusion** (www.volusion.com), another e-commerce provider, has
    also added a Facebook application that allows you to add a social store
    tab to your Facebook Page. Sun & Ski Sports launched its storefront,
    showcasing just eight products, as shown in Figure 4-15.

  ✔ **Payvment** (www.payvment.com), a free solution, Payvment's Facebook
    app is a completely integrated shopping solution. The service allows you
    to build and manage your storefront from within a tab on your Facebook
    Page and adds your products to a directory of Facebook stores.

National flower delivery service 1-800-Flowers.com was one of the first to offer
a complete shopping experience within Facebook, as shown in Figure 4-16.
But, before Facebook members can even browse its inventory, they first need
to install an application and like its Facebook Page. The service is provided by
Alvenda (www.alvenda.com) and even allows for same-day delivery service
on certain products.

Although e-commerce within Facebook is still in its infancy, Facebook is
developing its own payment solution — Facebook Credits. Seen as a potential
PayPal competitor, Facebook Credits allows Facebook members to securely
store their credit card information, to simply make purchases. One thing is
certain, social shopping will have a profound effect on Facebook's future.

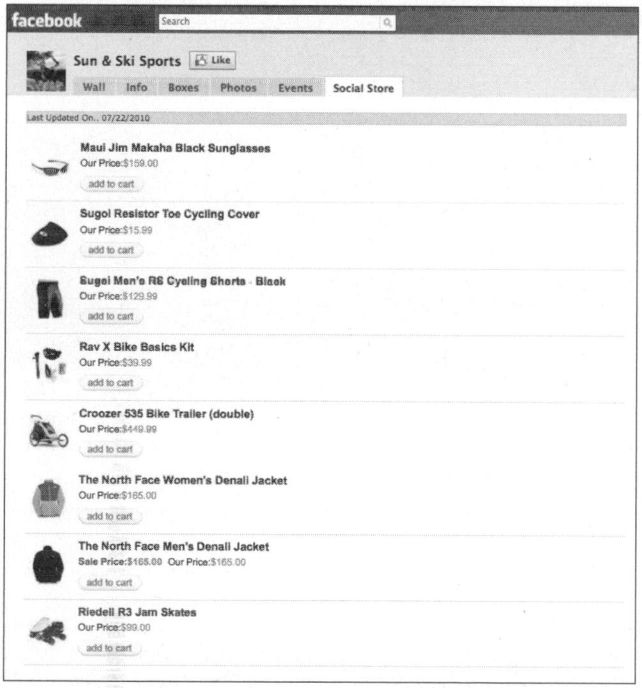

Figure 4-15:
Sun & Ski
Sports
features
just eight
products
and sends
customers
to the
company's
Web site to
complete
the
transaction.

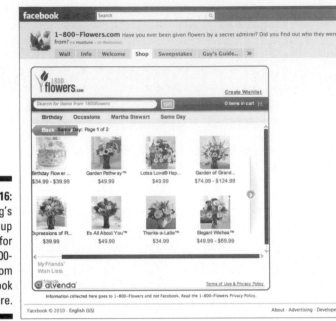

Figure 4-16:
Everything's
coming up
roses for
the 1-800-
Flowers.com
Facebook
store.

Chapter 5

Implementing a Content Strategy

*F*acebook marketing is all about content, but figuring out what content consumers want — that's the challenge. As a Facebook marketer, you need to act more like a publisher than a traditional marketer, bringing your brand to life through sharing and interacting with content.

Whether that interaction is a promotion or status update, you need to have a coherent content strategy to achieve your marketing objectives. Your *content strategy* is your plan for creating, publishing, and managing the information you put out there; it's your roadmap to navigating new marketing terrain, identifying what content needs to be produced and deciding who will create the content with what resources, when, and most importantly, why.

In this chapter, you discover why a content strategy is central to your Facebook marketing plan. We walk you through the basic elements that go into creating and implementing a content strategy, from knowing what and when to share to measuring your success. You also discover how to get the most engagement from your fans with updates and the importance of consistency from a messaging and timing perspective.

Making Content Matter

In the new Facebook marketing paradigm, organizations are just waking up to the fact that, in addition to the products and services they sell, information is one of their core offerings. And, in fact, information may just be the most important one. Facebook marketing starts with giving valuable information to your customers; it's a social media marketer's new currency.

Creating, aggregating, and distributing information via your Facebook Page helps build trust between you and your customers; however, it can also weaken that trust, depending on the content you serve. Providing relevancy is the key. For example, if you sell antiques, don't post links to blog posts about scrapbooking, even if that's a hobby of yours. That is an extreme example, of course, but you get the idea. And, of course, on Facebook, you can always ask your customers what type of content they like to consume, what media (such as videos) they prefer, and what will make your Page more useful to them.

Keep in mind that creating relevant content that resonates with your audience is part science, part art:

✔ On the science side stands Facebook Insights, a set of metrics that quantify how people interact with your content. If something works based on the response it receives, by all means, produce more content similar to it.

✔ On the art side of the equation, your content strategy also requires an element of creativity. Even if you simply *aggregate* — repurpose other people's content by linking to articles or videos — that reuse requires an editorial eye to determine what's worth posting and a copy writer's creativity to best rephrase the headline.

For example, by posting links to relevant and entertaining videos found on YouTube, Chad Raney — motivational speaker and author — provides his fans with engaging content that's right for his audience (see Figure 5-1).

Knowing your audience

The first commandment in Facebook marketing is to Know Thy Fans. Before you can deliver content that's relative to your customers' lives, you need to understand the psychographics and demographics of your audience. Who are these folks? What interests and motivates them? What can they learn from you that will make them more valuable to their organization?

Anyone with a Facebook Page, whether a business, nonprofit, celebrity, or personality-in-training, needs to understand who their intended audience is. On Facebook, that also means knowing how your audience consumes information. For example, do they log into Facebook from their mobile phone? Do they log in at work or only on the weekends?

Before you start posting content, do some research to define your audience and the Facebook culture. Research competitors' Pages and determine what information they have available and how they present it. Think about ways to create content that stands apart from the competition. Engagement comes from providing something useful to your audience. Without a full understanding of your audience, you'll have a difficult time creating content they want to consume.

Content and conversations can significantly contribute to making a *conversion* — that is, getting a user to take a specific call to action, such as signing up for a newsletter or liking a Page.

Figure 5-1:
Linking to
relevant
YouTube
videos is a
good way
to share
information
that's enter-
taining and
valuable
to your
audience.

Staying on message

Based on the traditional marketing model, from awareness and knowledge come desire and action; however, with Facebook, the rules have changed. Everyone and everything is connected, so any engagement you do through your Page doesn't go away after it posts on your Page. Fans may take away and utilize advice or tips you post or pass on any videos that you upload. Therefore, you have to maintain a common message, or theme, throughout all your updates to ensure that you always accomplish the goals you set out for yourself in your Facebook marketing plan, whether they're brand aware-ness and/or increasing sales.

Make sure you use the appropriate voice and tone based on your audience and content type. For example, if you're posting quick tips or human interest sto-ries, you may want to use a more conversational tone. However, if you're offer-ing more technical or research-driven content for a B2B (business to business) audience, a more serious, almost clinical tone may be more appropriate.

Here are some questions you need to ask to decide whether your content is on message and matters to your audience:

✔ Does the content address your audience's questions, concerns, or needs?

✔ Does it inspire or entertain your intended audience?

✔ Does it help users complete a specific task?

✔ Will it help influence a decision?

✔ Does it motivate the user in some way?

    ✔ Does it bring your brand to life or add a positive spin in some way?

    ✔ Does it build or break the trust you've entered into with your fan?

Publish content based on what the reader needs or wants, not about the company. Using the antiques example mentioned earlier, you don't want to always publish content about sales your company is having or how you got in a new shipment that they should stop by and check out. Make a point to include links to articles and blog posts about, say, caring for antique furniture or how to keep antique copper items from tarnishing.

Defining Your Posting Goals

People are drawn to Facebook content for various reasons. Some folks come for the discounts. Others consume and recommend (or *like*) content that informs or entertains them. And still others are attracted to more anecdotal or everyday life updates. One thing is for sure: Even within a group of like-minded individuals, people have differing opinions as to the kind of content they enjoy and share.

But compelling content doesn't magically appear. It requires planning, creativity, and an objective. Content without a goal doesn't help you sell more products, build awareness for your cause, or promote your brand.

Your content needs to align with the business goals of your organization. Some basic goals may include

    ✔ Driving traffic to your Web site

    ✔ Building your brand

    ✔ Improving customer service

    ✔ Generating leads

    ✔ Increasing ad revenue

    ✔ Adding e-commerce to your online marketing efforts

If your content strategy includes incentives — such as coupons, free giveaways, and promotions — you need to translate that into a very clear and straightforward call to action (or goal). You may have several converging goals behind your posts, such as to let people know about an event as well as provide an incentive for those who RSVP that they'll attend it.

The following sections examine some motivational goals to consider when you publish content to your Facebook Page.

Getting fans engaged

Engagement is the name of the game on Facebook. By *engagement,* we mean to solicit a response or action by your fans. This engagement from your fans could be commenting on a post, liking something, contributing to a discussion topic, or posting photos and videos. You want fans to interact with your Page for several reasons:

✔ You can build a relationship with fans through dialogue and discussion.

✔ The more activity generated on your Page, the more stories are published to your fans' news feeds, which drives more awareness to the original action and creates a viral marketing affect.

How do you get your fans to engage with your Page? That all depends on your audience and the subject matter of your Page. Here are some helpful hints to encourage fan engagement through your content:

✔ **Show your human side:** All work and no play makes for a very dull Page. People like to share the more human side of life. For example, many people take part in "take your child to work day" or even "take your dog to work day." If you participate in one of these, post a picture of your child or pet, and then add a note that they're doing a great job at helping Mom or Dad at work. Ask your fans if anyone else takes advantage of this opportunity and encourage them to post pictures as well.

✔ **Ask your fans what they think:** In the Facebook paradigm, Page admins actively solicit feedback from those connected to their Page. Be direct and ask fans what they think of your organization, new product, or position on a topic. For example, the Brain Aneurysm Foundation regularly asks its fans to share their personal experiences with the disease, as shown in Figure 5-2.

✔ **Tell your fans how much you appreciate them:** Don't underestimate the goodwill to be gained by saying thank you. Thanking your fans for their questions or complimenting them on their comments can go a long way in social media circles. The clothing retailer Lands' End is known for its exceptional customer service, and its fans aren't afraid to tell everyone about it! Lands' End participated in National Customer Service Week, and the fan response was incredible. As shown in Figure 5-3, Lands' End thanked its fans for the response.

✔ **Highlight a success story:** Another tactic that appeals to vanity is to highlight a peer's success — she'll be sure to thank you for the attention. Your other fans will appreciate hearing about one of their own making good. Many companies on Facebook run a Fan of the Month promotion and foster engagement by soliciting entries.

Figure 5-2:
The Brain
Aneurysm
Foundation
asks fans
about their
personal
experiences.

Figure 5-3:
Clothing
retailer
Lands' End
thanked fans
for their kind
words as it
celebrated
National
Customer
Service
Week.

✔ **Share your tips and insights:** People are always looking for information that helps them do their jobs better. Don't underestimate your knowledge and what you have to share that's valuable. Sharing helpful tips is some of the best engagement around. Technology blog Mashable does a great job at providing a steady stream of tips to its Facebook fans, as shown in Figure 5-4.

Figure 5-4:
Mashable
updates its
fans with
a steady
stream of
tech tips.

✔ **Provide links to relevant articles and research:** You don't have to be a prolific writer to be valuable to your fans. By posting links to relevant articles, videos, resources, and research, you build your credibility as a content aggregator.

✔ **Ask your fans what they think of something and test their knowledge using quizzes and polls:** Again, appealing to the ego factor, quizzes and polls are popular tactics on Facebook. Mentos, the popular chewy fruit candy, regularly creates light-hearted polls using the popular Facebook Poll Daddy Polls app. One of these polls, "In the Fruit Pack of Mentos, Which Flavor Do You Save for Last?" is shown in Figure 5-5. This poll served the double purpose of allowing their fans to share their opinions, and it showed the company whether one flavor was preferred. Its marketing team can utilize this information to better target future Mentos Page content and promotions.

Driving conversions

So you've created your Page, promoted it, built a sizeable fan base, and engaged regularly with your fans. Now, you want to get down to business and take the next step with your audience. This next step is a *conversion* — getting visitors to like your Page, sign up for e-mails, or even call a sales person for a demo. Whatever your conversion goal is, it needs to be communicated clearly to your fans and mixed into your total content strategy.

One of the most effective ways to drive conversions is to offer something of value in return for members liking your Page and an incentive for folks to come back often. For instance, Einstein Bros. offers coupons to people who like their Page, as shown in Figure 5-6. A free bagel in exchange for becoming a fan and ongoing discounts for return visits are powerful motivators that appeal directly to your palate, not to mention your wallet.

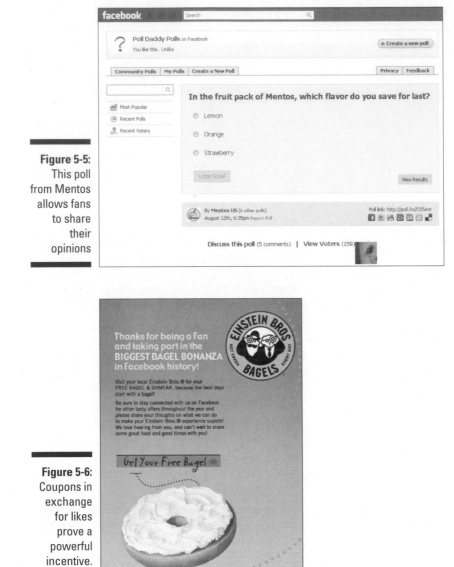

Figure 5-5:
This poll
from Mentos
allows fans
to share
their
opinions

Figure 5-6:
Coupons in
exchange
for likes
prove a
powerful
incentive.

Consider what incentives will keep your fans coming back. If you offer some sort of value for members to become fans of your Page, you need to also have an incentive for fans to keep coming back, such as access to special content, deals, coupons, insider tips, and so on. Only after you build a certain amount of trust with your fans can you try to sell them on your wares.

If a fan has to click more than three times to reach your contact form or email sign-up page, it's worthless. Base your Facebook content around this rule as much as possible. Keep the call to action simple and straightforward; for example, make it easy for them to reach your Web site's contact form by posting the direct link on your Page.

Fostering community

Great Facebook fan communities don't happen by accident; they take a great deal of care and feeding. Employee resources necessary to manage and maintain fan communities are the biggest expense for companies on Facebook. Posting content regularly isn't enough. Facebook marketers can't rely on the "if you post it, they will come" idea. Content must be fresh to make sure fans not only come, but come back again and again.

By adhering to some basic principles, you can cultivate a thriving community around your Facebook Page. Here are some helpful tips to leverage content that fosters community:

- ✔ **Manage the quality and quantity of your posts:** You have to walk a fine line between publishing on a steady basis and not publishing too frequently to your Page. If your content appears too often on your fans' News Feeds, they might hide your feed, or worse, unlike your Page.

- ✔ **Post relevant and fresh content:** Keep your posts relevant to the community on your Facebook Page. Find out what type of content the community values and then provide more of it.

- ✔ **Set the right tone:** When entering into a dialogue with your fans on Facebook, use a conversational tone; avoid marketing speak.

- ✔ **Encourage sharing:** Make sure that you frequently end your posts with a question to solicit a response from your fans. For example, if you mention an upcoming sale on shoes at your store, end the post by asking the question, "What is your favorite brand of shoes?"

- ✔ **Respond to comments:** In this always-on Internet, Facebook fans expect a response within 24 hours when they write on your Wall or Discussions tab. Taking too much time to respond, or simply ignoring them, could come at your peril. For more information, see the section, "Developing a Strategy for Responding to Comments," later in this chapter.

- ✔ **Be simple and direct:** Include a specific request for action that creates value for your fans. This could be in the form of a coupon, promotion, or suggested video to watch, but all need to be easy to enact from the fan's perspective. Too many clicks as part of the process, and people won't take the desired action.

- ✔ **Manage the kind of Page that people like:** Although this might seem obvious, people want to interact with Pages that they perceive as cool, interesting, or unusual. Manage the kind of community that you'd want to be part of.

Using Facebook for customer care

Increasingly Facebook, and social media in general, have turned into a customer care medium for many companies. For example, AT&T reaches out to customers who have problems with service through its Facebook Page, as shown in the following figure.

Facebook is a great environment to reach out and connect with customers and solve their problems quickly. However, if you use Facebook for customer care, make sure you have a strategy to respond to customer problems. Also, just because you add a customer service channel doesn't mean you should take away your other customer service channels. Facebook, Twitter, and other social media outlets shouldn't replace your existing customer channels, but rather complement them.

Customer Service response

Developing a Strategy for Responding to Comments

When you use Facebook marketing to build lasting relationships with your customers, you need to map out ahead of time, whenever possible, who in your company is responsible for responding to what comments, and in what time period. In part, this strategy depends on how active your fans are on your Page.

Examining general guidelines for responding to comments

Here are some points to keep in mind when putting together your strategy for responding to comments:

- **Typically, fans expect a response within 24 hours.** A lack of response could discourage fans and drive them to seek out other Pages.

- **Whenever possible, direct the conversation.** Don't let a conversation get out of hand. You can continue the conversation on the Wall or, if more appropriate, seek the customer's e-mail address and contact her in a more closed environment if the situation is more sensitive. Staying involved in your fans' conversations will make them want to stick around because they know they're being listened — and responded — to. Your goal should always be for your fans to look to you as a trustworthy source for any information and advice they seek.

- **Respond to your fans in the same method that they lodged their message.** If a fan reaches out to you in a positive manner via a comment on the Wall, by all means, keep the conversation going within that post. If someone asks a question, don't direct him to your Web site for more information; instead, respond in the moment. Don't provide him with your e-mail for offline follow-up unless the question requires a more personal approach.

    Answering comments on the Wall also triggers a Facebook notification for that user, along with all others who have provided comments under that original post or liked the post. By commenting under the original thread, the conversation stays alive on your Page where others can benefit from the discussion; it also allows others to continue commenting and liking the post, which generates stories in users' News Feeds.

    If your Page gets a lot of updates from fans during an event, for example, don't worry about responding to every comment. Prioritize and focus on the posts that have the highest number of comments, or group similar comments together and respond singularly to the group.

- **Address your customer's needs before your business needs.** Marketers often talk about understanding the voice of the customer — that is, what the customer values — but nowhere is this more important than in Facebook. Because Facebook is ultimately the expressions of its members, it makes sense to hear their needs before listening to the needs of your business. Ultimately, your voice is determined by your customers.

✔ **Be honest.** Inside Facebook, the most powerful message is one delivered by one friend to another friend. This means that you need to ensure that every communication is as open and honest as possible.

When posting or commenting on your Wall, be as authentic as possible and disclose any relationship that could be seen as borderline unethical. A relationship that can work against you undoubtedly will, so be careful.

A very public and notable example of this was the WalMartingAcross-America.com blog. The issue wasn't that the founders of the blog weren't real brand enthusiasts of Wal-Mart; the issue was that Wal-Mart paid them to blog. The relationship was quickly discovered and worked against Wal-Mart. The point here is to disclose any relationship that would make you feel uneasy if printed on the front page of the newspaper. This goes beyond Facebook — it's a tenet of all good social behavior.

The lesson learned is that if you want to build trust and have a loyal following on Facebook, you have to become an active member of the community. Start discovering your voice by putting the needs of the community first, building content that gains their trust, and then engaging in honest dialogue.

✔ **Keep a consistent experience throughout your posts.** For example, if you post a lot of videos, use the same video format. If possible, keep the video on your Page, or better yet, on a customized Video tab on your Page. If you know your fans are more likely to comment from their mobile phones, stick to text-based postings because many formats aren't compatible with a wide range of mobile handsets.

✔ **Stick to a regular broadcasting schedule for your updates and content releases.** Your fans appreciate knowing when and how often to expect updates from your Page, and your content team appreciates knowing what scheduling guidelines to keep. Don't disappoint your fans and lag off for a week or two if you've been publishing on a more regular basis.

You might be surprised to hear that according to a recent study by Dan Zarrella, who writes The Social Media Scientist blog, the weekend is the best time to post content on Facebook and generate engagement from your fan base. In fact, the study shows that posts published on Saturdays get up to 40 percents higher engagement levels than posts during the work week. Perhaps many company policies banning the use of Facebook during work hours impact engagement on Monday through Friday.

If you post on your Page as the admin, you are *not* notified by Facebook if someone comments on the post — you need to go back daily and check for comments and respond. However if you comment on your post (or someone else's), you get a notification that someone else has commented on the post as well.

Knowing when and when not to respond

Although generally you want to respond to comments within 24 hours, in some cases — such as with an irate customer who is never going to be happy with anything you might say — you may be better off not responding at all. Trying to decide when and when not to respond can be tricky, so here are some tips to help you make this decision:

- ✔ **If a mistake was clearly made on your part, respond and correct the situation quickly.** Apologies can go a long way as long as you explain that steps are being taken to correct the situation.

- ✔ **If someone leaves a negative comment about something that never actually took place or is based on incorrect facts, correct him.** Always be polite because often people don't realize they've made an error. If you don't respond, however, this misconception could spread and escalate.

- ✔ **Try to salvage a bad situation.** If you made a mistake and think you can put a positive spin on a bad experience or convince the customer to give you another chance, a response is appropriate to right the perceived wrong.

- ✔ **An irate person may never be satisfied, so you may be better off not doing anything.** Sometimes people direct their frustration with the world toward you and your Facebook Page. If you're dealing with such a person — you can figure out if you are based on other comments she's made — it's often better not to enter a fight you're never going to win. Instead, invest your time and efforts where you can have a positive result.

- ✔ **Don't engage in a fight you can't win.** Sometimes, a response does more harm than good. A negative comment or review can have a devastating effect on a company's online reputation. However, you don't want to engage in a back-and-forth that will uncover more cracks in the armor, so to speak. Often in these situations, it's best to take a passive role as opposed to going for the jugular.

- ✔ **Don't let anger derail your response.** Although the saying "it's not personal, it's just business," is good in principle, it's a lot harder in practice. Disparaging Facebook comments can really make you angry. Rather than rattle off a negative response, either have someone else who is less emotional about the situation respond or sit on the sidelines and wait until your emotions calm before responding. An angry response can go a long way in damaging your relationship with the customer and can have a spill-over effect on all who read it.

In developing your response strategy, try to map all the potential positive and negative comments visitors might leave and then plan appropriate responses to those comments in advance. By being aware of the potential pitfalls, you can at least prepare well-thought-out responses before you get blindsided by them.

Developing internal approval processes

Because Facebook Pages are public, many companies require a process to manage the approval of their content. Although smaller organizations might involve a single person responsible for maintaining the company's Page, other more corporate structures need to define who's ultimately responsible for every company word posted.

In developing an approval process, remember to keep everyone in the loop — from management to sales to marketing and even legal, depending on your corporate structure. But this process must be quick and efficient because getting a response approved often can take too long and derail the entire discussion.

Chapter 6

Building Your Fan Base

*W*here you now tread, many great ones have tread already. Many of today's most popular public figures and commercial products, from President Barack Obama to Coca-Cola, already have Facebook accounts. And scores of other local businesses, brands, actors, politicians, and musicians have done the same. You can create an outpost for your business on Facebook, as well.

With a Facebook Page in place (see Chapter 4 for details on creating a Facebook Page), you can turn your attention to building a strong fan base for your Page. Social networking is a quantity game — the amount of time you spend networking has a huge effect on the amount of results you receive. For example, if you attend a networking event, such as a Chamber of Commerce meeting, you might meet a handful of people. But if you make repeated appearances at these meetings, you'll most certainly build your credibility in the group and add to your number of contacts.

Think of Facebook, or any social network, like the Chamber of Commerce meeting, except the meeting is ongoing and you can meet an endless number of people (that's a big virtual meeting!). Also, at the Chamber of Commerce meeting, imagine you walk up to each group of people that you see, interrupt them, hand them your business card, and ask them to visit your store down the road right now. That approach wouldn't go over very well in that setting, and it doesn't work for you on Facebook.

In this chapter, we cover a few Facebook-friendly tactics that generate conversations, rather than interruptions. These tactics help to build awareness of your brand, drive your sales, form a community of people who share your values, and give you a way to listen to feedback from your customers.

We discuss how to generate the best Wall stories by writing text updates, adding photos and videos, and starting discussions. We also show you how to leverage your existing friends and customers, both within and outside of Facebook, and how to find new business prospects within the Facebook community.

Keeping Your Fans Engaged

If you build a Page, will they come? Not if nobody knows about it. The same viral elements that have helped make Facebook profiles so popular are also hard at work behind Facebook Pages. No, we're not talking about nasty computer viruses; we're talking about a way of spreading your reach. When fans interact with your Facebook Page, their actions become *social stories* and publish to their News Feeds. Then their friends may very well see these social stories when they log into Facebook, and those stories can influence other users to take a similar action. The stories link to your Facebook Page, generate social interactions in the News Feeds of your fans' friends, and drive more traffic to your Page. With Facebook, you can leverage each person's social graph — meaning that, through Facebook, users can discover new Pages of interest to them.

You want to create actions that generate social stories, such as starting a discussion, adding a photo, uploading a video, throwing an event, changing your Page settings, or writing on a Wall — even your own Wall. You can also add your company's RSS feed, any feeds from a company blog, or a feed of items from a feed reader that covers your industry.

As with so many other forms of social media, to keep your Facebook Page vibrant, you need to add fresh content regularly. You can't add any old content, either; you need to make the content interesting and relevant to your readers. Content truly is king because users who return to your Page regularly are more likely to become customers over the long haul. Moreover, existing customers who return often to your Page are more likely to keep coming back if you offer appealing content, so you owe it to your company to keep the content flowing.

You have several ways to make regular updates:

✔ **Find content that's relevant to your audience from any content aggregator or blog search engine, such as Digg (http://digg.com) or Technorati (http://technorati.com).** By taking the time to search on these sites every day, you can find interesting information to repost so that you can keep your site fresh and keep the conversation rolling. Just type a keyword that's applicable to your business and watch how many interesting articles are returned. A good place to start your search is with any keywords you use to make your Web site and blog more search engine optimized.

Technorati makes it even easier by having a special Tags page that lists the most popular tags used on the site over the last month. Technorati even lists them in alphabetical order, making your search even quicker.

- **Vary your tactics.** If you find a clever blog post about something you think is relevant to your audience, post it as a status update. For example:

  > Just read this post from ABC on 123, and here's the link: XYZ. They are on to something!

  Or even something like:

  > A colleague of mine asked me about 123 today, and I thought it'd be a great topic to start a discussion on!

- **Find something you don't agree with and post it in your Discussions tab to ask your fans what they think about it.** If you see a clever comment in a blog post, you can post the comment to your Wall and add a link to the blog post where you found it. For example, if you come across a story about the recently announced Baseball Hall of Fame inductees and you just so happen to be in the business of sports collectibles, post a link and ask your fans whether they agree with the selections.

You can keep your Page engaging and fresh by using the simple Facebook features we discuss in this chapter, including adding photos and videos, generating interesting discussions, hosting an event, and more. These Facebook marketing tactics help you keep your fans engaged and coming back for more.

Every time someone reaches out to engage with your Page, engage with that person in return. Failing to reciprocate can potentially backfire or cause less revenue. When fans ask you a question or are interested enough in what you're saying to post a comment on your Wall, they have invested time in the interaction. Not responding or acknowledging them in some way makes it seem like you're ignoring them. Who wants to give their money to a company that ignores them even before a sale takes place? If a user asks you a question, respond to it. If you receive a compliment, thank the person and reinforce your commitment to creating exceptional customer experiences. If you receive a negative comment, ask how you can improve the overall experience.

Adding New Updates to Your Page

Maintaining a steady stream of content helps you attract new members from the Facebook community, as well as interact with them. This fresh content also helps keep your existing fans interested and engaged. Every time you update your Page with the status update box (the What's On Your Mind? text box), Facebook posts a *social story* (a written account of the action that occurred) on your Wall.

You can choose from two types of features that post content to your Wall: the Update feature and the Notes feature. You need to decide when and how to use them, so we discuss the uses of each one in the following sections.

Updating your status with the status update box

You can easily use the Update feature by entering a status update in the status update box. You're limited to 420 characters, including spaces, which is about 4 to 5 lines of text (just slightly longer than a Twitter post). Be sure to click the Share button to post the status update to your Wall.

If you want to add a message and a link to an article or news item of interest for your fans, follow these steps:

1. **Click the Link button, which is the leftmost button directly below the status update box.**

2. **Enter your message in the status update box.**

3. **In the text box to the left of the Attach button, enter the URL for the content you want to share.**

   Always *stay on brand,* meaning make sure the content relates to your business in some way. And consider keeping your links on the positive side. No need to associate negative news with your business.

4. **Click the Attach button.**

   A short summary of the article appears below your message, as shown in Figure 6-1. If your article has any images, you can select a thumbnail to accompany the post or just click the No Thumbnail box if you don't want one.

5. **Click the Share button to publish your link and message.**

Figure 6-1:
Include a link when you use the Update feature.

Using the status update box is also a quick and easy way to post events, videos, and photos to your Wall simply by clicking one of the icons to the left of the Share button. The only difference between using the status update box instead of going through the tabs at the top is you can take a picture using a Webcam that you hook up to your computer when you choose a photo upload.

The biggest benefit of choosing this route to upload items is that it saves some time, especially if you only have one photo or video to upload. Whichever way you choose the end results are the same: New content published to your News Feed!

Using Notes for your message

The Update feature (discussed in the preceding section) allows you to quickly post short bursts of information. But if you want to share a more complete story, including a photo and tags, use the Facebook Notes feature.

Of all the content-creation tools that you can use to share a post in Facebook, the Notes feature offers you the most flexibility. Notes have a title and body copy, much like an e-mail or blog post, and Facebook doesn't restrict the length of notes. (However, it does restrict the title to 128 characters, including spaces.) You can even add photos to your Notes, either by choosing from an existing Facebook album or by uploading a new one.

To add a note to your Page, follow these steps:

1. **Open the Notes tab.**

   If you don't already have a Notes tab visible on your Page, click the plus sign (+) at the right end of the tab bar, and then click Notes in the list that appears.

2. **Click the Write a Note button, as shown in Figure 6-2.**

   The Write a Note page appears.

3. **Compose your note by entering the following:**

   - *Title:* Add a title up to 128 characters in length.

   - *Body:* Type as much body text as you want, as well as HTML commands.

   - *Tags:* If you mention any of your friends in your note, you can tag them by typing their name and then choosing the correct person from the options that pop up.

Figure 6-2:
Click the
Write a
Note button
to compose
your note.

4. **If you want to import a photo, click the Add a Photo button and then click the Browse button to navigate to the image you want to upload. If you want to use a photo from a Facebook album, click the Add a Photo button and select the photo.**

   You can also enter a caption in the Caption box to the right of the photo.

5. **If you added a photo, tag someone in it by clicking the Preview button at the bottom of the notes section and then clicking the photo you want to tag.**

   A screen appears where you can tag the photo by clicking, yes you guessed it, Tag This Photo, on the right of the screen.

6. **When you're finished, click the Back to Note link on the top left to return to the preview your note.**

7. **Click the Publish button to publish your note.**

   Fans can subscribe to your notes much like they do to a blog.

Using Notes to import your company blog

If you have a company blog, you definitely don't want all your hard work to go unnoticed on Facebook. Facebook lets you import your external blog to your Page by using Notes so that you can keep your fans and their friends up-to-date.

You can import posts from only one blog, and the posts appear as notes on your Wall. Facebook automatically updates your notes whenever you add a new blog post. However, you can't edit imported blog posts.

To import your blog by using the Notes tab, follow these steps:

1. **Click the Notes tab on your Page.**

   If you don't already have a Notes tab visible on your Page, click the double-arrow sign (>>) at the right end of the tab bar, and then click Notes in the list that appears.

2. **Click the Edit Import Settings link in the bottom of the left column.**

   The Import a Blog Page appears.

3. **In the Web URL text box, enter a Web address or an RSS or Atom feed address.**

4. **Select the check box to verify that you have the rights to use or reproduce this content on Facebook and that the content isn't obscene or illegal.**

5. **Click the Start Importing button.**

   A preview of some of your blog posts appears.

6. **If you like what you see, and the blog imported correctly, click the Confirm button. If not, click the Back button on your browser and retry the import.**

   You can't edit imported blog posts.

 If you import too many blog posts in a day, Facebook might block you from writing or importing new notes, which can result in Facebook disabling your account. A good rule of thumb is to only post content that you think your Fans can read that day. After all, you don't want to bombard them with too much information in one shot.

Uploading Media: Photos, Videos, and MP3s

A simple strategy to encourage interaction on your Facebook Page involves providing photos, videos, and even MP3s. When you upload media, a link to that media appears on the Wall of all your fans.

If you throw an event (see Chapter 7 for details) and shoot photos or video at the event, upload the media to Facebook and tag the people who attended. You can share the photos with your fans, but also appear on the Wall of all your fans' friends, which gives you immediate credibility with those friends.

Adding photos

The Photos tab lets you upload photos for your Page. Use this tab to upload photos that you want to organize in albums to share with your fans.

Facebook allows you to upload an unlimited number of albums and up to 200 photos per album to your Facebook Page. You can reorder photos, rotate them, and acknowledge a Facebook member by *tagging* (identifying) them in the photo. We explain how to tag a photo later in this chapter.

To use the Photos tab to upload a photo, follow these steps:

1. **Click the Photos tab at the top of the page.**

2. **Click the Create a Photo Album button.**

   Facebook prompts you to select the images you want to upload and then allows you to name the album and enter the location of where they were taken, as shown in Figure 6-3.

   Use images and photos that communicate who you are and what your business is about, and that inject personality into your Page. Be sure you select photos you want potential customers to see — not the holiday party where everyone had a few too many cocktails!

3. **Click the Create Album button.**

   Here you can add a caption to the photo, tag other people in it, organize your album, change the album's details like the name and location, and delete the album altogether.

Figure 6-3: Creating a new photo album for a Page.

> **Upload Photos**
>
> Create your album while you wait.
>
> Name of album: Facebook Marketing Event
> Location:
> Quality: ⦿ Standard   ○ High Resolution (takes ~10x longer)
>
> [Create Album] [Cancel]

In the example in Figure 6-4, discount retailer Marshalls regularly posts photos on its Wall for the Tuesday Shoesday event. With a clever name and scheduled postings, Marshalls not only draws shoppers to its stores in the hope of finding that perfect pair of shoes, but it also encourages fans to post Tuesday Shoesday finds of their own which is a great Facebook Wall conversation starter!

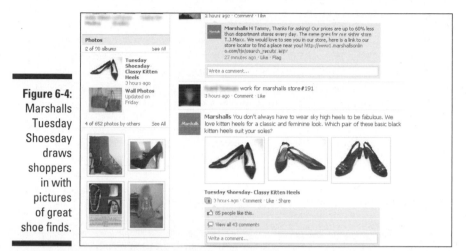

Figure 6-4:
Marshalls
Tuesday
Shoesday
draws
shoppers
in with
pictures
of great
shoe finds.

You can take a photo with a camera and immediately upload it to Facebook if you have that camera attached to your computer or a smartphone equipped with a camera. The first time you use your Webcam with Facebook, it asks you to give permission for Facebook.com to access your camera and microphone.

Adding videos

You can add a video to Facebook just as easily as you can add a photo (which we discuss in the preceding section). You can either upload or record a video. Adding videos is a great way to, for example, introduce yourself and your employees through short interviews or footage from your most recent company party or trade show. Again, be sure that anything shown on the video shows your company in a positive light!

You can add a video to your Wall by uploading one from your hard drive, a CD, or other storage device. All video must be less than 1,024MB and shorter than 20 minutes. You also need to agree to the Facebook Terms of Service, which stipulate that you made the videos you're placing on Facebook.

Recording a video requires that you have a Webcam attached to your computer or a smartphone from which to record and upload the video. Apple's Mac has a built-in Webcam — but don't despair if you don't have a Mac because you can easily connect a Webcam to your PC by using the provided cables.

To upload a video to your Page, follow these steps:

1. **Click the video camera icon underneath the status update box.**

   If you don't already have a Video tab visible on your Page, click the double-arrow sign (>>) at the right end of the tab bar, and then click Video in the list that appears.

2. **Click the Upload button and then browse your hard drive to find the video file that you want to upload.**

   While the file uploads, you can tag people as well as add a title and description.

3. **Click the Save Info button.**

   As the video uploads, you get a message that it's processing, and you're given the option to be notified when it's done. At this point, you can edit the info you entered, delete the video, or go back to the Video tab.

If you want to record your own video, you need a camera integrated into your computer system and a good microphone either in or attached to that computer. If your computer has what it takes, follow these steps:

1. **Click the Video tab.**

2. **Click the Record button.**

   A message box appears asking for you to give Facebook access to your camera and microphone.

3. **Click Allow and then click the Close button to close that window and access the camera window.**

4. **Press the Record button again to begin filming.**

   The Record button is red with a white dot and is right underneath your video screen.

5. **When you're finished, click the Stop button, which is the black button with the white square.**

6. **Click Save or Reset.**

   Clicking Save takes you to the screen where you can choose to edit settings, such as adding tags, a title, and description for your video as well as choosing a thumbnail that will represent the video on your Page.

7. **When you're finished editing the settings, click the Save button.**

   Your video is posted to your Page for all your fans to enjoy!

Adding a music player

If you're creating your Facebook Page to market a band, musician, or comedy act, you may want to add the Music Player tab, which lets your fans listen to your recorded MP3 tracks directly on your Page. (See Chapter 4 to find out how to add tabs and applications to your Page.) You can add as many tracks as you want — Facebook doesn't impose a limit. Keep in mind that the file size must be smaller than 15MB, and the track won't play automatically (the user must click the blue button with the arrow to play it).

Facebook allows you to display a maximum of six tabs on your Page, and you must add a track before the Music Player tab will show with the rest of your tabs.

Follow these steps to use the Music Player on your Page:

1. **Click the Edit Page link on the left side of your Page.**

2. **Select Applications from the menu on the left and click Go to Application under Music Player, as shown in Figure 6-5.**

   The Music Player application is at the top and is already installed on your Page, but you have to access it this way the first time you upload a track. After you add your first track, the tab shows up at the top and you can access it that way from then on.

3. **Click Add a Track.**

   You're presented with a box that lays out all the legal requirements for uploading music. Be sure to read through everything and know whether you're in compliance because you're asked for your electronic signature before you can proceed!

4. **Browse your hard drive to find the track you want.**

Figure 6-5:
To place music on your Page, go through the Music Player application.

5. **In the box that appears when the upload completes, enter the song's title, artist, and album.**

6. **(Optional) Add a link where your fans can buy this music.**

Now that you've uploaded your first track, you have a new Boxes tab on your Page. If you click that tab, you see your Music Player and the tracks you've uploaded.

Tagging for success

Tagging (identifying and labeling the name of) a fan in photos, videos, or notes directly links your Page to an individual Facebook user. If you throw an event (as described in Chapter 7) and shoot photos or video at the event, be sure to upload the media to Facebook and tag the people who attended. When you tag someone, the person who's tagged then receives an e-mail notification about it. By tagging, you not only share with your fans, but also appear on the Wall of all those fans' friends, which gives you immediate credibility with the friends of your fans. For more information on tagging within notes, see the "Using Notes for your message" section, earlier in this chapter.

To tag a friend or fan in a photo or video, display the photo or video and then follow these simple steps:

1. **Click the Tag This Photo (or Video) link below and to the right of the image.**

   The cursor turns into a plus sign (+).

2. **Click the face of the person you want to tag.**

   A pop-up menu displays a list of your friends, as shown in Figure 6-6.

3. **Select the name of the friend who appears in the picture or video, and then click the Tag button.**

Tagging has some limitations, however. Facebook allows you to tag only people you know. For people you know (such as your friends) or current customers who are engaged with you (such as your fans), tagging is a helpful way to recognize them. Be sure to take as many photos as possible at in-person events and shoot as many videos as you can so that you can post and tag them accordingly.

If you're tagging members who aren't Facebook friends, you can enter their e-mail addresses to send them e-mail notifications and links that give them access to the image in which they appear.

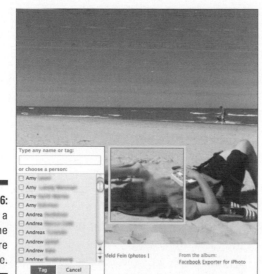

Figure 6-6:
Tagging a
photo on the
BeachStore
Page.

You can obtain a suitable photo to include on your Page by conducting a promotion to find the best new product or service idea or even the most creative use of your products. Then, take a photo of the winner with your company's CEO and tag the winner in the photo on Facebook. (To find out how to host your own Facebook promotion, see Chapter 7.)

When you tag a fan in a photo, that person can delete the photo from his profile by clicking the Remove Tag link next to the profile name.

Starting a Discussion

The Discussions tab lets you engage your fans to express their ideas, questions, and suggestions. Discussions let you know exactly what your fans and customers think and want from your company. Think of the Discussions tab as a community section.

All discussions on Facebook Groups and Pages are *public,* meaning that search engines, such as Google, can search them. Oddly enough, however, folks can't search for them in the Facebook search utility.

A discussion is broken into two parts: the topic and the post. The topic is limited to 120 characters, including spaces, and the post is limited only by your imagination, from a size perspective. Unlike the Notes feature, which is similar in look to the Discussions feature, you can't add a photo to a discussion. (For more about Notes, see the "Adding New Updates to Your Page" section, earlier in this chapter.)

To use the Discussions tab, follow these steps:

1. **Click the Discussions tab.**

   If the Discussions tab is not visible on your Page, click the plus sign to the right of the tabs and then click Discussions to add the tab.

2. **Click the Start New Topic button.**

3. **Type a title for the topic and the content of the post, as shown in Figure 6-7.**

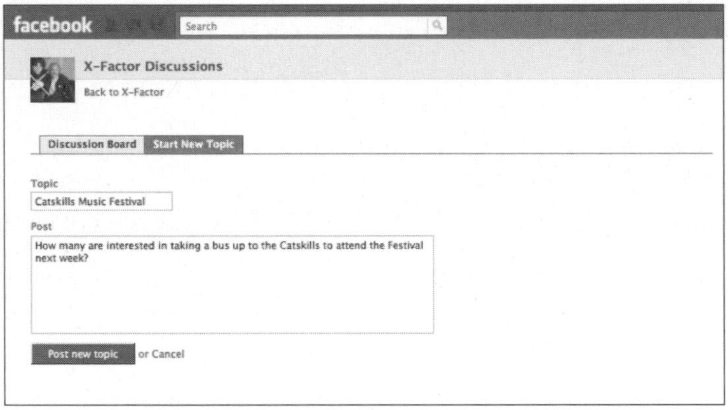

Figure 6-7:
Starting a new discussion topic.

Keep your discussion short and to the point. Use a provocative title, provide some content that helps explain your position on the topic, and then watch what happens. Be sure to monitor the conversation at least daily and respond to as many comments as you can.

4. **Click the Post New Topic button.**

Because discussions can grow to contain many topics, Facebook provides you with a topic view so you can see the entire discussion. Find the topic you want, and then click the topic name to see the complete topic view and reply to any comments.

Dell Computers has a Social Media for Small Business — Powered by Dell Page that puts the discussion board idea to good use. The Dell discussion board (as shown in Figure 6-8) features more than 70 topics, varying from discussions about home-based businesses to how to get more fans to your Page.

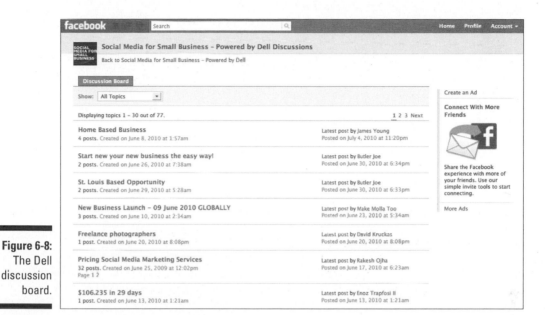

Figure 6-8:
The Dell
discussion
board.

Sharing Your Page

The Share button, which appears at the bottom of the left column on any Page, lets you invite Facebook friends or a list of Facebook friends to check out your Page. Additionally, you can input e-mail addresses of folks who may not be on Facebook so that they receive an e-mail invitation to view your Page with a link they can click to view your Page.

Suggesting a Page to your friends

People you have recently become friends with you on Facebook may not know you have a Page set up specifically for your business. Facebook makes it easy for you to let them in on the good news.

To do so, follow these steps:

1. **Choose the Suggest to Friends link underneath your photo on the left side of your Page.**

   The Suggest to Friends dialog box appears, as shown in Figure 6-9.

2. **Either scroll through your friend's pictures and click those you want to invite or type their names in the Find Friends box at the top to find a specific friend quickly.**

   You can add a personalized message here as well.

Figure 6-9:
Sharing
your Page
with a
friend.

3. **Click the Send Invitations button at the bottom of the dialog box.**

   The Your Invitations Have Been Sent dialog box appears letting you know your request was sent successfully. Now get ready for all your new likes to come rolling in!

Any recipients who aren't already Facebook members need to join Facebook first to be able to like or comment on your Page.

Promoting a Page via your profile

The Share button, which appears at the bottom of the left column on your Page, lets you post any Page (even if you haven't created it) to your personal profile to let all your Facebook friends know about it, and you can express how you feel about that Page by adding a personal message. If your target customers are businesses, for example, what better way to showcase your work than by promoting the Facebook profiles of the businesses you have worked with. Take it a step further and add a message, such as

> I had the pleasure of working with ABC Company on the corporate photography for their XYZ product — what a great, knowledgeable bunch!

Follow these steps to post a Page to your profile:

1. **Click the Share button at the bottom of the Page.**

   The Post to Profile dialog box appears, as shown in Figure 6-10.

2. **Input a message about the Page.**

   Your message can be up to 827 characters in length.

3. **Click the Share button.**

Figure 6-10:
Posting a
Page to your
personal
profile.

Making Your Page Easier to Find

Anyone, whether a Facebook member or not, can access your Facebook Page. People can find your Page by using Facebook's internal search, as well as search engines, such as Google and Microsoft's Bing. But what you might not know is that a Facebook Page can actually improve your search engine rankings, so people can more easily find both your Facebook Page and your Web site.

By publishing a steady stream of links to your company's blog posts and other pages of your company's Web site within Facebook, you allow search engines to more easily find you, which is also known as *search engine optimization (SEO)*. Simply by having a Facebook Page, you increase the number of relevant links into your site and therefore your site's SEO. But you can do a whole lot more than just add a bunch of keywords to make your Page easier to find.

All Facebook Pages are public, and therefore, search engines like Google can index them. So viewers outside Facebook can provide additional traffic to your Page. Make sure that these new visitors land on a landing page within your Facebook Page (as described in Chapter 4) to ensure that they get the pertinent information about your business right off the bat. This is the time to catch their interest! Build a positive image for your brand and engage readers so that they engage with you and return often.

Be sure that your Page contains many uses of the keywords that can best help you appear in the search engines. For example, if you're a professional photographer, make sure you use keywords like *wedding photography* or *photography in Atlanta* to help capture the people who are specifically in the market for your services. Some good places to use these keywords are in your Info tab as well as in any notes you post. Also, be sure that you provide all the necessary contact information, such as directions to your offices, as well as your company's Web site and blog addresses. If people who haven't joined Facebook find you through a search engine listing for your Facebook Page, make it easy for them to contact you without having to join Facebook first.

Chapter 7

Setting Up Groups, Promotions, and Events

So, you've created a Facebook Page to promote your company (see Chapter 4) and developed a content strategy (see Chapter 5) to keep a steady stream of information flowing. Now you need to give people a reason to visit your Page. What can you do to cut through the clutter and attract a Facebook fan base? Increasingly, marketers turn to creating their own Facebook Groups, as well as hosting promotions and events for the answer.

This chapter discusses how you can use groups, promotions, and events to motivate and grow your audience by promoting brand awareness and building community. We show you how to create your own group on a topic that engages potential business clients, and how to promote the group to attract members and prospective customers. Plus, we show you how to launch a promotion on Facebook. Finally, we discuss creating an event, promoting it to your fans, listing it, managing it, and following up afterward.

Discovering Facebook Groups

A great option for marketing your business on Facebook is Facebook Groups. With *Facebook Groups,* you can join and create up to 300 groups that can be based around shared interests, activities, or anything you like. Groups are different from Pages or profiles because they're less about the business or person, and more about a shared interest or cause. Groups can be a more personal option for marketing your business because you relate to an audience around a cause or local issue that your business cares about; therefore, people are more inclined to get involved.

You might have several reasons why you want to join a Facebook group to help promote your business; conversely, you might even want to have your own Facebook group as a standalone to discuss a topic outside your business interests or to coexist with a Facebook Page for your business. For example, Figure 7-1 shows the Facebook Marketing group, which was created to give marketing professionals a place to share ideas on how to utilize Facebook as a marketing medium. This is a great group to join to meet fellow business owners and marketing professionals, gain more insight into Facebook marketing, and trade tips for marketing success.

Figure 7-1:
A Facebook group provides members with an online hub to share opinions about a topic.

A good place to start marketing your business is with a Page, but a more advanced marketing tactic may be to start, join, and be active in groups that match your business in some way.

The following sections go into more detail about the differences between Groups and Pages as well as how to find, join, and participate in groups to help market your business. (For the lowdown on starting a group, check out the section "Creating Your Own Facebook Group," later in this chapter.)

Distinguishing Facebook Groups from Pages

For a Facebook Page, only an official representative of a business, public figure, nonprofit organization, artist, or public personality can create a Page and serve as its administrator (admin). Pages are designed to provide basic information about a business, feature community-building blocks (such as discussions and comments), upload user-generated content, and post reviews.

By contrast, any Facebook member can create a Facebook group about any topic. Groups serve as a central hub for members to share opinions and discussions about a topic.

When an admin updates a group's page, the News Feed story includes the name of the group's admin. Pages, however, attribute updates to the Page and never reveal the admin's name. Groups even allow you to post updates via the status update box. Just like with Pages, you can post links, videos, and photos and even set up an event directly from the status update box.

The following are some key differences between Facebook Groups and Facebook Pages:

- **Groups make it easier to recruit Facebook members.** Group admins can send messages to all group members' individual Inboxes, provided the group has fewer than 5,000 members. Page admins, however, can't send messages to all fans. With Groups, you can send invites quickly and easily to all your Facebook friends requesting they join your group or attend an event. The messages appear in the members' Inboxes.

- **As the admin of a Facebook group, you can dictate how open you want your group's membership to be.** Group admins can restrict membership access by requiring a member approval process, whereas Pages can only restrict members from becoming a fan based on age and location requirements. You can make your group open to *all* Facebook members; *closed* so that only Facebook members approved by the group's admin can see it; or *secret* so that it's invitation-only and not visible in a Facebook Groups search.

- **You can't add apps to a group like you can to a Page.** Whereas Pages allows for a high degree of interaction and rich media with the addition of applications (apps), Facebook Groups doesn't allow for the addition of apps. You're less able to take advantage of some of the more interactive features of a Facebook Page.

- **Your friends can easily send an invite to all their friends to join your group simply by clicking the Invite People to Join link underneath the group's picture on the left side.** This lets you invite your existing friends by clicking their pictures as well as invite people via an e-mail message.

You might want to consider a Facebook group if you want to have a serious discussion — perhaps around a cause or a topical media issue that you want to enlist support on — that members can really get involved in. For example, you may choose to start a group if you have strong feelings and opinions regarding Facebook privacy issues and any changes, and you want to have an ongoing discussion with fellow marketers on the topic.

The key is to keep the discussion flowing with the group members. You might be better off joining a few groups to see how it's done before jumping in to create your own. In the next section, we discuss how to find groups that might be relevant to your business.

Finding a group

Finding a group isn't difficult; just follow these steps to use the search box to find a group:

1. **In the search box at the top of your screen, type a name or title that interests you and then click See More Results For at the bottom of the list.**

   For example, if your business designs custom t-shirts, you can search for a group related to fashion. Use the search terms *fashion, designer clothes, haute couture,* or *trends* to yield some groups that you might want to join and be part of.

2. **Click the Groups tab on the left side of the search results page so that you look only at groups.**

   For example, the typical Facebook search for *t-shirt* displays the results shown in Figure 7-2.

Figure 7-2:
Results of
a search
for t-shirt
groups.

3. **Search the results until you find a group you want to visit, and then click either the image or the group name's link.**

   In the search results, be sure to note the number of members, the type of group, and any recent activity so that you have some indication of how active the group is.

When the group's landing page opens, note at the top of the page any recent activity posted by the group admin on their Wall. Also, look for dates of any photos or videos that have been uploaded as well as any recent discussions on the Discussions tab. At this point, you may decide you want to return to the search results page and browse any related groups or try your search with a different search term.

The most important part of the group are the Wall and the Discussions tab. These are really where the action is. But you need to join the group to get a sense of how active that group is and whether you want to contribute. See the section "Joining a group," later in this chapter, for details on joining a group (makes sense, right?).

If you find a group that matches with your business and are thinking about reaching out to its members in an attempt to sponsor the group, don't. That's a good thought, but that option no longer exists. Facebook did away with sponsored groups in favor of targeted ads (see Chapter 10).

Joining a group

After you identify a group that matches your interest and has an activity level that matches your objectives, join the group and interact with the other members.

All you need to do is navigate to the group's page you wish to join and click the Join button next to the group name at the top, as shown in Figure 7-3. (See the "Using the Facebook search box" section, earlier in this chapter, for the low-down on finding a group.) Keep in mind that you can join up to 300 groups.

Click to join

Figure 7-3: Joining the Facebook Marketing group.

Accessing groups you've joined

After you join groups, you want quick access to them. To do so, open your News Feed page and then follow these steps:

1. **To access groups that you've already joined, click the See All link in the center of the menu on the left side.**

   This takes you to the Groups page (see Figure 7-4) where you have access to all the groups you've joined.

2. **Click the group's name link to access that group's page.**

Figure 7-4: Access the groups you've already joined.

Participating in a group

One of the Golden Rules of social networks and other forms of social media is to spend some time observing and listening to the conversation. Get a feeling for the rhythm of the group's conversations before you barge in and change things.

You'll find that only a portion of the group actively participates; many members just lurk in the background. That's okay, and don't let that discourage you from participating. If you truly want to know more about groups, take the first step and jump into the conversation. That really is the best way to figure out how social networks operate.

A good place to start is to find a discussion topic that you happen to know a lot about and offer answers to any questions other conversation participants may ask. This is not only an easy, casual way to get started in group participation, but it also goes a long way to establishing yourself as an expert on the subject. Mention that you own a business that's related to the topic at hand to help cement the fact that you actually do know what you're talking about. Do not, however, try to sell your goods and services directly. Nobody appreciates a hard sell in this arena, and you may even be labeled as a spammer.

 You might find that in some of the larger groups, people try to hijack the conversation by posting links to their own groups or related Web sites. Don't try this tactic. Technically, this is spam, and Facebook members have a very low tolerance for spammers. Any member who's considered a spammer can and will have his profile shut down by Facebook. Although the rules on spamming aren't published anywhere on the site, it's widely considered taboo by the members of the group, the group admin, and of course, Facebook.

Creating Your Own Facebook Group

When you get the hang of how a group works, you might want to start your own group to support your business. Creating a group is actually quite simple, and a group contains elements that are similar to those on a Facebook Page.

Securing your group's name

Before jumping in and creating your group, search for the name of the group you want to start so you can see whether any existing groups or Pages have that same name. (See the earlier section "Using the Facebook search box," in this chapter, for details.) Having a name that's never been used on Facebook isn't required, but a unique name helps you distinguish yourself. Also, Facebook doesn't let you own a name in the same way as when you reserve a Web site address (URL). Other people can use a name that's similar to or even identical with other names on Facebook.

Setting up your group

After you choose a group name that you want to use, create your group:

1. **Click the Create Group tab in the navigation bar on the left.**

   The Create Group dialog box appears, as shown in Figure 7-5.

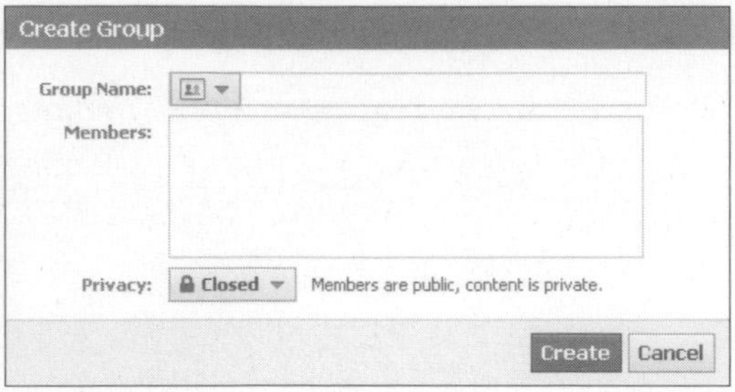

Create Group

Group Name:	[⊞] ▼
Members:	
Privacy:	🔒 Closed ▼ Members are public, content is private.

Create   Cancel

Figure 7-5:
The Create
Group
dialog box.

2. **Provide the following basic information about your group:**

   • *Group Name:* Because you did the research in the earlier section, "Securing your group's name," go ahead and plug in the name you chose.

   • *Group Icon:* These optional icons are found in the drop-down list next to the group name and can help specify the type of group you have. For example, if you had an animal-related group, you may want to select the paw print or the dog bone icon.

   • *Members:* Here is where you invite your friends to become members of your group. Just start typing a name into the box, and Facebook brings up your friend's name that matches.

   • *Privacy:* Your group can be Open, Closed, or Hidden. Open groups can be found by anyone on Facebook when doing a search. Anyone can join the group and anyone can see the Wall, discussion board, videos, and photos in it. Closed groups require approval by the group admin to join them. Anyone can see the basic group description information, but only members can see the Wall, discussion board, videos, and photos in it. And secret groups can't be found by using a search or even in member profiles; they truly are secret. Membership is by invitation only; therefore, only members can see the Wall, discussion board, videos, and photos in it.

   Facebook no longer allows you to set settings to control who posts what on your group's Wall. All members can post comments, photos, videos, links, and events as well as create documents, which is essentially a group's version of creating a note. Keep this in mind when setting your privacy levels.

   Depending on your need or the development of your group, you might want to keep the group closed until you're fully ready to launch.

3. **Click the Create button.**

   Congratulations! You've created your first group! The last step you need to take before posting content to your group's Wall is to set up your group's custom e-mail address. Any messages sent to this address are sent to the entire group.

To set up the e-mail address:

1. **Click the Edit Group button on the top-right side of the page.**

   You may recognize that this is the basic information you provided earlier, but this time you can set up a group e-mail address.

2. **Click the Set Up Group Email button.**

   Here you can choose a personalized e-mail address. All group e-mail address end in `@groups.facebook.com`. For example, if your group name is East Coast T-Shirt Designers, you want a similar e-mail address, so maybe you'd choose `ECShirtDesigners@groups.facebook.com`. Note that you only have 50 characters to work with, so choose wisely.

3. **After choose an address, click the Create Email button.**

   You return to the Basic Information page.

4. **Click the Save Changes button to finish.**

Deleting a group

Removing or deleting a Facebook group is relatively easy. To do so:

1. **Click the Edit Group button on the top right of your group's main page.**

2. **Click the Members tab on the left menu.**

3. **Click the X button next to the name of all the members you want to delete, including yourself.**

   You receive warning box that reads: `Are you sure you want to leave this group? Since you are the last member, leaving now will also delete this group.`

4. **Click the Delete Group button.**

Facebook runs a periodic sweep of groups aimed to remove empty groups, so it takes care of deleting the group a short time after you remove the members and admin(s).

Creating a Facebook Promotion

Promotions, sometimes referred to as contests, and giveaways have traditionally played a vital role in consumer marketing. From cereal companies to fashion retailers, to automobile dealers, and so on, the promise of winning something of value for free is a tremendous lure. Whether backed by a media campaign, promoted on a product's packaging, or announced at an employee sales meeting, promotions have the power to motivate and drive engagement.

And the same incentives that served marketers before Facebook, such as raffles and drawings, still apply on Facebook. Promotions with high-value prizes tend to be more active. Celebrity appeal and limited edition offerings always help, too. But if you don't have access to costly prizes, you can still offer an appropriate reward (we've filled out a form for the chance to win a t-shirt, but only if it's really cool).

The best part about marketing on Facebook is that you don't have to be a major brand to host a successful promotion (although it doesn't hurt). And you don't have to have a boatload of money to pull off a successful promotion (although that doesn't hurt, either). Anyone with a Facebook Page can create and promote a promotion. Although Facebook doesn't offer a promotion application, you can check out some of the third-party promotion applications (apps) to find a solution that works best for your promotion. You can either search Facebook's own app directory for *promotions,* which turns up results like the Sweepstakes app, or you can do an Internet search for *promotion applications that integrate with Facebook.*

Understanding Facebook rules for promotions

The Facebook Promotions Guidelines page spells out the rules surrounding the use of promotions within the Facebook Platform. In an effort to eliminate spam from promotions, the guidelines serve to protect the user's profile data from being used by brands for their own benefit. Facebook also limits the way companies can use the Facebook brand name and logo in association with the promotion.

If you employ promotions and promotions on your Facebook Page regularly, it's a good idea to stay up-to-date with Facebook's guidelines. You can find the most updated guidelines at www.facebook.com/promotions_guidelines.php.

There are some things to keep in mind when running a promotion and using Facebook's name in it. You have to use special wording that you can find at the link provided in the preceding paragraph. Facebook clearly states that you must include the exact wording right next to any place on your promotion entry form where personal information is requested. You must tell the entrant exactly how her personal information will be used; for example, that you're collecting her e-mail address for marketing purposes. Finally, the person entering your promotion must know that the promotion isn't run or endorsed by Facebook.

Facebook marketers can no longer do the following:

✔ Have photo promotions that require entrants to make changes to their profile in any way, such as upload a photo

✔ Have status update promotions that require posting status updates for entry

✔ Automatically enter people in a promotion after they become a fan

Another recent change that has marketers up in arms is that Facebook must approve all promotions. In other words, to run any promotion on the Facebook Platform (and they all have to be on the Facebook Platform), you must have written approval directly from Facebook. How do you go about getting that, you ask? Through an account representative. If you've already been in contact with a representative for another reason, you can utilize that person to get started. If not, you must use their provided contact form found at www.facebook.com/business/contact.php to get the process started.

After you're established with a Facebook representative, that person ensures that your company creates promotions on the Facebook Platform and through a certified application. Some examples of popular apps are Promotion Builder by Wildfire Interactive (www.wildfireapp.com), Fan Appz (http://fanappz.com), and Vitrue (http://vitrue.com/apps). We discuss all three of these in more detail later in this section. To get started with any of these, all you have to do is head on over to their Web sites and sign up.

Of course, you can always link from your Facebook Page to a promotion that is hosted on your own Web site, outside the Facebook guidelines. However, you still need to be mindful of how you use the Facebook name, and it's probably best not to use the Facebook name at all in association with your promotion if not on Facebook.

Setting up a promotion

Facebook offers a compelling environment from which to host a promotion or giveaway on your Page. You can use your Page as a starting point with a link to your Web site for promotion entry details or have the entire promotion contained within the Facebook community.

Promotions can be very creative and challenging, or can simply require a simple yes/no answer. They can motivate users to upload a video or simply complete a contact form. Some promotions require a panel of esteemed judges to determine the winner; others select winners randomly. Still other promotions allow the users to vote for the outcome.

Although promotions are as unique as the companies that host them, we offer some tips that can improve your chances of success. Following are some best practices for creating Facebook promotions and giveaways:

✔ **Offer an attractive prize.** The more attractive the prize, the more response you'll get. A box of Cracker Jacks isn't going to garner much interest. For a prize to be attractive, though, it doesn't necessarily have to cost a lot. The best prizes tend to be those that money can't buy, such as a chance to meet a celebrity, to participate in a TV commercial, or to attend a product's prerelease party. There's no better way to get people to try your products or services than by offering them as prizes, too.

✔ **Use your existing customers and contacts to start the ball rolling.** Getting those initial entries is always the toughest part of running a Facebook promotion. This is when you need to reach into your network of family and friends. Reach out to your mailing list of customers with a friendly invitation. Promote the promotion on Twitter, LinkedIn, MySpace, and of course, your Facebook Page. Wherever you have contacts, use whatever social network, e-mail exchange, or instant messenger you have to get them to participate.

✔ **Cross-promote via your Web site.** You need to promote your Facebook promotion across all your channels to gain maximum participation. That includes your Web site. Adding a promotional banner with a link to your Facebook Page is a good start. But you can do so much more to promote your promotion. For example, issue a press release via one of the many news wire services. Add a message to your phone answering system. The possibilities are endless.

✔ **Keep the promotion simple.** This goes for all aspects of a promotion: Don't overcomplicate the rules. The fewer the questions on a form, the higher the rate of completion. Keep first prize a single, valuable item and then have several smaller second-place prizes. And remember, the fewer the clicks to enter the promotion, the better.

✔ **Don't set the bar too high.** If you ask the participants for an original creation, keep the requirements to a minimum. For example, don't place a minimum word count on an essay promotion. Or don't require a video for the first round of submissions because videos are a lot of work.

✔ **Run promotions for at least one month.** Things like word-of-mouth marketing require time. The more time you promote the promotion, the more entries you get. The more you build up the excitement by keeping the promotion in front of your fans, the more often they take note of it and look forward to the big day when the winner is announced.

✔ **Integrate your promotion with a media campaign.** Facebook ads are an ideal complement to any promotion. By combining a Facebook ad campaign with a promotion, you maximize the viral effect and amplify the number of engagements. (See Chapter 10 for more on Facebook advertising.)

✔ **Make your promotion fun, interesting, and uniquely you.** The main thing to keep in mind when planning a Facebook promotion is that members want to be entertained. Promotions should offer an outlet to self-expression, engage members, encourage them to share with friends, and communicate something unique about your brand.

Using third-party promotion apps

Although Facebook doesn't offer a promotion application, several third-party promotion applications are available. Some are free, and some cost money to power more sophisticated promotions and sweepstakes.

Promotion Builder by Wildfire Interactive is a Facebook promotion app available for less than a dollar per day; it provides a direct solution for marketers looking to offer a promotion or giveaway on their Facebook Page. This is another way that viral marketing comes into play. When a fan enters your promotion, she's given the opportunity to share the promotion with her friends, potentially bringing in even more fans and promotion entries. The app provides everything you need to create and host a promotion on your Facebook Page (see Figure 7-6). Head to its Web site at `http://wildfireapp.com` to find out more and sign up.

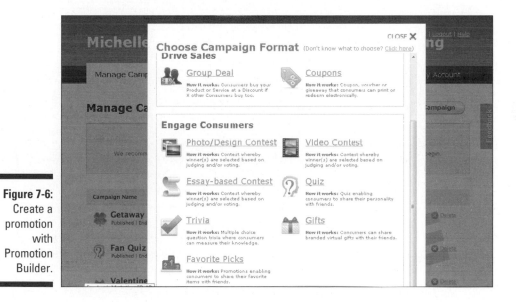

Figure 7-6: Create a promotion with Promotion Builder.

Another option when you're searching for a promotion app for your Page is Fan Appz (`http://fanappz.com`). In addition to being able to run promotions, you can also create quizzes and polls that can then be posted on your fan's Wall so their all their friends can see . . . and possibly take your quiz (or poll), too. What a great way to drive traffic to your Page! Finally, there's Vitrue (`http://vitrue.com/apps`). Its suite of applications offers options for promotions but also other apps for fan engagement. It's like a one-stop shop for all your Facebook marketing needs.

Hosting a Facebook Event

Facebook Events is a great way to get people together virtually or in person to support your business, brand, or product. Events is also an economical way of getting the word out beyond your normal in-house marketing list by inviting fans of your Facebook Page or members of your Facebook group. Fans can also help you promote your Facebook event by sharing the event with a group of their friends when it's valuable.

When you create a Facebook event, it lives on forever, long after the actual physical (or online) event ends. Facebook Events allows you to stay in touch with those who attended, and even the ones who didn't, by posting a steady stream of photos, videos, and updates recapping the event. By encouraging attendees to post their own pictures, videos, and comments, you make it a much more interactive and richer experience for all those on your guest list.

Creating an event

Facebook Events helps you with the fine points of creating and throwing your own event. Generally, Pages should list any event you'd normally post to your business Web site. If it's good enough for your corporate Web site, post it to Facebook. First, decide what the purpose of your event should be. A good place to start is with networking events to get people introduced and interacting with each other outside the Facebook world. After you establish yourself as a great business event creator, you can branch out to other marketing-related events like a new product or service launch party or a welcome gathering if you've hired new employees to your sales team. This serves the double purpose of promoting your brand and giving these new employees a chance to network with current and potential customers.

After you create an event a time or two, you can create events quickly and easily. If you want to throw an event for your Page, go to your Page and then follow these steps to create the event:

1. **Click the Events tab on your Page.**

   If this is your first event, you may need to click the + sign to access the Events tab.

2. **Click the Create Event button in the upper-right corner to display the Create an Event page.**

   The Create an Event page appears, as shown in Figure 7-7.

3. **Fill in the following details about your event:**

   • *When:* The date and time of the event

   • *What Are You Planning:* The purpose or reason for the event

   • *Where:* Where the event will be held

   • *More Info:* Any additional details you want to provide

   Use as many rich keywords in the What Are You Planning and More Info boxes because Facebook events are indexed by search engines, which could mean extra traffic for your event.

4. **Click the Select Guests button to invite guests to your event.**

   Inviting friends to the event isn't mandatory; you can simply publish your event and hope for the best. However, Facebook makes inviting friends to your event so easy that it's hard not to. Plus, it's a good idea to get the ball rolling because you're holding an event to promote your business in some way. So why would you not invite people to get the word out to promote your event?

5. **In the Select Guests dialog box that appears, as shown in Figure 7-8, invite friends in any of the following ways:**

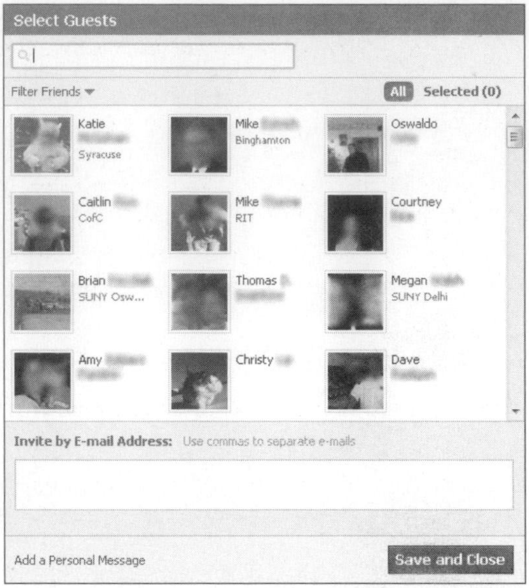

Select Guests

Filter Friends ▼		**All** Selected (0)
Katie Syracuse	Mike Binghamton	Oswaldo
Caitlin CofC	Mike RIT	Courtney
Brian SUNY Osw...	Thomas D.	Megan SUNY Delhi
Amy	Christy	Dave

Invite by E-mail Address: Use commas to separate e-mails

Add a Personal Message   **Save and Close**

Figure 7-8:
Sending
your first
batch of
invites.

- Select friends directly from the filter list.

- Search for friends with the search box on top of the list.

- Invite an entire Friends List you created. (See Chapter 2 for a full discussion of creating a Friends List.)

- Invite non-Facebook members to the event by typing their e-mail addresses (separated by commas) into the Invite by E-Mail Address box.

- After your event posts to your Page's Wall, your fans can sign up right then and there.

Inviting non-Facebook members to an event means they need to register with Facebook before responding to your request, so be judicious about using this option. If you think some non-Facebook users that you have invited will be hesitant to sign up for an account just for this purpose, make sure to include an alternate way for them to contact you to RSVP.

After you publish your event, it appears on both the Wall and the Events tab of your Page. You can also invite all your fans by clicking the Update Fans of *[Your Page Name]* link under your events name on its page. You're given the option to send the update to all fans or to target the update to only select fans based on demographics. To do this, click the Target This Update box. Doing so expands your options, so you can target by city or state, or leave it at the Everywhere option, which is the default. Here you can also target either men or women (the default is Both), and by age. This is a good way to narrow down the selected invitees in case, for example, this is an adults-only event where alcohol will be served.

6. **After you select your list of invitees, click the Add a Personal Message link to add a quick message to the invitee and then click the Save and Close button.**

   In the Add a Personal Message box, provide something compelling for the reader and make sure the value that invitees can derive by coming to your event is front and center in your message. You can invite your first 100 people with this invite method.

   Facebook allows you to invite an unlimited number of attendees to an event in increments of 100, with no more than 300 outstanding invitations at a time.

   After you click Save and Close, you return to the Create an Event page.

7. **On the Create an Event page, select or deselect the remaining two options:**

   - *Show the Guest List on the Event Page:* Allows the guest list to be seen. By selecting this check box, your guest list is visible on the event's page.

   - *Non-Admins Can Write on the Wall:* Allows invitees to write on the Wall. By selecting this check box, your guests can add their own content on the Wall.

   Next, you want to liven up your event's page with an image that can get some attention. If no image is chosen, a question mark displays.

8. **Click the Add Event Photo button on the left side of the Create an Event page.**

   The Add Event Photo dialog box opens, as shown in Figure 7-9.

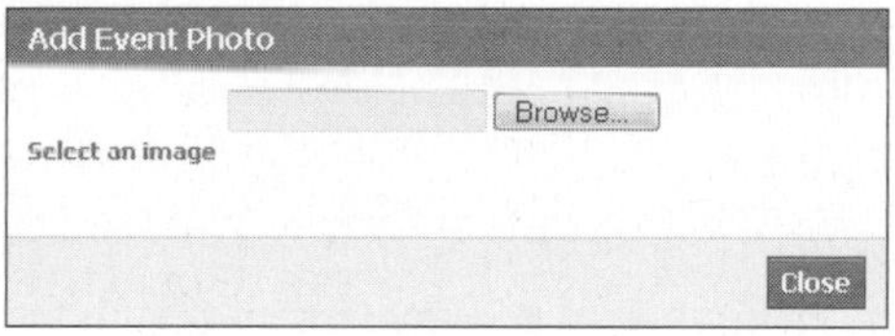

Figure 7-9:
Uploading a
picture for
your event.

> Add Event Photo
>
> Select an image [   ] [Browse...]
>
> [Close]

9. **Click the Browse button to search your computer for a graphic file, select the picture that you want to use, and click the Close button.**

   Add a photo that best describes your event. Logos can be boring, so take the time to find an image that visually represents your event in a way that makes people want to attend.

   With all images on Facebook, be sure you have the right to distribute the image. The Internet offers plenty of sources for royalty-free images, such as iStockphoto (www.istockphoto.com), so be sure to use one if you don't have a proprietary image from your business.

You're taken to the event page where you or your fans can dress up the event even more by adding comments photos, videos, and links to the event's status update box.

10. **After you enter all the pertinent details about your event, click the Create Event button.**

Your event appears on your Wall.

Editing your event

Making changes to your event's page is easy. Simply click the event's name then click the Edit Event link found under the event's name. You can change nearly everything about the event, including the location. You can also notify everyone of any changes by posting a message on your Wall or by sending them a message via the Update Fans of *[Your Page Name]* link at the top of the event page.

Following up after an event

Wise marketers use Facebook Events after the event occurs to build a post-event community and extend the value of that event. If you had a very healthy debate with lots of questions, you could post a transcript in your Notes section for attendees or even non-attendees. If some questions weren't answered because of time constraints, you could write the answers and send them to the attendees, too.

At the very least, a short thank you note either via e-mail or Facebook mail to those that attended is just good form. As well, sending a sorry you couldn't make it note to those that didn't attend, perhaps with a recap, is also good form. Taking several photos of the event and posting them is the single best way to reach out. By taking photos, tagging them with the attendee's name(s), and posting them, you can leverage the viral power of the Facebook Platform. (See Chapter 6 for the lowdown on adding and tagging photos.)

Chapter 8

Cross-Promoting Your Page

In This Chapter

▶ Working Facebook into your marketing plans

▶ Using other online communication to drive fans to your Facebook Page

▶ Promoting your Facebook Page via offline marketing

▶ Making your Facebook Page search engine–friendly

*T*he best kind of Facebook promotion takes advantage of existing marketing activities to cross-promote your Facebook Page. Keep in mind that visitors from your Web site and other sources are just as valuable as working directly in Facebook when it comes to building your fan base. Driving users to your Facebook Page from other marketing vehicles allows you to take advantage of the Facebook Platform, which provides an ideal environment for building relationships with your customers and prospects.

Many marketers drive visitors from their Web sites to their Facebook Pages so that those marketers can take advantage of Facebook's ability to create an instant community around their brand with virtually no infrastructure cost. Cross-promoting your Facebook Page via your company Web site also helps improve your *search engine optimization* (which affects the ranking of your site in search engines). By creating more relevant links from your Facebook Page to your Web site, you allow users to find both more easily if they use search engines.

In this chapter, we cover the tactics that you can use to promote your Facebook Page outside of Facebook. Consider how best to integrate your Facebook Page into your existing marketing programs. We examine how companies are adding Facebook to their e-mail marketing campaigns, Web sites, and blogs; we also discuss search engine marketing tricks and tips.

Making Facebook Part of Your Marketing Mix

After you set up your Facebook Page, you need to start promoting it to your existing customers so that you can build your Facebook fan community. For marketing purposes, Facebook lets you create a network that you can leverage when you have something to share. You can create brand awareness for your business by sharing or publishing a steady stream of informative, relevant, and engaging content that keeps your fans coming back, which can eventually lead to future sales.

Encourage your customers to interact with and like your Facebook Page. When a user *likes,* or becomes a fan of, your Facebook Page, she opts-in to receive information about your business, sort of like if she asks to be included in your e-mail list. Additionally, the more fans who interact with your Page, the more stories your Page generates and distributes to your fans' News Feeds, which their friends see on their own News Feeds, resulting in a viral effect.

The following sections give you the lowdown on how to get started cross-promoting your Page.

Choosing your own Facebook username

Before you go about promoting the very long and abstract URL that Facebook has assigned to your Page, consider creating a custom name — *username* — for your Page. This name appears after `www.facebook.com/` when someone views your Page. For example, the username for Dell Computer's Page is simply `dell`:

```
www.facebook.com/dell
```

Originally, Facebook required a Page to have more than 1,000 *fans,* or people who like the Page, to qualify for a custom username or vanity URL, but now that Facebook has dropped the fan count to 25, most Page owners can obtain a username. Your fans can remember and find your Page faster if you have a custom address, and that address allows you to more easily market a memorable Facebook name offline.

You must have registered to have a username for your profile before getting one for your business Page. You do so simply by visiting the Username page described in the following steps.

Follow these steps to claim your own Facebook username for your Page:

1. **Log into Facebook and go to the Username page at `www.facebook.com/username`.**

   A page similar to Figure 8-1 appears.

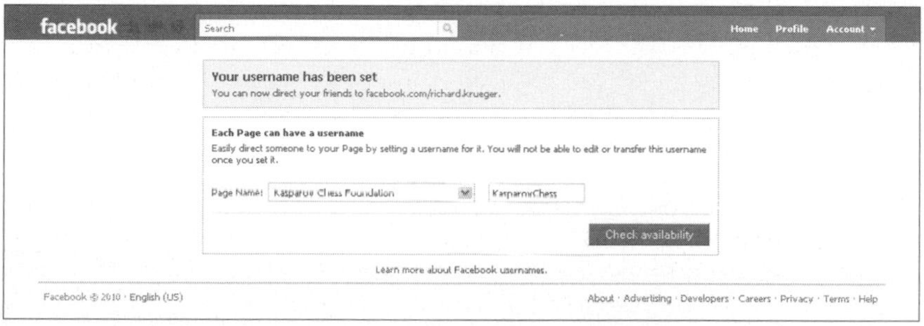

Figure 8-1:
Setting a
vanity URL
for your
Facebook
Page.

2. **Click Set a Username for Your Pages.**

3. **From the Page Name drop-down list, select the Page (if you're an admin for multiple Pages) for which you want to create a username.**

4. **In the empty text box to the right of the Page Name, enter a username that makes sense for your brand and to your fans, and then click the Check Availability button.**

   Choose your name carefully. After you choose a customized username for your Facebook Page, you can't change it under any circumstances. If you make a mistake in choosing your name, you can't delete your Page and start over — so make sure you choose a name that best describes your business or organization. The best option is, of course, the name of your business, but if that's not available, consider trying an industry-related keyword.

   Facebook may take some time checking the availability of the name.

5. **If you see a message that your name is available, as shown in Figure 8-2, click the Confirm button to claim that name.**

   If you don't qualify, you haven't obtained the minimum number of fans (25), you've already registered this Page for a username, or someone else has already taken your name.

   If you did everything right, you see a Success dialog box, similar to the one shown in Figure 8-3. Now, you can let the world know about your Facebook Page URL, as described in the next section.

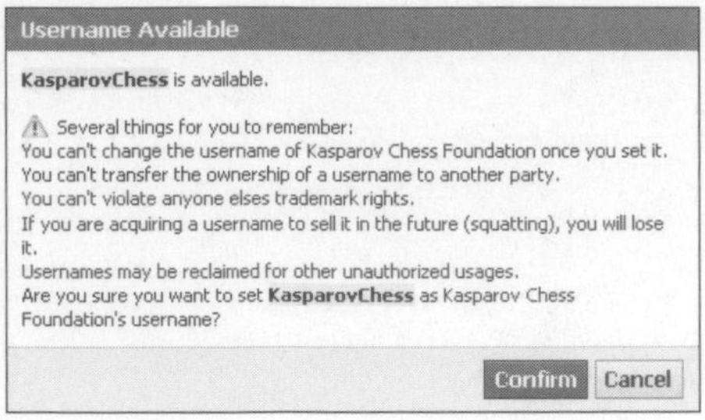

Figure 8-2:
Getting
confirmation
on a
username
for your
Facebook
Page.

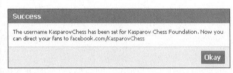

Username Available

KasparovChess is available.

⚠ Several things for you to remember:
You can't change the username of Kasparov Chess Foundation once you set it.
You can't transfer the ownership of a username to another party.
You can't violate anyone elses trademark rights.
If you are acquiring a username to sell it in the future (squatting), you will lose it.
Usernames may be reclaimed for other unauthorized usages.
Are you sure you want to set **KasparovChess** as Kasparov Chess Foundation's username?

[Confirm] [Cancel]

Figure 8-3:
You
successfully
registered
your
username.

Success

The username KasparovChess has been set for Kasparov Chess Foundation. Now you can direct your fans to facebook.com/KasparovChess

[Okay]

Cross-promoting your Page

Your Facebook URL, or Web address, is a new touch point for your customers. But if no one knows where to find you on Facebook, your Facebook marketing efforts can't help your business. That's why you need to plaster your Facebook URL everywhere, online and off: on your Web site, on your printed marketing materials, in your store window, on your drum set (if you're a musician) — basically, wherever people look, you should promote your Facebook address.

Cross-promoting makes a lot of sense from a branding standpoint, as well. By having a Facebook presence, you add credibility to your organization in much the same way a Web site does. Your customers appreciate knowing how to get in touch with you on Facebook. You've taken a lot of time and energy building your Facebook presence; now, you need to let your existing customers know about it through your existing channels.

Consider this scenario: You have a blog for your business, a Twitter feed, a new Page on Facebook, and oh yes, a Web site. You've put a lot of effort into tapping all these new forms of media, but how can you expect everyone to know about all these sites if you don't cross-promote them?

Social media can really boost your company's visibility and brand aware-ness, but it does have a downside: Many businesses end up with fragmented media. Therefore, you need to establish a strong policy of cross-promoting these sites, which you can do in a variety of ways.

Be sure to cover at least the basics when it comes to letting everyone know about your various sites. Here are some ways you can get the word out:

✔ In your e-mail signature and on your Web site home page, list all the ways that the reader can connect with you.

✔ On your blog, list your Page in a special Social Links section or with Facebook's latest Like Box plug-in, which can pull updates to your blog directly from your Page. (See Chapter 15 for details.)

The preceding options are ideas on how to cross-promote your Facebook Page by getting users to discover your various sites, which then pulls them back to your Facebook Page. Facebook also provides a variety of applications that can plug your blog feed, Twitter feed, FriendFeed, Delicious bookmarks, and RSS feeds into your Page. (See the next section for details about how to integrate your Twitter feed with your Page.)

Facebook also allows you to use Facebook social plug-ins on your Web site, adding many of the same capabilities that have made Facebook so popular, such as commenting, the Like button (discussed in detail in Chapter 14), and the ability for visitors to log in by using their Facebook ID and password. Refer to Chapter 15 for more information on Facebook plug-ins.

Integrating Twitter into your stream

If your company has a presence on other social media platforms — such as Twitter, YouTube, Flickr, foursquare, and hundreds more — cross-promote your company's content by leveraging all these channels, playing to the strengths of each respective platform. By cross-promoting, you increase your content's exposure, meaning that you can reach a potentially larger audience and mindshare for your brand. In addition to exposing your content to more people, you also increase the chances that those people will share your content within their own circles of influence, which broadens your exposure even more.

Today, numerous tools help you integrate your content across social-media platforms. For example, many people connect a company Twitter account to the company's Facebook Page, often by using one of Facebook developer Involver's many free social media integration apps. Involver has apps that can integrate with your YouTube channel and Flickr account as well.

By using Involver's Twitter for Pages app, you can relatively easily set up your own Twitter tab on your Facebook Page and have your tweets magically appear on the Page. Although we get in to how to install Involver's Twitter app in the following steps, installation for their other apps is just as straightforward.

To integrate your Twitter stream into your Facebook Page, follow these steps:

1. **Visit Involver's gallery on the Web at www.involver.com/gallery.html.**

2. **Click the blue Install button below the Twitter app description, as shown in Figure 8-4.**

   Your Facebook account opens, displaying the applications permissions page.

3. **If you have more than one Facebook Page, select the Page where you want to install the Twitter tab from the Add This Application To drop-down list, as shown in Figure 8-5.**

4. **Click the Add Twitter for Pages button to install the app.**

5. **On the application's Settings page that appears, enter your full name, e-mail address, phone number, and Twitter username and select the Terms of Service check box.**

6. **Click Save Changes.**

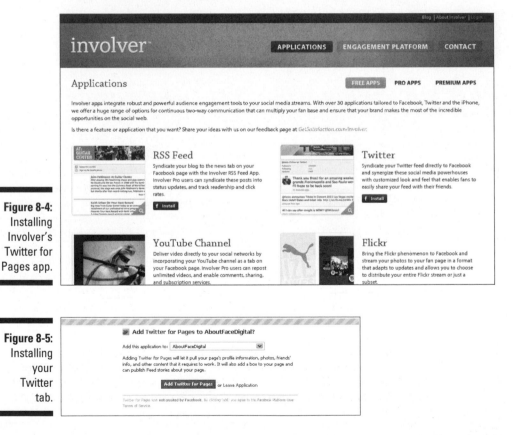

Figure 8-4: Installing Involver's Twitter for Pages app.

Figure 8-5: Installing your Twitter tab.

7. **On the Last Step page that appears, click Continue to Fan Page to complete the process.**

8. **Go back to your Facebook Page, click the plus sign (+) at the far right of the tab bar, and then select Twitter from the drop-down list that appears.**

   A new Twitter tab is added to the menu bar, as shown in Figure 8-6. If you don't see the tab, type **Twitter for Pages** in the Search Available Tabs text box.

Click for Twitter profile   Share Page with friends

Figure 8-6:
Your new
Twitter tab.

Most recent tweet

Congratulations, you've just integrated your Twitter feed into your Facebook Page. The Twitter tab shows your recent tweets; includes a Follow on Twitter link, which takes fans to your Twitter profile; and provides a sharing option for your fans. To use the Like button, a user enters a friend's name in the text box shown in Figure 8-6 and then clicks the Send Page Invitation button. Involver wisely includes this feature in the app so that your current fans can easily promote your Page to your Facebook friends, as well as via e-mail.

When you add a Twitter tab to your Facebook Page, you syndicate your Twitter content, allowing fans to view your Twitter stream without having to follow you directly on Twitter. Your fans can also obtain access to your Twitter profile, and you maximize your Page's viral potential by offering a Like button.

Feel free to move your Twitter tab to anywhere on the tab menu by simply clicking and dragging the tab to the desired position.

Leveraging Your Facebook Presence via Your E-Mail, Web Site, and Blog

Most likely, more than half of the people you e-mail for your business have Facebook accounts. Because all Facebook Pages have their own URLs, you can copy and paste your Page's URL into your corporate e-mail, inviting customers and prospects in your database to sign up as fans.

Better yet, you can add a Facebook badge or Like button to an HTML e-mail, as well as on your Web site or blog, as described in the following sections. Additionally, we give you the lowdown on creating a Facebook Like button in the section "Using the Facebook Like button," later in this chapter.

A number of third-party apps, such as WiseStamp, help you inject a little Facebook into your e-mail signature by automatically adding your latest Facebook status update to the bottom of your e-mails. Find the instructions on how to do this here: `http://wisestamp.com/goodies/how-to/create-your-personal-facebook-signature`.

You get to decide what you want to include in your online communications, but explain the value of checking out your Facebook Page to fans by encouraging them to make use of these social features. The more ways you allow your fans to share and consume content, the more content they will consume and share! Integrating Facebook into your e-mail and Web site marketing offers you a viral distribution channel like no other.

Creating a Facebook badge

Facebook badges allow you to *embed,* or add, a snippet of code on a Web page, blog, or even in e-mail, and badges appear in the format you choose, along with your Page's profile image. You can create a Facebook badge for either your profile or Page.

To create a badge for your Page, follow these steps:

1. **Click the Edit Page link on the left side of the Page, just below the photo.**

   The Settings page appears.

2. **Click the Marketing link on the left side of the settings page and then click the Get a Badge link, as shown on the right in Figure 8-7.**

   Your Page's main photo appears in the preview window on the left. On the right side of the window, you can choose where you want to add the badge; your options include Blogger, TypePad, and Other (which offers an HTML embed code that you can cut and paste into most Web pages).

Figure 8-7:
Start here
to get
badges
for your
page.

3. **Click Edit This Badge.**

   The Page Badges Edit page, shown in Figure 8-8, appears. On this page, you can design your badge the way you want.

4. **Choose what information to include on your badge. You can adjust the following badge settings:**

   - *Layout:* Vertical, Horizontal, and 2 Columns

   - *Items:* Name (the name of your Page), Status (the current status on your Page), Picture (your Page's picture), and Fans (the number of fans your Page has)

   When you select different options, your badge changes accordingly on the right side of the window.

5. **When you're satisfied with your design, click the Save button at the bottom of the page.**

   The original Page Badges page reappears, displaying a message that the badge was successfully updated.

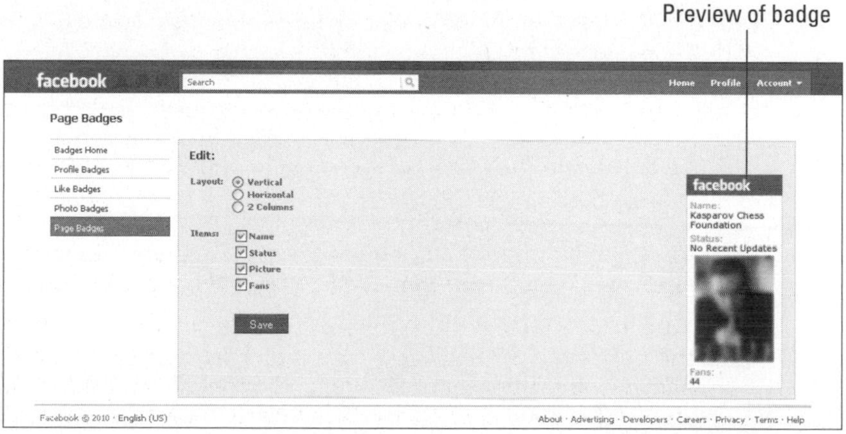

Preview of badge

Figure 8-8:
Editing a
Facebook
badge for
your Page.

6. **To embed this badge into an HTML e-mail, newsletter, or Web page, click the Other button (as shown in Figure 8-9), copy the code that appears in the text box below the button, and paste it into the location where you want it to appear in your e-mail, e-newsletter, or Web page.**

Figure 8-9:
Getting
the HTML
embed code
for your
customized
Facebook
badge.

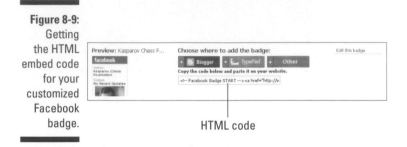

HTML code

You can also create a different type of badge by choosing from the buttons on the left side Page Badges menu. In addition to the Page Badges, you can create the following:

- *Profile badges:* This links to your Facebook profile page and shows your current profile picture.

- *Like badges:* This shows that you have liked a particular organization's Page. You can choose which Page to like when you create the badge.

- *Photo badges:* This shows up to six photos that you've posted on your profile.

Integrating the Like button

The Like button is automatically at the top of everyone's Page, and of course, your goal is to get people to click it! When someone clicks a Like button, a notice is placed on her Wall that she's liked this particular Page. This means that everyone on her Friends List can see that she's liked a Page . . . and hopefully it's yours! This is great exposure for your Page and is essentially what makes Facebook such a viral marketing powerhouse. The more people clicking your Page's Like button, the more people exposed to your Page. For more information on using the Like button to your advantage, see Chapter 14.

You can embed Facebook's Like button in your e-mails, Web site, or blog, which allows the reader to share your Facebook Page with other members and friends, or post it directly to his Facebook profile. Similar to creating a badge (as discussed earlier in this chapter), the Like button involves creating and customizing embeddable code that you can find on the Like button page.

To create a Like button, go to the plug-in page at `http://developers.facebook.com/docs/reference/plugins/like`. Figure 8-10 shows the options that you can select when creating your button. We discuss the process in detail in Chapter 14.

Figure 8-10:
Creating a
customized
Like button.

Promoting Your Facebook Presence Offline

Companies invest a lot of their marketing budget in offline activities, such as events, direct marketing, and outdoor advertising. Increasingly, offline efforts are driving online results. Do all that you can to promote your Facebook Page in the real world, such as including your Facebook Page URL in your offline communications.

Everyone, from politicians to celebrities to small business to the Fortune 500, are leveraging the offline world to promote their Facebook presence for a simple reason — Facebook's social features make it a great place to interact and build relationships with consumers in unprecedented ways. The viral aspects of the Facebook platform are also ideal for spreading a message beyond the original point of contact.

Although this chapter discusses many great online tactics to enhance your Facebook presence, you can also promote your Page in offline ways, which may be more in line with your traditional marketing efforts — not to mention more effective for many of the small businesses, stores, restaurants, and local community groups that are marketing on Facebook. Closing the loop between marketing online and offline can be as simple as hanging a sign in your store window saying you're on Facebook and give your Page's name.

Some businesses go to great lengths to promote their Facebook Page offline. Check out Figure 8-11 and Figure 8-12 for some ideas.

Figure 8-11:
Crandon, Wisconsin's Chamber of Commerce promotes its Facebook Page by using an oversized billboard.

Figure 8-12:
Tom's of Maine toothpaste promotes its Page on all its product packaging.

Networking offline

Grow your network in the real world, as well as online: Join business networking groups, attend conferences and trade shows for your industry, and get involved in local organizations that hold frequent events. By joining professional organizations and attending industry events, you can establish your credibility in your particular niche. You can also connect to the other influencers and industry movers and shakers. Always network, whether through professional events or casual get-togethers because what better opportunity is there to be able to hand out your business cards that include your Facebook Page URL?

If people want to find out more about your business, direct them to your Facebook Page. Let them know about all your business's social-media out-posts — not just Facebook, but Twitter, YouTube, Flickr, SlideShare, and so on. Invite your real-world social network to connect with you online.

Placing the Facebook logo on signs and in store windows

If you own a restaurant, retail store, or professional office, why not put up a decal in your window or a sandwich board on the checkout counter that asks your customers to visit your Facebook Page? Make sure that anyone who visits your establishment can see the sign, like in the example shown in Figure 8-13. Let your customers know that you offer them something of value on your Page. Encourage them to like your Page and become a fan.

Tell your customers that you plan to reward them for visiting your Page. Give them a discount, a coupon, or special content (for example, recipes if you're a restaurant). Often, the people with whom you engage offline everyday are your best potential Facebook supporters. Invite your real-world customers to connect with you on Facebook — and don't forget to reach out and connect to them by rewarding them for their continued support.

Figure 8-13: A local deli hangs a sign asking people to like its Facebook Page.

Referencing your Page in all ads and product literature

Spread the love — and your Facebook Page URL — wherever you can. Put your Facebook Page address on all company printed materials. Display the Facebook logo and your Page link on your business cards; letterhead; direct-marketing campaigns; print, radio, and TV ads; catalogs; product one-sheets; customer case studies; press releases; newsletters; and coffee mugs, umbrellas, T-shirts, mouse pads, and holiday gifts. Basically, wherever eyes might look, you want to place your Facebook URL.

Don't forget to get employees involved in spreading the word about your Facebook presence. Make sure you inform the people who work for your business about your Facebook Page because they can become your biggest brand ambassadors.

Optimizing Your Page

It's very important to optimize your Page so that it shows up at the top of Facebook's internal search results as well as on Google. A poorly indexed Page can result in a lot of missed opportunities because visitors just can't find your Page.

Facebook is quickly becoming a fenced-off garden, where Google and other search engines capture little activity inside Facebook. So Page administrators take the time to make their Pages and social networking activities easier to find via Facebook's members-centric search engine. Facebook search results now include a member's friends (and Pages that she's a fan of) status updates; photos, links, videos, and notes that match your search query; along with profile, Page, group, and application results.

If other users have chosen to make their content available to everyone, members also can search for their status updates, links, and notes, regardless of whether they're friends. Search results continue to include people's profiles, as well as pertinent Facebook Pages, groups, and applications. Users can filter the results so that they see only friends' News Feeds or News Feeds for everybody who has made their privacy settings accessible to all. For example, Figure 8-14 shows the results of a Posts by Everyone search for the phrase *Facebook Marketing*.

Figure 8-14:
Facebook's
internal
search
displays
search-
related
News Feed
stories.

Using search engine optimization to drive traffic

Pages hosted by Facebook tend to rank well when searched for and then displayed in other search engines, including Yahoo! and Google, particularly when users search for businesses or people. In addition to making your content easy to find on Facebook's internal search, consider making your content *search engine–friendly* — meaning easy for Google and the others to find and index.

For internal searches, Facebook shows search results as a mixed bag, including links to related profiles, Facebook apps, groups, Pages, and Web pages outside of Facebook. By optimizing your content with rich descriptions and information — referred to as *search engine optimization (SEO)* — you can improve when and where your Page shows up in the results.

Here are some practices to help you optimize your Facebook Page across all search engines:

✔ Choose your Page name and username wisely. For example, if you own a pizza shop, "Pete's Pizza," it's going to get you buried far down in search results. However, naming your page something like "Pete's Pizza-Minneapolis" will bump you to the top of the search results for people looking for pizza in Minneapolis. (For details on how to change your username, see "Choosing your own Facebook username," earlier in this chapter.)

✔ When you write your description and the overview section of your Page's Info tab, use descriptive keywords that people are likely to search for. For example, to go along with the preceding pizza example, you want to make sure you mention what your restaurant is known for, so maybe something like "We have the best New York-style pizza, the hottest wings, and the coolest staff in all the Twin Cities! Stop by one of our three metro locations: St. Paul, Minneapolis, or our newest shop near the Mall of America in Bloomington."

✔ Add custom content by using iFrames or HTML. Include relevant keywords that complement your description and Info sections. Include relevant links in the code.

✔ When adding content such as photos, discussion topics, and status updates, use appropriate keywords in the titles. For example, if your pizza shop recently donated food to a local school, post pictures of the kids enjoying the special treat with the caption "Pete's Pizza staff enjoying some pizza with the kids at Main Street Elementary School."

✔ Add one or more of Facebook's social plug-ins (see Chapter 15) to your Web site or blog. Integrate Facebook buttons, Share buttons, and Like buttons to increase the number of links back to your Facebook Page. (See "Leveraging Your Facebook Presence via Your E-Mail, Web Site, and Blog," earlier in this chapter, for details on how to create these buttons.)

✔ Whenever you create an update on Facebook, such as a discussion topic on a Page, choose topics that your intended audience is likely to search for. For example, if you want to know whether your fans would be interested in a whole-wheat pizza crust option, post that question on the discussion board and point out some of the health benefits of using whole-wheat crust, such as it can help people get more fiber in their diets.

If you take the time to optimize your content, you see the benefits in your Page traffic and fan engagement. If people can quickly and easily find you in search results because you've posted interesting, engaging information, they're more likely to return to your Page in the future. Future visits mean interested fans and fun interaction!

Facebook Questions

Facebook has recently released *Facebook Questions,* a way to harness members' social graphs to ask and answer questions. Facebook Questions offers marketers an excellent opportunity to boost their presence by either asking or answering a question. Keep in mind that the more likes you get for your Facebook Question, the more likely it will show in search results, so make it likeable — use descriptive works, look at ways to encourage interactivity, and promote it throughout your network. At the time of this writing, this feature is still in beta. However, you can find out more information at www.facebook.com/questions/.

Driving more likes to your Page

Are you doing all you can to encourage people to like your Facebook Page? Okay, you're not CNN or Lady Gaga, but you can think like a marketer and increase the number of fans and level of engagement and interaction by employing some best practices in fan-building.

Here are five ways for attracting more fans to your Facebook Page:

✔ Use the Facebook Like Button social plug-in on your Web site. (See Chapter 14 for details.)

✔ Create a customized landing page that encourages visitors to click your Page's Like button. For example, when new visitors go to the EzineArticles.com Page, the landing page in Figure 8-15 appears. The arrow at the top of the Page encourages visitors to Like the Page. (Landing pages are described in detail in Chapter 4.)

✔ Run promotions on your Page by using a customized tab. For example, if you're a photography studio, use a third-party app like Promotion Builder from Wildfire Interactive (www.wildfireapp.com) to allow your fans to upload photos for a Fall Colors photo promotion you run. By adding a promotions tab to your Page, you draw people's attention and they'll want to click it to see what's going on. (See Chapter 4 for details about creating a customized tab.)

Figure 8-15: Be creative in getting people to like your Page.

✔ Integrate Facebook's Activity Feed and Recommendations plug-ins on your Web site to engage your visitors more effectively by keeping your content in front of them in multiple formats. If you have regular events, add Facebook's Live Stream plug-in to your Web site and Webcast the event for all to see and become a fan of. (You can download social plug-ins at `http://developers.facebook.com/plugins`; see Chapter 15 for details.)

✔ Review your Page's Insights on a regular basis to understand how your visitors are engaging with your content, and to keep track of what's resonating and what's not. (See Chapter 9 for more on Insights.)

Stories posted in the early morning or just before bed have higher engagement rates. This is because people typically check their Facebook feeds either when they first get up, first get to work, or are winding down for the night.

Chapter 9

Measuring Your Page Activity

• •

In This Chapter

▶ Using Facebook Insights to gain insight into your fans

▶ Getting Page updates in your e-mail

▶ Enabling third-party analytics

• •

*F*acebook Insights is a suite of tools that helps you — the Page owner — make informed decisions about how your fans interact with the content on your Page. Insights is also your tool to gauge your Facebook advertising and custom application's effectiveness. Facebook Insights is the eyes and ears on your Page, monitoring traffic and demographics, profiling data, and getting conversions down to the sale.

Insights gives you access to standard metrics such as the number of Page visitors; demographic metrics about people who visit your Page, such as where they live geographically; profile metrics detailing the interests of your fans; and even conversion metrics, such as how many visitors signed up for an e-newsletter or completed a sale. Stats are updated within a 24-hour period, so you can quickly identify what's working and what's not, and then adjust your content strategy accordingly.

In this chapter, we show you how to use Facebook Insights for your Page. We explain what the different metrics are and how to use them to realize your content goals. We also offer tips on how to integrate third-party analytics into your Page.

Using Facebook Analytics: Insights

Understanding your Page analytics is key to being a successful Facebook marketer. Facebook has such rich data on its users that you can learn quite a lot through Facebook Insights for your Page. Through Insights, you can identify and analyze trends within your Facebook Page and get a better sense of how your audience consumes and engages with your content. It's important to pay attention to your fans' activities on your Page so you can find out what content resonates with your audience. For example, if you see that fans react to a certain type of post, you can adapt your content strategy and give them more of what they like.

The following sections discuss how to access and interpret Insights data.

Accessing Insights

You (as a Page admin) can find your Insights Dashboard by visiting www.facebook.com/insights (see Figure 9-1). If you manage more than one Page, click the corresponding tab on the left navigation bar to view the Page Insights for that respective Page.

You can also access your Page Insights directly via your Page. Facebook includes an Insights section in the left column, just below your Page's Information section, as shown in Figure 9-2. You can see a brief overview of your stats, including your monthly active users, daily new likes, daily post views, and daily post feedback simply by visiting your Page. Click the See All link at the top of the Insights section to access your complete analytics.

Select your Page here.

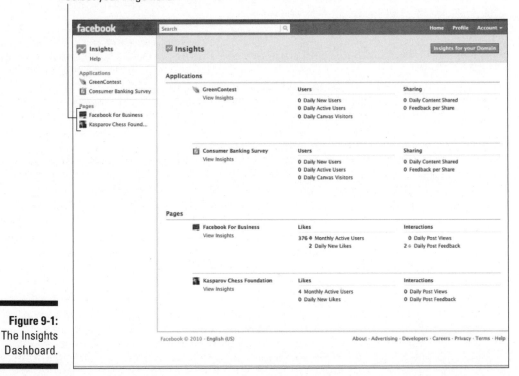

Figure 9-1:
The Insights
Dashboard.

Figure 9-2:
Only Page
admins can
see key
metrics when
viewing the
Page.

Insights

Only Page admins can see the Insights section when they visit the Page, and you must have at least 30 fans before you can do so.

Interpreting the data from Page Insights

Facebook Insights for Pages focuses on two key areas: your fans and your *interactions,* such as when users comment, like your Page, or write on your Wall, as shown in Figure 9-3. Insights allows you to drill deeper into each area, shedding more light into your Page's performance.

Facebook breaks down its analytics into two subsections: Users and Interactions. You can switch between the two sections by clicking the appropriate tab in the left navigation bar. Or you can click the See Details link next to the Users or Interactions headings on your Insights Dashboard to see a detailed breakdown of user activities and demographics.

Figure 9-3:
Insights
allows
you to drill
deeper to
reveal more
information
about how
users
interact
with your
content.

Users

The first section of Facebook Insights (refer to Figure 9-3) focuses on your users. To access more detailed information on your users, click the Users tab in the left navigation bar. The initial chart you're presented with shows the total monthly active users, daily new likes, and total likes, as shown in Figure 9-4. You can also see how your numbers have increased or decreased over the past three weeks or so.

Your *monthly active users* is the most important metric when looking at visitors to your Page. Focus on the monthly active users metric to get a sense of how well your Page engages your users. For example, Figure 9-4 shows that the monthly active users for our Page is 386 and has risen 2.7 percent over the last three weeks. This means that our fan interaction has increased because fans appreciate the type of content we've been posting, and we should keep it up.

On the Users page, you find a counter showing your monthly active users, daily new likes, and total likes. A top chart shows daily new likes and unlikes, as shown in Figure 9-5. If you click the Total tab on this chart, you see total likes and users who have hidden your Page from appearing in their News Feeds, as shown in Figure 9-6.

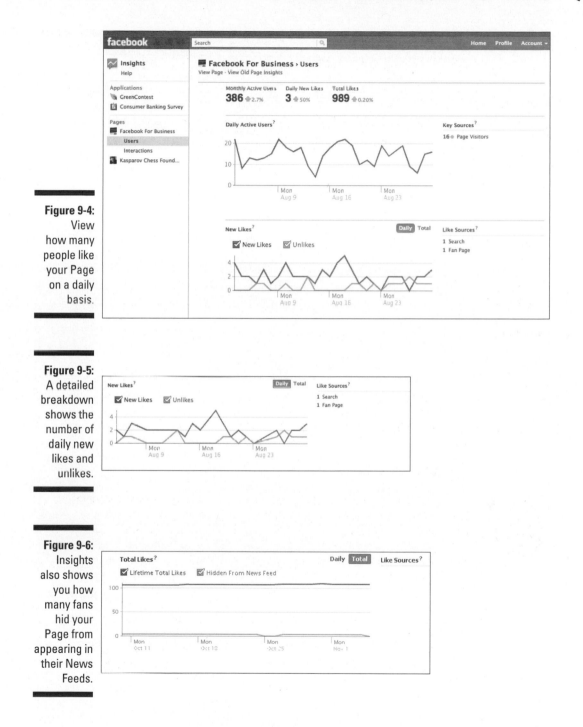

Figure 9-4:
View how many people like your Page on a daily basis.

Figure 9-5:
A detailed breakdown shows the number of daily new likes and unlikes.

Figure 9-6:
Insights also shows you how many fans hid your Page from appearing in their News Feeds.

Exporting data from Facebook Insights

Facebook has added some features to help you look at the data you collect from Insights in new ways. You can

✔ Export the data as an image file by right-clicking the graph you want to save and selecting Save Image.

✔ Export the data as an Excel or CSV file for viewing in your spreadsheet program, as shown in the following figure. This way you can view the data as one page simply by clicking the Export button on the top-right corner of the page (refer to Figure 9-3).

Daily Active Users	Monthly Active Users	Daily New Likes	Daily Unlikes	Lifetime Total Likes	Daily Logged-in Page Views	Daily Logged-in Page Views	Daily Stream Impressions	Daily Likes and Comments
Daily Users who have engaged with your Page, viewed your Page, or consumed content generated by your Page (Unique	Monthly Users who have engaged with your Page, viewed your Page, or consumed content generated by your Page (Unique Users)	Daily New Likes of your Page (Total Count)	Daily Unlikes of your Page (Total Count)	Lifetime Total Likes of your Page (Total Count)	Daily Page Views from users logged into Facebook (Total Count)	Daily Page Views from users logged into Facebook (Unique Users)	Daily Impressions of stream stories generated by your Page (Total Count)	Daily Number of likes and comments created on your Page's content (Total Count)
1	13	0	0	108	9	1	0	0
1	13	0	0	108	8	1	0	0
1	14	0	0	108	19	1	0	0
1	14	0	0	108	12	1	0	0
3	14	0	1	108	19	3	0	0
1	13	0	0	109	6	1	0	0
1	13	0	0	108	1	1	0	0
3	13	0	0	108	64	1	0	3
2	12	0	0	108	19	1	0	2
1	12	1	0	108	4	1	0	0
1	11	0	0	107	1	1	0	0
2	12	0	0	107	4	2	0	0
1	11	0	0	107	2	1	0	0
2	11	0	0	107	5	2	0	0
1	10	0	0	107	6	1	0	0
1	10	0	0	107	1	1	0	0
1	10	0	0	107	1	1	0	0
1	10	0	0	107	5	1	0	0
2	10	0	0	107	6	2	0	0
2	9	1	0	107	9	2	0	0
0	8	0	0	106	0	0	0	0
1	9	0	0	106	2	1	0	0
2	13	0	0	106	2	2	0	0
0	13	0	0	106	0	0	0	0
1	13	0	0	106	1	1	0	0
1	13	0	0	106	2	1	0	0
2	13	0	0	106	8	2	0	0
1	12	0	0	106	1	1	0	0
2	12	0	0	106	6	1	0	0

Key metrics / Lifetime Country / Lifetime Gender and Age / Lifetime City / Lifetime Lo

When you dig deeper into the users' data, things get interesting. By looking at a daily account of unlikes and how many fans have hidden your updates, you get a sense of how well your content resonates with your fans. If you see an unusually large number of unlikes or fans that hide your updates on a particular day, your content may be turning them away for some reason. Likewise, if you see a spike in likes on a particular day, look to repeat your success.

Interactions

The second part of Insights focuses on *interactions,* detailing how many times users like, comment, and post on your wall, as shown in Figure 9-7. The goal is to grow these numbers on a consistent basis.

Figure 9-7:
The
Interactions
page details
how many
likes and
comments
your Page
generates
on a daily
basis.

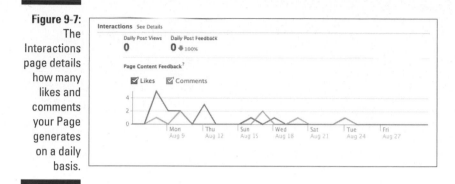

Click the See Details link next to the Interactions heading on your Insights
Dashboard to go to a page featuring two charts, as shown in Figure 9-8:

✔ **Daily Story Feedback:** This chart shows how users interact with your
content daily: They can like your Page *(Likes),* make a comment on your
post *(Comments),* or unsubscribe *(Unsubscribes)* from receiving your
updates in their News Feed.

Pay close attention to the number of unsubscribers because this metric
speaks directly to the content you publish to your Page. If you notice
a spiking trend in unsubscribers, reevaluate your content strategy and
change direction.

Figure 9-8:
Daily Story
Feedback
and Daily
Page
Activity
charts help
you gauge
how much
your fans
interact with
your Page.

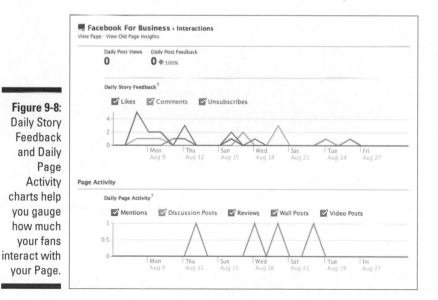

✔ **Daily Page Activity:** This chart details ways that your *fans* — the people who like your Page — engage with your Page in other ways, such as mentioning your Page on their Wall *(Mentions)*, contributing in your discussion area *(Discussion Posts)*, writing a review on Pages that have a Reviews tab *(Reviews)*, updating to your Page's Wall *(Wall Posts)*, or posting a photo or video *(Video Posts)*.

If you deselect any of the check boxes in the Daily Story Feedback and Daily Page Activity charts, the charts appear without that data.

Pay attention to how many likes you get. If you see spikes in fan growth, try to understand what contributes to those increases.

Demographics: Understanding your audience makeup

Insights also reveals demographic data about your fans, such as gender, age, and location. To find the demographics charts, go to your Insights Dashboard and click the See Details link next to the Users heading at the top of the page. You can find the demographic data on the Demographics chart of your Users page, as shown in Figure 9-9.

This chart shows a breakdown of your users' location (country and city), language, gender, and age. With this information, you can quickly determine what age groups your Page attracts and where your users are based.

Figure 9-9:
This chart includes gender, age, and geographic data, such as country, city, and language.

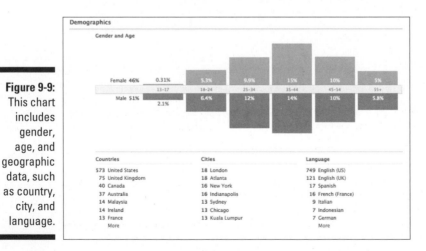

If you see that your audience trends to older users, tailor your content and advertising (if you use Facebook Ads) to this audience. Likewise, if your Page strikes a chord with an audience from a particular country, think about delivering content that specifically appeals to this region of the world. After all, Facebook has a global audience.

Viewing Weekly Page Updates via E-Mail

Facebook sends a weekly e-mail to all Page admins highlighting some key metrics and providing direct links to important Page admin functions. If you're admin to more than one Page, stats for each Page are represented in the e-mail. This e-mail is a big timesaver because even a quick glance gives you some insight into your Page's performance, as shown in Figure 9-10.

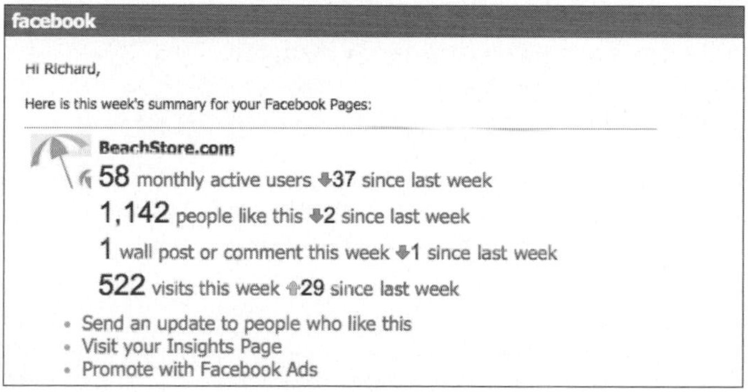

Figure 9-10: This weekly e-mail summarizes key performance indicators.

facebook

Hi Richard,

Here is this week's summary for your Facebook Pages:

BeachStore.com

58 monthly active users ⬇37 since last week

1,142 people like this ⬇2 since last week

1 wall post or comment this week ⬇1 since last week

522 visits this week ⬆29 since last week

- Send an update to people who like this
- Visit your Insights Page
- Promote with Facebook Ads

The e-mail includes the following information:

- ✔ The number of monthly active users and increases/decreases over the previous week
- ✔ The number of people who like the Page and increases/decreases over the previous week
- ✔ The weekly number of Wall posts or comments, and increases/decreases over the previous week
- ✔ The total weekly visits and increases/decreases over the previous week

The e-mail also includes the following helpful links:

> ✔ Send an Update to People Who Like This
>
> ✔ Visit Your Insights Page
>
> ✔ Promote with Facebook Ads

These links make it easy to access some important features that often require a lot of digging to find. But to get the weekly e-mail, you must opt-in first.

To opt-in to the e-mail, go to your Facebook home page and follow these steps:

1. **Choose Account⇨Account Settings in the top-right corner of the page.**

2. **On the My Account page that appears, click the Notifications tab at the top.**

   On the right side is a list of links under the View Settings For heading.

3. **Click the Pages link to go directly to the Pages section of this long list.**

4. **Select the Weekly Page Updates for Admins check.**

   That's all there is to it!

Integrating Third-Party Analytics

Although Facebook Insights is an invaluable tool to measure the most important metrics for tracking your Page activity, sometimes you may want to have additional information at your disposal, such as what keywords were used to find your Page and the average amount of time people stay on your site.

Facebook recently made its Page Insights data available to third-party analytics through its Open Graph protocol. A number of companies have already integrated this data into their existing services. Leading analytics companies, such as Webtrends and Coremetrics, have begun to roll out new offerings with Facebook data, alongside their existing Web site analytics.

> ✔ **Webtrends:** A very detailed analytics package that you can use via self-installation or with the Webtrends services team. This is a paid service, and you must contact Webtrends for package pricing based on your needs. See Figure 9-11. (`www.webtrends.com/Products/Analytics/Facebook`)
>
> ✔ **Coremetrics:** In addition to traditional Web site analytics, Cormetrics' solutions help you track your Facebook return on investment (ROI). You can request a demo and speak with a salesperson by clicking the Request a Demo button on the top right. See Figure 9-12. (`www.coremetrics.com/solutions/web-analytics.php`)

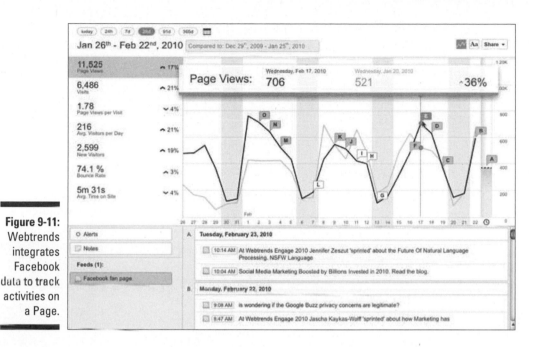

Figure 9-11:
Webtrends
integrates
Facebook
data to track
activities on
a Page.

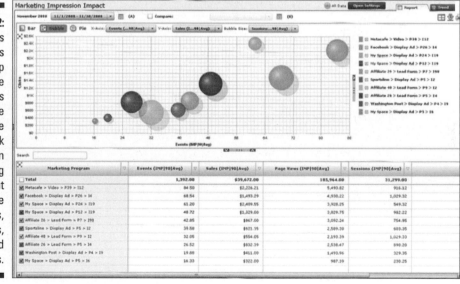

Figure 9-12:
Coremetrics
integrates
data to help
Web site
owners
determine
the role
Facebook
plays in
influencing
subsequent
Web site
visits,
behaviors,
and
conversions.

- ✔ **SociafyQ:** In addition to tracking Facebook Page stats, SociafyQ also takes care of your other social networking accounts, such as Twitter and YouTube. A free account offers limited tracking capabilities, but paid subscriptions start at about $4.00 and offer more analytical capabilities as well as exporting functions. (www.sociafyq.com)

- ✔ **ObjectiveMarketer:** ObjectiveMarketer goes a step further than just showing you analytics of people landing on your Facebook Page. If you plan on running any promotions, you can integrate those into your tracking as well. There is a free 15-day trial, and then you can upgrade to a paid subscription. (www.objectivemarketer.com)

Additionally, social media management platforms from companies such as Buddy Media and Involver incorporate Facebook Page Insights analytics, providing Page admins with a one-stop service for posting, monitoring, and measuring their Facebook activities.

Part III
Engaging in Facebook Advertising

The 5th Wave   By Rich Tennant

"I hope you're doing something online. A group like yours
shouldn't just be playing street corners."

In this part . . .

Part III discusses strategies for advertising your products and services on Facebook. You discover how to target your ads to a very specific audience and then create and test those ads to ensure their success. We explore the Facebook tools that help you measure and optimize your advertising campaign and then obtain insight into your customers from their interactions with your Page.

Facebook ads can be a new source of revenue for your business and enable you to further promote your products or services. And best of all, Facebook advertising is a great way to build a fan base for your Page quickly.

Chapter 10

Checking Out Advertising Options and Strategies

*W*ith more than 500 million members worldwide, Facebook can reach an audience nearly four times the size of the Super Bowl's television viewing audience. The social network's ability to target to a desired age, sex, location, relationship status, education, and interest marks a major paradigm shift in mass media advertising. You can reach a highly defined consumer market and pay only when one of those consumers clicks through an ad to your Facebook Page or other Web destination.

Facebook provides a self-service advertising model akin to Google's. Just like Google, Facebook allows you to easily create your ad, select your target audience, set your daily budget, and measure results. Ads can be purchased based on cost per impression (CPM) or cost per click (CPC). However, unlike Google, Facebook ads for Pages come with a built-in Like button, and event ads offer an in-ad RSVP capability, allowing consumers to interact with ads in entirely new ways.

In this chapter, we show you how to use Facebook ads to your advantage. We introduce you to the different options available — what they are and how to use them to fulfill your advertising goals. We offer tips on evaluating your advertising budget, targeting your audience, writing ad copy, uploading an effective image, and designing an ad. Finally, we help you create your landing page strategy and evaluate its effectiveness in fulfilling your marketing goals.

Introducing Facebook Ads

The stakes are high for Facebook to have a winning advertising strategy. Advertising represents Facebook's largest source of revenue and is expected to grow exponentially over the next five years. The self-service option has improved steadily and offers many targeting options, such as being able to reach engineering students at Ivy League schools or engaged women between the ages of 21–35. The Facebook advertising platform shows tremendous potential and true innovation for both large and small advertisers. Figure 10-1 shows Facebook's advertising launch pad from which you can create a new ad or manage an existing ad campaign.

Figure 10-1: The Facebook advertising launch pad.

Facebook offers an incredibly *sticky* — as in users come back often — site for advertisers. In fact, with a 50-percent daily return rate, consumers spend more time on Facebook's News Feed pages than they do on Yahoo!'s, MSN's, and MySpace's combined. Facebook has even surpassed Google as the most popular site based on the number of minutes spent on it.

But more importantly, Facebook provides the infrastructure for you to form a sustained relationship with potential customers. By linking to internal Facebook Pages, you can keep the user engaged within the Facebook environment; it's a self-contained marketing ecosystem unto itself. Just as you'd approach any marketing initiative, follow your predetermined marketing strategy when advertising on Facebook. (See Chapter 3 for the lowdown on putting together a marketing plan.)

You can place three types of ads directly through Facebook:

- ✔ A traditional **text ad.**
- ✔ A **display ad,** which includes text and an image, as shown in Figure 10-2.
- ✔ A unique Facebook **engagement ad,** which needs to be ordered via a Facebook advertising sales rep and requires spending at least $30,000. (For details, see the section "Placing Ads through a Sales Rep," later in this chapter.)

Facebook ads appear in the far-right column of the user's page in the *ad space.* Up to four ads can appear in the ad space, but you can't control the order in which your ad appears.

The following sections go into more detail about how you can reach a specific audience with a Facebook ad and how to decide on a budget.

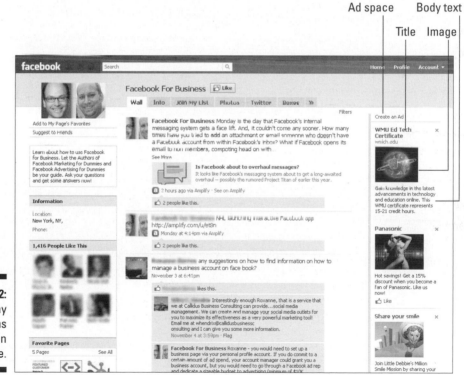

Figure 10-2:
A display ad contains text and an image.

Targeting your audience

Facebook focuses its advertising strategy around its vast member data, allowing advertisers to target an audience segment precisely. In contrast, Google AdSense is *where* your ad displays, whereas Facebook is all about *who* sees it. In fact, Facebook offers advertisers the ability to reach their exact audience — from a broad demographic, to a geographic preference, and to a more granular interest.

Targeting your audience is as important as the message. Develop *personas,* or personality characteristics, to represent your target audience. Find out what they're interested in — their educational background, relationship status, and where they live. Reach only the audience you desire by targeting to meet your business's ideal customer profile.

Facebook advertising isn't directly *contextual* — ads don't necessarily correlate to the content displayed. An advertiser can't pinpoint where on the site her ads should appear. Google AdSense, on the other hand, is a contextual-based advertising platform. Google's text-based ads tie in directly to the keywords queried, whereas Facebook ads are based on who you want to target.

Here are some ways that you can find the right audience for your Facebook ad:

- **Targeting by location:** Facebook allows for precise location targeting, based in part on your profile data and the IP address of the computer you log in with. Most cities in the United States, Canada, and the U.K. allow you to expand the targeting to include surrounding areas of 10, 25, and 50 miles if you want to reach specific regional markets.

- **Targeting by interests and likes:** Facebook leverages its members' profile data to allow advertisers to drill down to specific keywords. These keywords represent a member's interests. Topics that users are passionate about — such as their musical tastes, television preferences, religious views, and other valuable psychographic data — can be used to further micro-target your audience. Never before has there been a mass medium that allows for this kind of precise targeting. By adding keywords to your targeting, you can reach consumers based on the interests listed on their profiles.

- **Targeting by connections:** Connections are an interesting ad targeting parameter for Facebook advertisers. You can target people already connected to your Facebook Page or connected to another Page of yours. You can also target ads only to people who aren't already connected; therefore, your existing fans aren't shown your ad. And you can target the friends of people who are already connected to your Page. This is a powerful targeting capability because friends of fans are more likely to become fans themselves.

With micro-targeting, you limit the total reach of your campaign. By casting a wide net, on the other hand, you might be reaching outside your target audience.

Setting your budget

Facebook employs a bidding structure for its advertising inventory based on supply and demand. If there's greater demand to reach a specific demographic, the ad typically has higher bids. The company also provides a suggested bid for you based on the approximate range of what other ads reaching this demographic have historically cost.

Facebook's ads are based on a *closed bidding system*; you can't see what others pay for ads, nor can they see your bid. Facebook provides a recommended bidding range when you create your ad and updates that range throughout the life of your campaign. As a strategy, setting your bid initially on the low side of the suggested range is a good idea. You can monitor your campaign to see whether the ad performs at your given bid. You can also set a daily maximum budget. (For details, see "Managing Your Ad Campaigns with Ads Manager," later in this chapter.) Although Facebook allows you to bid as little as one cent, expecting a bid at that price to deliver any impressions is unrealistic.

You don't have to follow the Facebook pricing guidelines, but if you bid too low, your ad won't appear.

Your purchase strategy should be based, in part, on your goals. Facebook allows you to purchase ads based on two types of pricing:

- ✔ **Cost per click (CPC):** With CPC, you pay each time a user clicks your ad. If your goal is to drive traffic to a specific page, paying based on CPC will probably be the best performer for you.

- ✔ **Cost per impression (CPM):** With CPM, you pay based on how many users see your ad. If your objective is to get as many people within your target demographic to see the ad but not necessarily click through, ads based on a CPM basis may be your best option.

Test your ads on a CPM basis because using a CPM model allows you to identify the best performing ads and gives you a good idea of your cost per click. Therefore, when you run your campaign, you know the best model to purchase your ads.

Creating Winning Ads

Facebook offers advertisers unique ways to interact with Facebook members. From becoming a fan of a company's Page to confirming attendance at a Facebook business event to installing an application, these actions are automatically turned into stories that appear in your fans' News Feeds. Marketers who maximize these interactions by giving fans reasons to participate transform their fans into brand advocates, often without them even realizing it.

Before we go into detail about how to actually create an ad on Facebook, we want tell you how to create compelling ads that drive clicks. In the following sections, we discuss ways to write effective ad copy and choose the optimal image. We also discuss the importance of knowing your audience and delivering incentives that are right for them. Finally, it's important to know the restrictions that govern Facebook ad guidelines so your ads are approved.

Copywriting tips

Facebook is about making connections. Ad copy needs to reflect this spirit and maintain a familiar, conversational tone. With a friendly attitude in your headline and body, social stories generated around your ad have a more natural flow within the fan's News Feed.

Given a 25-character limit on the title and a 135-character limit on the body, you can't waste a whole lot of words. Be direct, straightforward, and honest with your objective. Keep in mind that Facebook is also about building trust, and your copy must show an openness and willingness to share and connect with your audience.

Facebook ads should entertain, if the subject calls for it. Ads with a humorous message deliver higher rates of user engagement. For example, the Facebook ad in Figure 10-3 uses a funny juxtaposition between image and headline.

Following are five guidelines when considering your Facebook ad copy:

- ✔ **Pose a question in your headline or in the body of the ad.** Don't be afraid to use a question mark where appropriate.

- ✔ **Reference your target audience.** By relating to your audience, you're more likely to grab their attention. Consider giving shout-outs, such as "Hey, Housewives . . ."

- ✔ **Be direct.** Tell them explicitly what you want them to do. For example, "Click here to receive your free t-shirt."

- ✔ **Use influencer's testimonials.** To establish credibility, consider highlighting an endorsement, such as "Voted South Jersey's best pizza."

✔ **Speak to their dreams.** As with most advertising, appeal to your audience's desires, hopes, and ambitions. For example, Figure 10-4 is a Facebook ad for a home guitar course that targets Jimmy Buffet fans and asks, "Want to Play Like Buffet?" in its headline.

Figure 10-3:
This ad
uses humor
to attract
interest.

Figure 10-4:
This ad
targets
Jimmy
Buffet fans.

Choosing the right image

Ads accompanied by images overwhelmingly perform better than text-only ads. Therefore, we strongly recommend that you include an image in your Facebook ad. If you use a photo, include a high-quality picture with the maximum allowed size of 110 pixels wide x 80 pixels tall with an aspect ratio of 4:3 or 16:9. Image files can't exceed 5MB.

Preferably, use images that are easily recognizable, aren't too intricate in detail, and feature bright colors without the use of the blue that's so strongly identified with the Facebook logo and navigational color scheme.

Here are five other ideas to select the right image to get your Facebook ad noticed:

✔ **If your image includes people, they need to reflect the demographic you're targeting.** People like to see people who look like themselves.

✔ **Test different images with the same copy.** When you test a single factor, such as the ad's image, you can easily tell the stronger performing image.

✔ **An amateur photo style sometimes works better than stock photography.** A more personalized approach can help you stand out in the crowd.

✔ **Use a smaller image or one with a solid background color.** The maximum size for an ad image is 110 x 80, but sometimes smaller images stand out among the rest of the full-size images people are used to seeing in Facebook ads. For example, using a dark background in the image makes the ad in Figure 10-5 stand apart from the rest on the page.

✔ **Make your image stand out with a decorative boarder.** Consider adding a branding element around the image or making the ad current (for instance, if it's holiday season, add decorative holiday border).

Figure 10-5: The image is the most important element in your ad.

Selecting your target audience

One of the Golden Rules of marketing is to know thy audience like you know yourself. For Facebook advertisers, that saying has added weight because Facebook makes it very easy to target your desired audience. In fact, selecting your target audience is central to the Facebook self-serve advertising platform. You can target by location, age, relationship status, education, company, job position, and interests. You can even target by language because Facebook is available in 80 languages with many more in development.

Knowing your audience also means knowing what motivates and speaks to them. Your ad's *call to action* — the desired result you want from the ad, such as getting the user to click through to your Web page or like your Page — needs to be in line with their expectations.

Simplifying your offer

Time spent on Facebook is typically not focused on viewing ads. In fact, Facebook advertising is usually at the tip of the marketing funnel in which you need to attract your audience's attention before you can garner interest. You have a short amount of space from which to communicate your offer via your Facebook ad. Don't waste words or over-complicate things. Your call to action needs to be direct, clear, and easy to follow. Multiple directions serve only to confuse your audience. Sometimes clever and wit isn't as effective as using the simplest word choice possible, as shown in the ad in Figure 10-6.

Figure 10-6:
Sometimes the simplest way to say something is the best.

Understanding ad restrictions

To maintain a high standard of content, Facebook places strict guidelines on advertisers. All ads require a review period, which can take up to 24 hours. Ads that are approved can be served immediately thereafter. Unapproved ads can be found on your Ads Manager page below Status Unapproved. (We discuss the Ads Manager in detail later in this chapter.)

When you create your ad, make sure to review Facebook's guidelines, which you can find at www.facebook.com/ad_guidelines.php.

Ten common ad mistakes are

- ✔ Incorrect use of capital letters
- ✔ Incorrect grammar, spelling, and use of slang
- ✔ Inaccurate ad text
- ✔ Deceptive claims
- ✔ Inappropriate images
- ✔ Misguided targeting
- ✔ Improper sentence structure
- ✔ Language deemed inappropriate
- ✔ Incorrect usage of punctuation
- ✔ Symbols exchanged for words

Creating a Facebook Ad

Creating your ad in Facebook is quick and easy. Whether you create a text or *display* ad (text and image), or build in social actions, such as a fan request, getting your ad up and running in Facebook requires some basic steps. To get started:

1. **Scroll to the bottom of your screen and click the Advertising link.**

   The Facebook Ads page appears (refer to Figure 10-1).

2. **Click the Create an Ad button on the upper right of your screen.**

   The Advertise on Facebook page appears, displaying the options for designing your ad (see Figure 10-7).

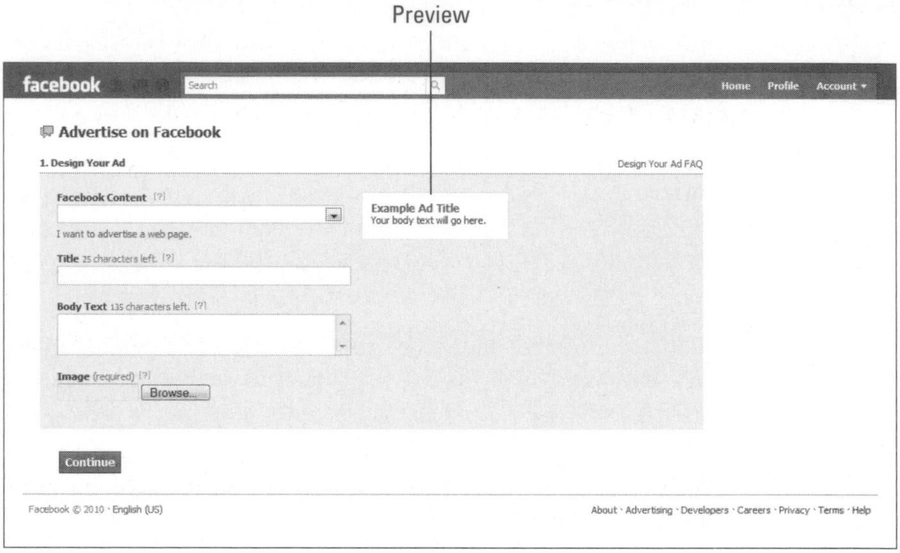

Figure 10-7: Designing a Facebook ad is fast and easy.

The following sections explain how to fill in the information for Facebook's three-step process for creating an ad: Design your ad; target your ad; and figure out campaigns, pricing, and scheduling.

Step 1: Design Your Ad

When designing your Facebook ad, keep it simple. Focus on one simple objective and be direct. Ads with images generally perform better than text-only ads. And if your image features people, the chances are even greater that someone will click through. (For more information on designing your ad, see the "Creating Winning Ads" section, earlier in this chapter.)

Before you create a Facebook ad, decide what you want the *landing page* — the page a user is taken to when he clicks your ad — to be. You can either link to a destination within Facebook (such as your Page, an event, or a group) or to an external Web site. However, we recommend that you link to a destination within Facebook, as we outline in the following steps. (See the later section, "Devising a Landing Page Strategy for Your Ads," in this chapter, for more on choosing between an internal or external destination.)

Follow these steps to design your ad (refer to Figure 10-7):

1. **Below the Destination URL box, click the I Want to Advertise Something I Have on Facebook link.**

   A list of your Facebook Pages, events, and/or groups that you manage appears depending on what you've designated for your business.

2. **Select the appropriate internal destination and then click the Continue button to reveal the targeting options.**

   You can either enter an internal Facebook address or *external* Web site (a Web address outside of Facebook) as your landing page.

3. **In the Title text box, type a title or headline for your ad.**

   You are limited to 25 characters and must adhere to the Facebook formatting policies. If you are advertising a Page, the page title is the default title, and you can't change it.

   As you build your ad, you see a near real-time preview on the right (refer to Figure 10-7).

4. **In the Body Text box, add body copy with up to 135 characters.**

   Using all caps or title case caps is prohibited under Facebook's guidelines. For example, the title, Shop At Big Al's For Your Shoes, would not be prohibited because it uses title case caps.

5. **In the Image section, click the Browse button and then navigate to the image you want to use in the ad.**

6. **Click the Continue button.**

   The Targeting options appear, as we describe next.

Step 2: Targeting

After you design your ad, you need to target your audience by selecting the Targeting criteria, as shown in Figure 10-8. You can think of targeting in terms of an archer's bull's-eye. The closer you get to the center, the narrower the circles; the farther out you go, the wider the area. (For more information on targeting your ad, see the "Targeting your audience" section, earlier in this chapter.)

On the right of Facebook's Targeting section, you see a number that represents the approximate number of people who would be exposed to your ad, as shown in Figure 10-8. You can see the audience size change as you add or remove targeting factors in the following steps.

If you reach too small of an audience, your ad might not generate any click-throughs. Widen some factors, such as age range, or add surrounding locations to your geo-targeting.

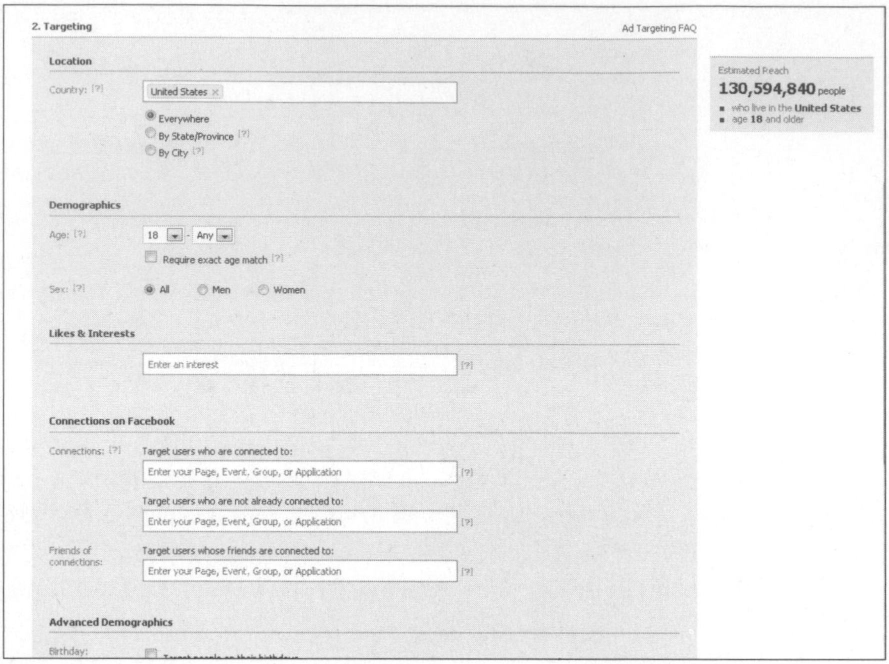

Figure 10-8:
Target your
audience's
primary
language.

Follow these steps to target a specific audience for your Facebook
ad campaign:

1. **In the Country text box, type the location of the user you want your ad
   to be seen by.**

   There are nearly 100 countries from which to target, and each ad can
   reach up to 25 countries. You can also drill down to the state/province
   or city level. For many cities, you can even specify among 10, 25, and
   50 miles surrounding the city.

2. **From the Age drop-down lists, choose the age range of the audience
   you want to see the ad.**

   If you know your audience's approximate age range, this is a great way
   to target them. For example, if you sell retirement homes, you can target
   people 55 and older. To reach the widest possible audience, leave this
   at the default setting: Any. Keep in mind, Facebook doesn't allow you to
   target members younger than 13.

3. **Select All, Men, Women for the gender of your audience.**

   You can target just men, just women, or both. All is selected in the default
   mode, making the ad available to the widest amount of members possible.

4. **In the Likes & Interests text box, type any keywords you want to
   target specifically.**

Keywords are based on the information that members choose to include in their Facebook profiles. When you start typing a term, a range of possible words appears. You can click one of these words without completing your term. If the keyword you enter isn't identified in enough Facebook members' profiles, it's not statistically large enough to target. You can enter as many keywords as are relevant. Keep in mind that targeting based on Likes & Interests is optional and not required.

When using keywords of interest to target an ad campaign, it's always a good idea to include those keywords in the ad copy.

5. **In the Connections on Facebook text box, enter your Page, event group, or application whose fans you want to target specifically.**

You can also target users who aren't fans of your Page, event, group, or application. This could be a good option if your goal is to acquire new fans. And there's even an option to target users who are friends of people connected to your specific Facebook Page, event, group, or application. Keep in mind, friends of existing fans may be an attractive audience for you to target because friends tend to have similar interests.

6. **Click the Show Advanced Targeting Options link to reveal advanced demographics.**

Advanced demographics allows you to target based on a number of unique factors. This section is in part what makes Facebook's targeting so interesting for certain types of advertisers. Because Facebook has so much information on its users, only Facebook can offer exact targeting to this level.

7. **If you want to target people on their birthdays, select that check box.**

8. **Select which gender your target audience is interested in: All, Men, or Women.**

9. **Select the audience's relationship status.**

You can choose among All, Single, In a Relationship, Engaged, and Married. For example, if you're a wedding dress designer, you can target people with Engaged as their marital status.

10. **Type the target audience's language preference.**

Facebook allows you to target people by their native language. Reaching a specific culture, such as Chinese-speaking Americans or Spanish-speaking people in Florida has never been easier. If your business is particularly culture-based, this is a highly effective way for you to target your audience.

Facebook has 40 languages listed and nearly 100 countries, and it keeps growing. Facebook offers a truly global campaign from one centralized management platform.

11. **Select the desired educational level of your audience.**

Your options are All, College Grad, In College, or In High School. You can choose to reach just college graduates, current students at a particular school, or just Harvard Business School graduates. This is a great tool for recruitment because you can target people with the right schools and degrees you're interested in hiring.

12. **Target down to the workplace.**

As you start to type the workplace, you see a range of workplace possibilities with those letters appear. If the workplace you're entering isn't statistically large enough to support an ad, it remains blank.

For example, say you're a business to business (B2B) marketer and want to reach folks at Fortune 1000 companies. Why not just target a specific company, such as IBM, with an ad and landing page just for it? It's now possible and very cost-effective via Facebook ads.

13. **Click the Continue button to proceed to the Campaigns, Pricing and Scheduling section, which we describe next.**

Step 3: Campaigns, Pricing, and Scheduling

The final step to creating your ad is to set your daily ad budget, bid, and schedule (see Figure 10-9).

The following steps detail how to set your Facebook ad budget:

1. **In the Campaign Name text box, type the name of your campaign.**

Campaign refers to a group of ads that all share the same daily budget and schedule; it can consist of many separate ads. By grouping ads under a single campaign, it's easier to manage various campaigns and determine how each group of ads performs.

2. **In the Budget text box, set your daily maximum budget.**

You can also choose to set a lifetime budget and enter the amount you want to spend for the entire life of that campaign.

The minimum daily spending amount is $1; you can run a Facebook ad for as little as $1 a day, albeit to a very small number of people.

3. **In the Schedule section, choose from two options for when the ad runs:**

   • *If you want the campaign to start today and run indefinitely,* select the Run My Campaign Continuously Starting Today check box. Then select a time in the At text box.

   • *If you want to choose a specific date range,* enter the starting time and the ending date and time.

4a. **If you're satisfied with the suggested bid per click in the Pricing section, proceed to Step 7.**

4b. **If you want to go with a different bid, click the Set a Different Bid (Advanced Mode) link.**

5. **Select the radio button next to the type of pricing structure you want to go with: Pay for Impressions (CPM) or Pay for Clicks (CPC).**

Facebook allows you to either bid based on CPM or CPC. If you select Pay for Impressions (CPM), remember your bid represents every 1,000 *impressions,* or ad views.

6. **Enter the maximum amount you're willing to pay per click or impression.**

The minimum amount you're allowed to bid for CPM is $0.02 and for CPC is $0.01, although Facebook often rejects bids that are too low.

Facebook gives you a suggested bid range. As a strategy, we suggest setting your bid on the low side of the suggested range initially.

7. **Click the Review Ad button near the bottom of the screen.**

The Review Ad page appears and recaps your ad's creative elements, targeting, type of bid (CPC or CPM), bid price, daily budget, and duration of ad *flight* (the time period an ad runs).

8. **After you review your ad, click the Place Order button.**

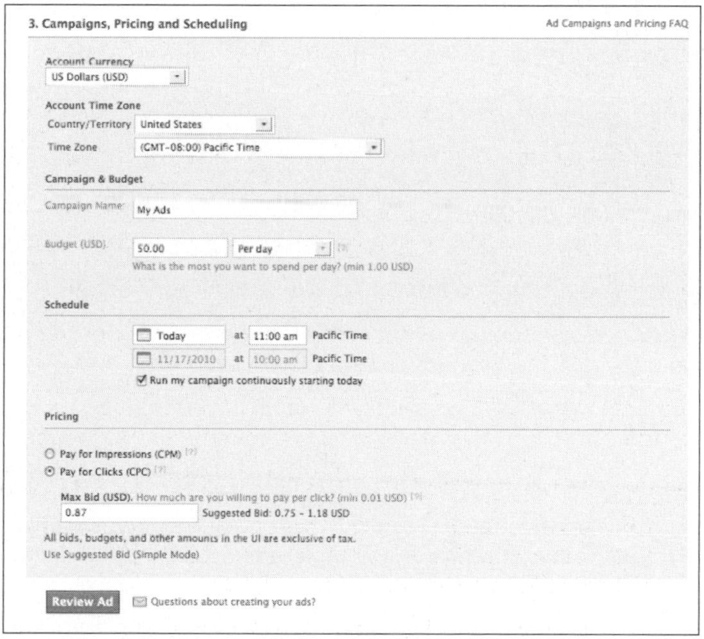

Figure 10-9:
The
Campaigns,
Scheduling,
and Pricing
step.

---

3. Campaigns, Pricing and Scheduling   Ad Campaigns and Pricing FAQ

Account Currency
US Dollars (USD)

Account Time Zone
Country/Territory United States
Time Zone   (GMT-08:00) Pacific Time

Campaign & Budget
Campaign Name: My Ads

Budget (USD)   50.00   Per day
What is the most you want to spend per day? (min 1.00 USD)

Schedule
☐ Today   at 11:00 am Pacific Time
☐ 11/17/2010 at 10:00 am Pacific Time
☑ Run my campaign continuously starting today

Pricing
○ Pay for Impressions (CPM)
◉ Pay for Clicks (CPC)

Max Bid (USD). How much are you willing to pay per click? (min 0.01 USD)
0.87   Suggested Bid: 0.75 - 1.18 USD

All bids, budgets, and other amounts in the UI are exclusive of tax.
Use Suggested Bid (Simple Mode)

Review Ad   ✉ Questions about creating your ads?

Creating Multiple Campaigns

Facebook makes it easy for you to duplicate an existing ad, change a number of variables, and launch multiple multi-faceted ad campaigns. An advertiser has several reasons for doing this:

- ✔ **To tailor each ad to a specific region:** Because economical, educational, and personal preferences vary from region to region, the ad copy and image may need to reflect these differences.

- ✔ **To reach multilanguage audiences:** You can use Facebook's language targeting on an ad-by-ad basis.

- ✔ **To test which variables in ads perform better:** By changing variables, you can optimize the campaign to the better performing ads.

- ✔ **To test different bids and models (CPC versus CPM):** This enables you to determine which are more economically efficient.

Facebook makes it easy to pattern a new ad after an existing one. When designing your new ad (as we describe in the section "Step 1: Design Your Ad," earlier in the chapter), you can copy an existing ad by selecting that ad from the Copy an Existing Ad drop-down list, as shown in Figure 10-10.

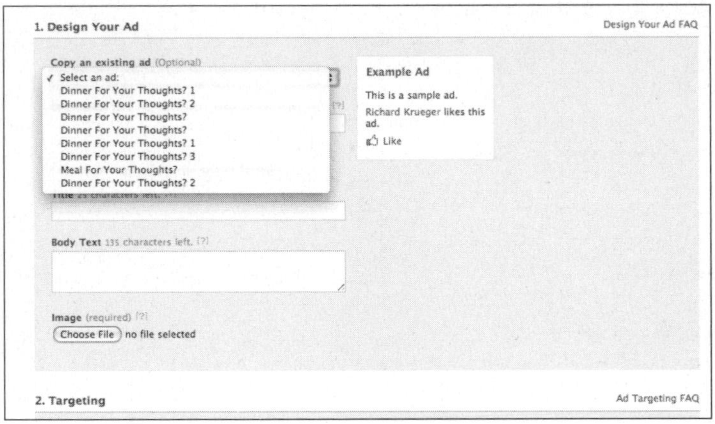

Figure 10-10:
Copy an existing ad to make multiple campaigns that target different audiences.

Facebook offers you a full range of metrics to measure success from within your Ads Manager. Because replicating an ad and creating different iterations for testing is easy, Facebook is quickly becoming the advertising platform of choice for savvy marketers. For a complete review of how to measure and test to improve your ad's success, see Chapter 11.

Devising a Landing Page Strategy for Your Ads

If you're familiar with interactive marketing, you understand the importance of making a good first impression with your ad link. Your *landing page* (as it is known in advertising) is the page that opens when users click your ad, and it can be an internal Facebook page or an external Web site. All engagement begins on the landing page. Successful landing pages provide an easy path to *conversion* — or realizing your goal. A conversion can include capturing user data via an input form, driving membership for your Page, or simply making a sale. Regardless of your objective, if your landing page doesn't deliver a desired result, your campaign is worthless.

Facebook allows you to create ads that link to either an internal Facebook location or an external Web site (URL), but only one per ad. The following sections explain how to choose a destination for your ad.

Landing on a Facebook location

As a best practice, when running a Facebook ad campaign, link your ads to an internal Facebook location as opposed to an external Web site. For internal Facebook ads, you can link to a Facebook Page, application page, Groups page, Events page, or Marketplace ad that you created or administer.

Furthermore, with the new Facebook tabbed format, you can link to specific tabs within your Facebook Page, delivering a more relevant Facebook ad that's optimized for your target audience. Conceivably, you can create a customized landing page within Facebook for each ad and audience segment. Figure 10-11 shows the Summit Mining landing page, which features a newsletter sign-up form.

 Everyone who sees your Facebook advertisement is a Facebook member. Don't take users away from the Facebook experience with your ad by leading them to an external page. Instead, bring visitors to your Facebook Page where they're just one click away from becoming a fan. Because you have access to your fans' profiling data, your fan base can become an extremely valuable marketing asset.

Landing on a Web site page

Facebook also allows you to refer your ad visitors to an external Web address (URL), provided it adheres to the company's advertising policies and guidelines.

If you choose an outside Web site, you aren't required to prove that you're the owner of the Web domain.

Figure 10-11:
The landing
page for
Summit
Mining.

You might want to send visitors to your Web site for several reasons. Linking to an outside Web site offers you greater control over your landing page's content, technology, and design. You might already have finely tuned landing pages that you prefer to drive ad traffic to, regardless of where the traffic originated. And, you can employ much more sophisticated Web analytics on your site than are presently available on Facebook.

Because ads can be purchased on a CPC basis, you can opt to pay only when a user clicks through to your page, regardless of whether it's an internal Facebook page or an outside Web site. In Figure 10-12, QualityHealth directs its Facebook ads to a landing page on its Web site that features the same offer that's highlighted in the ad.

Figure 10-12:
Quality-
Health's
external
landing
page.

Revealing content on your landing page

A new technique that's gaining a lot of favor with Facebook marketers is using a *reveal tab* for a landing page. A reveal tab is a great way to get your visitors to click the Like button and become a fan of your Page. With a reveal tab, you give visitors a reason to become a fan, by showing only part of the Page they land on, as shown in the Teesey Tees example in Figure 10-13. This technique, known as *fan gating,* is also effective when used with coupons and special promotions. Hide the information they need to redeem the promotion until they like your Page.

By adding a custom reveal tab, you can significantly increase the number of fans to your Page.

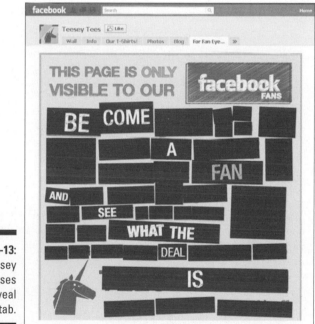

Figure 10-13: Teesey Tees uses a reveal landing tab.

Managing Your Ad Campaigns with Ads Manager

After you create an ad with Facebook, you want to keep tabs on that ad's performance. Facebook's *Ads Manager* is your personalized, central hub where you can view all your ad activities (see Figure 10-14). To access Ads Manager, visit www.facebook.com/ads/manage or click the Advertising link on the bottom of any Facebook page.

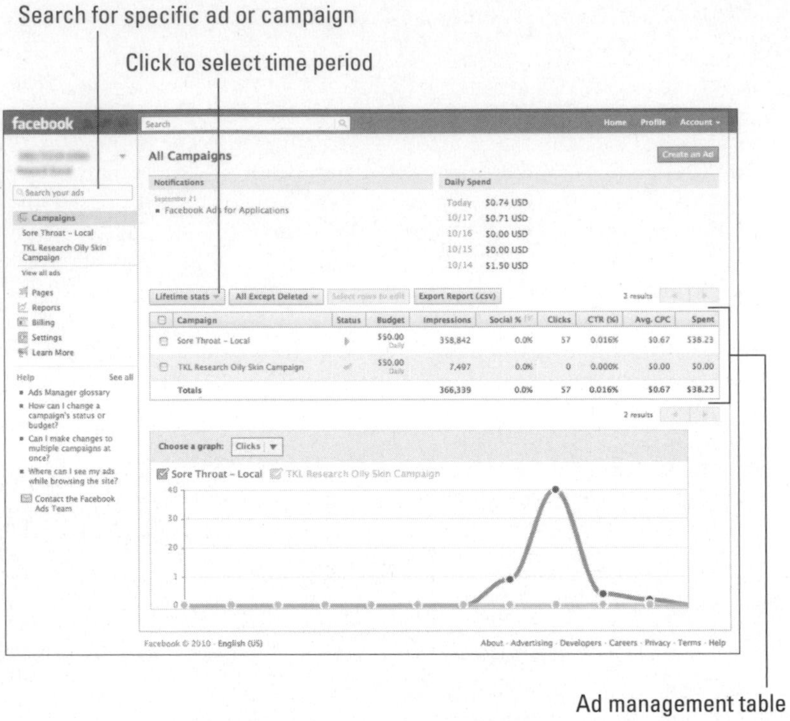

Search for specific ad or campaign

Click to select time period

Figure 10-14:
The
Facebook
Ads
Manager
shows
your ad
campaigns.

Ad management table

Viewing performance data

Facebook does a good job of balancing Ads Manager's ease of use with powerful digital marketing features. In the Ads Manager, you see Facebook *notifications* — typically messages from Facebook advertising updating you on new developments, which come fast and furious. You also see your daily spend for the previous five days.

The ad management section (refer to Figure 10-14) shows a table that features the most important data on your ads' performance. At a glance, you can view the following information:

✔ **Campaign:** The name you created for your ad(s)

✔ **Status:** Shows whether the ad is live or paused

- ✔ **Budget:** The maximum bid amount you entered

- ✔ **Impressions:** How many times the ad has been shown

- ✔ **Social %:** The percentage of your ad's impressions in which the viewer saw at least one friend who liked your Page, event, application, or ad

- ✔ **Clicks:** Number of clicks generated by the ad

- ✔ **CTR (%):** The percentage of people who clicked the ad compared to the total number who saw the ad

- ✔ **Avg. CPC:** The average cost you'd pay on a CPC basis

- ✔ **Avg. CPM:** The average cost you'd pay on a CPM basis

- ✔ **Spent:** Amount spent on the ad; default setting for the lifetime of the campaign

The default time period that's shown in the ad management table is Lifetime Stats. However, you can click the Lifetime Stats button's drop-down list to see additional view options: Today, Yesterday, Last Week, or Custom (in which you enter the desired dates).

The ad management section defaults to an All Campaigns view, regardless of how many campaigns you run concurrently. To edit multiple campaigns or ads, simply select the check boxes to the left of the ads or campaigns you want to edit. If you click the option to Edit *(number)* Row, you can change ad parameters like status and budget.

You can also drill into each ad further by clicking the campaign name. Here, you can view some of the data visually in chart form directly below your ad management table, as shown in Figure 10-15. The Choose a Graph drop-down list at the top of the chart allows you to view clicks, impressions, or CTRs.

You can also drill into each ad or campaign by clicking the ad name. If you have multiple ads within that campaign, the breakdown of ads within the campaign appears, as shown in Figure 10-16.

Because typical campaigns on Facebook deliver a click-through rate of approximately 0.15 percent, keep your audience reach as large as possible to get the most out of your ad spend.

Figure 10-15: Ads Manager allows you to manage multiple ad campaigns.

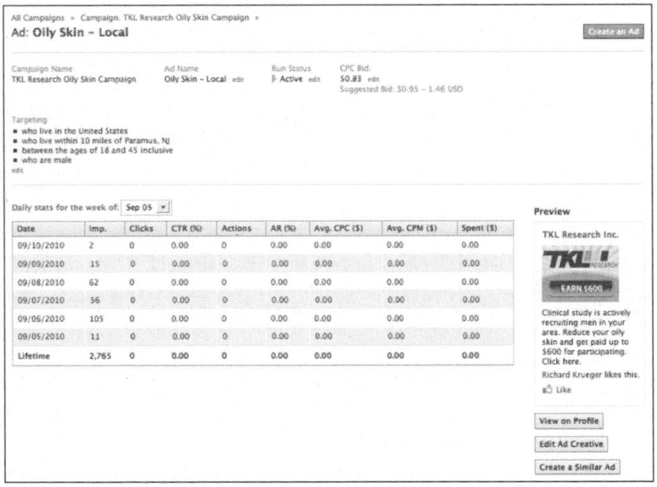

Figure 10-16: Ads Manager allows you to drill deeper into a campaign to view the ad's performance.

Making changes to your daily budget

When setting your campaign budget, you're wise to pay attention to your daily spend and performance results. Your *daily spend* is the maximum amount you've allocated to your campaign budget. Get some benchmarks for your campaign's performance. If you find that your CTR is greater than 1 percent, consider lowering your bid because a higher-performing ad gets preference over underperforming ones. The difference in a few cents can be significant, depending on your total spend, so constantly adjust your bids to maximize your return on investment (refer to Figure 10-9). For more information on setting a budget for your ad, see the "Setting your budget" section earlier in this chapter.

You can make changes to your campaign's daily budget from the All Campaigns view within Ads Manager in several ways:

✔ Click the budget amount for the campaign you want to change. A pop-up box appears that allows you to modify your daily budget.

✔ Select the check box to the left of any campaign you want to edit. Click the Edit *(number)* of Rows option above the list of campaigns to change the name, status, or budget of any checked campaign.

You can also change your campaign's budget from the individual campaign view by clicking Edit next to the Daily Budget listed at the top of the campaign details.

Changes are active within a few minutes of making the change. Any ad charges already accrued for the day are included in your new budget so your account is not overcharged.

Placing Ads through a Sales Rep

Like all major media companies, Facebook has a staff of competent sales professionals at the ready to assist you with your campaigns — for no extra charge. Purchasing ads directly through a Facebook representative has its advantages. A rep assigns you a campaign manager who oversees all aspects of a campaign, from creating an ad to targeting through bidding and optimizing your campaign. For those advertisers that can commit to spending a minimum of $10,000 per month over an initial three-month period, this is definitely a preferred option.

Although Facebook limits its handholding ad service to advertisers with a sizeable budget, there are significant advantages to this direction:

- ✔ You can choose to have your ads displayed on the coveted News Feed page where CTRs tend to be higher.

- ✔ You can participate in Facebook's newest type of ad unit, *engagement ads,* which bring interactions with your brand directly into the ad unit. Examples of engagement ads include the ability to RSVP to an event, add a video comment, become a fan (as shown in Figure 10-17), or take a poll. Facebook's engagement ads are ideal for driving consumer engagement, collecting data, and raising brand awareness.

Facebook claims that its engagement ads have a higher action rate than the industry average CTR of 15 percent. Facebook also offers extended reach by generating social stories around user's interactions with the ad, amplifying reach as they're seen on friends' News Feeds. If your budget is large enough and your objective is to generate engagement, engagement ads purchased via a Facebook ad rep are just the vehicle to meet your marketing needs.

Figure 10-17:
Facebook engagement ads allow social actions.

To get in touch with Facebook's advertising staff, you can complete a contact form at www.facebook.com/business/contact.php.

Chapter 11

Measuring and Optimizing Ad Activity

In This Chapter

▶ Checking out your ad campaign mid-flight

▶ Evaluating ad performance with Facebook reports

Although still relatively new, the Facebook advertising platform performs well for tens of thousands of advertisers. The platform's ability to target ad demographics is already legendary, and because prices are determined by a supply-and-demand–based bidding system, now is probably the best time to jump in. As we discuss in Chapter 10, you can purchase ads on a cost per impression (CPM) or a cost per click (CPC) basis — at extremely low price points while supply far exceeds demand. Whether you want to micro-target your audience or reach as broad an audience as possible, there's no better social networking platform for advertising than Facebook.

Facebook offers you a full range of metrics to measure success via the Web site's internal ad management and its exportable reports. In this chapter, we show you how to use the Facebook reporting tools to gauge the number of impressions and click rates as well as other valuable traffic data, including the number of fans added on a daily basis, the demographics of your fans, the number of visitors to the Page, and those that engaged in an activity while on your Page.

Testing Your Ad

As with all online advertising, it's a good idea to test several variations of your ad before you commit the bulk of your advertising budget. With Facebook, you can easily

- ✓ Copy an existing ad.
- ✓ Change the title, body copy, or photo of that ad.
- ✓ Target your desired demographic.

✔ Use the CPM/CPC pay model.

✔ Use the suggested bidding or enter your own bids.

✔ Change the referring page (either within Facebook or to an external Web page).

Or you can perform any combination of the preceding tasks. Because you can set an individual budget for each campaign and track its effectiveness, you can identify the better-performing ads. With some historical data, you can optimize your campaign by increasing the budget on better-performing ads and decreasing or eliminating the poorer-performing ones.

By running several tests and changing specific variables, such as the headline, you can compare key metrics, such as impressions, clicks, and click-through rates (CTRs), to determine the better-performing campaign. For example, in a recent campaign for a sore throat clinical trial, two campaigns were created in which the headline was the only differential. The first ad's headline stated, "Earn $600 and Feel Better," whereas the second ad's headline declared, "Got Sore Throat?" The second ad saw a dramatic increase in click-throughs as well as a lower CPM. This simple test helped to identify the better-performing ad; therefore, the company dedicated more of its ad budget to the second ad.

Testing variations of an ad

To test both CPC and CPM campaigns, follow these general steps:

1. Create an ad and then copy that ad by choosing it from the Select an Ad drop-down list on the Design Your Ad page (the first section on the Advertise on Facebook page). For one of the ads, select the Pay for Impressions (CPM) option under the Pricing section of the Advertise on Facebook page and set your bid. Dedicate a similar daily spend amount for each ad.

   See Chapter 10 for details on creating an ad.

2. After a short period of time, say several days or a week (long enough to get a sample of data large enough to make a decision, which should be more than 100 clicks), review your Ads Manager to determine which ad fared better by looking at your average CPC and CPM.

   The ad with the lower cost for both categories is your better-performing ad in terms of cost. (Typically, if CPC is less on one ad over the other, the CPM will always be lower for the same ad as well.) If a campaign focuses on an extremely narrow or highly targeted audience, CPC-based ads often deliver a more cost-efficient ad buy.

A campaign with a strong *call to action,* or offer, such as "Sign Up to Get Your Free Gift," is likely to have a strong response rate regardless of its purchase model. The call to action could be in the headline or in the body. Typically, to get the most response, the call to action should be in the headline, but that's not always possible with a 25-character limit. Please note, typical response rates on Facebook ads are generally in the 0.75 percent CTR or less, so don't be discouraged if your ad is being clicked by less than 1 percent of those who see it. That's why targeting a wider audience is always encouraged on Facebook because ads with low-performing CTRs could generate very little traffic to your referring Facebook Page, event, or application.

Today's savvy interactive advertisers live and die by performance metrics, including total impressions, clicks, and CTRs for a reason. They know that the best way to improve an ad's effectiveness is to understand the available data and make informed decisions.

Before you fully embrace or dismiss Facebook advertising, set some basic benchmarks to evaluate a campaign's success or failure. *Benchmarking* is a way to set expectations for your ad's performance. By running some test ads with a limited budget and shortened time period, you can approximate what you can expect when the ad is exposed to a larger audience. If, for example, your test shows a CTR of 1 percent on a CPM buy of $4, you can estimate how many people will click your ads if you spend $4,000 total on the campaign.

On Facebook, ads purchased on a CPC basis are more cost-effective at driving traffic to a given Web site or Facebook destination than if purchased on a CPM basis. However, if your goal is more of a brand awareness campaign and you want to gain exposure to as many people as possible, ads purchased on a CPM basis could be a more effective strategy.

Testing your ad's link page

Smart marketers continuously test their ad's referral link (*landing page,* as we discuss in Chapter 10). You can employ advanced tracking services to determine which landing pages are more effective in terms of getting the visitor to undertake a specific action, such as signing up for your newsletter or purchasing an item. And keep in mind that just a slight increase in their *conversion rate* (the number of consumers who complete a specific desired action like completing a form) has a dramatic effect on your campaign's overall return on investment. However, not every company has a budget that allows them to extensively test different iterations of a landing page. In that case, at the least, monitor your ad's performance, see what works, and replicate your successes where possible.

Understanding Facebook Ad Data

Facebook offers marketers ample reporting data to help make better decisions and gauge their ad's performance. Like all digital advertising efforts, our feeling is, the more testing, the better. When you run a test campaign, you get actual responses from real Facebook users, as opposed to a focus group or company insiders providing advice. The data generated through real-world testing of your ad campaign should provide valuable insights as to your ongoing ad performance.

Understand that any reporting data, such as click-through percentages and cost per click (CPC), from your test ad campaigns will vary somewhat from when you run your main ad campaigns. (Like the disclaimers you see in a financial commercial's fine print: Past performance is not a guarantee of future behavior.) The idea is to use the test campaigns to identify the most popular or most likely elements for success, as compared to other options that you've tried in your ads.

You can get to your Ads Manager (discussed in detail in Chapter 10) by clicking the Advertising link on the bottom of any Facebook Page. If you already have an ad running, you're automatically taken to your Ads Manager from this link. The following sections cover some of the key reports offered through Facebook's Ads Manager, to help you track your ad's performance and know what to look for as you design your main ad campaigns and make the final decisions.

Advertising Performance report

The most common report to review is your Advertising Performance report, which is available from your Reports screen within Ads Manager. This report (shown in Figure 11-1) details all the major statistics for any ad campaign you've run. As you review your campaign, look for results that stand out or give you an idea of what stood out among the various tests you may have run.

Impressions

Impressions refers to the number of times your ad was shown on a Facebook Web page to someone. Although impressions don't tell you about your ad's performance, it's important to spend a minute and take a look at the number of times your ad was "run" on the site, regardless of the actions the viewers took when they saw it.

Questions to ask yourself include

- ✔ Are the number of impressions enough of a good sample size to make a valid decision?
- ✔ What changes, if any, did you make to your ads if you see a big change in the number of impressions received on a given day or week?
- ✔ Are your ads generating a consistent amount of impressions per day, week, or month?

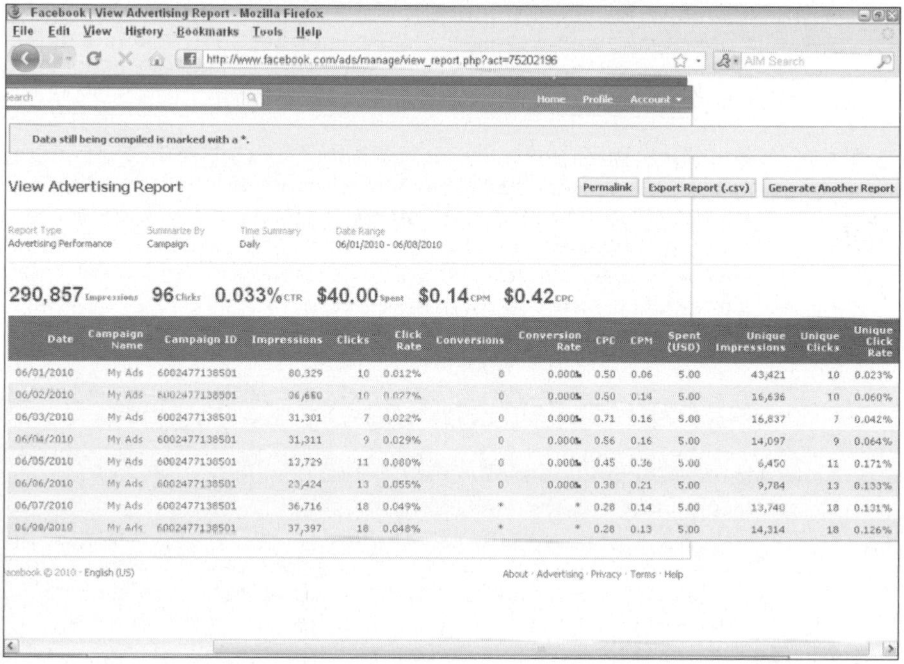

Date	Campaign Name	Campaign ID	Impressions	Clicks	Click Rate	Conversions	Conversion Rate	CPC	CPM	Spent (USD)	Unique Impressions	Unique Clicks	Unique Click Rate
06/01/2010	My Ads	6002477138501	80,329	10	0.012%	0	0.000%	0.50	0.06	5.00	43,421	10	0.023%
06/02/2010	My Ads	6002477138501	36,650	10	0.027%	0	0.000%	0.50	0.14	5.00	16,636	10	0.060%
06/03/2010	My Ads	6002477138501	31,301	7	0.022%	0	0.000%	0.71	0.16	5.00	16,837	7	0.042%
06/04/2010	My Ads	6002477138501	31,311	9	0.029%	0	0.000%	0.56	0.16	5.00	14,097	9	0.064%
06/05/2010	My Ads	6002477138501	13,729	11	0.080%	0	0.000%	0.45	0.36	5.00	6,450	11	0.171%
06/06/2010	My Ads	6002477138501	23,424	13	0.055%	0	0.000%	0.38	0.21	5.00	9,784	13	0.133%
06/07/2010	My Ads	6002477138501	36,716	18	0.049%	*	*	0.28	0.14	5.00	13,740	18	0.131%
06/08/2010	My Ads	6002477138501	37,397	18	0.048%	*	*	0.28	0.13	5.00	14,314	18	0.126%

Figure 11-1: Your Advertising Performance report shows all your major statistics.

Click-through ratio

The click-through ratio (CTR) is probably the most important indicator in determining the performance of your ad. By looking at the ratio between click-throughs over impressions, you can see which ads perform the best from your entire set.

Questions to ask yourself here include

- Are the highest-generating CTRs significantly higher than the other values to indicate a genuine preference, or obvious choice in ads? Or are a group of test ads scoring higher than other test ads?
- Are the highest CTRs good enough to justify a bigger investment in Facebook ads? In other words, are you getting enough of a return from your click-through ratio to justify the expense?
- If you made changes to your test campaigns while they were running, are the CTRs after the change significantly better or worse than before the change?

Avg. CPC

Regardless of the payment model you choose to run your test campaigns of Facebook ads, the site will calculate what your resulting average cost per click was for those campaigns. So, say for example, you choose to pay for impressions under a CPM model. If you received 100,000 impressions for $500 (at a

$5 CPM, or $5 for 1,000 impression rate), and those 100,000 impressions resulted in a 1 percent click-through rate of 1,000 clicks, your average cost per click would be the amount spent divided by the number of clicks, or $500/1,000 or $0.50 per click.

Therefore, knowing your average CPC gives you an idea of bidding ranges where your campaign will perform optimally. In the preceding example, if you're getting an average CPC of $0.48 through a CPM payment model and you're paying more than $0.50 if you run a CPC payment model, perhaps you'd consider changing your payment model going forward to take advantage of the CPM model and the lower costs.

Responder Demographics report

If you're more interested in the types of people that are looking at and responding to your ads, the Responder Demographics report is valuable data for you to review. Facebook groups together your ad viewers based on two of the filters you used when targeting your ad. So for example, you can pull up a report that shows you the responders to an ad or ad campaign based on gender/age, and then location by country or state. In the example in Figure 11-2, we ran an ad targeting male comic book fans aged 18+ in the United States, and the report showed the amount of impressions, clicks, and the click-through rate for each demographic segment. (A *segment* is a range of users, such as males aged 18–24 or males living in a particular state.)

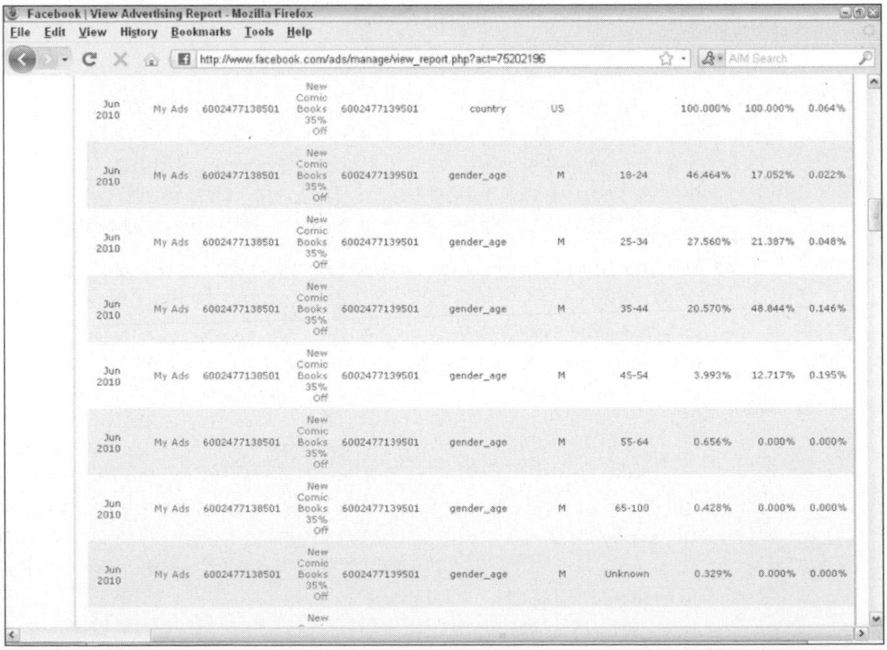

Jun 2010	My Ads	6002477138501	New Comic Books 35% Off	6002477139501	country	US		100.000%	100.000%	0.064%
Jun 2010	My Ads	6002477138501	New Comic Books 35% Off	6002477139501	gender_age	M	18-24	46.464%	17.052%	0.022%
Jun 2010	My Ads	6002477138501	New Comic Books 35% Off	6002477139501	gender_age	M	25-34	27.560%	21.387%	0.048%
Jun 2010	My Ads	6002477138501	New Comic Books 35% Off	6002477139501	gender_age	M	35-44	20.570%	48.844%	0.146%
Jun 2010	My Ads	6002477138501	New Comic Books 35% Off	6002477139501	gender_age	M	45-54	3.993%	12.717%	0.195%
Jun 2010	My Ads	6002477138501	New Comic Books 35% Off	6002477139501	gender_age	M	55-64	0.656%	0.000%	0.000%
Jun 2010	My Ads	6002477138501	New Comic Books 35% Off	6002477139501	gender_age	M	65-100	0.428%	0.000%	0.000%
Jun 2010	My Ads	6002477138501	New Comic Books 35% Off	6002477139501	gender_age	M	Unknown	0.329%	0.000%	0.000%

Figure 11-2: See the responder demographics to your Facebook Ads.

Exporting Ads Manager reports

You can easily export your data as an HTML, CSV, or Microsoft Excel (XLS) file. From your Facebook Ads Manager, click the Reports tab and then select what report you want to gener-ate, for which period, and in what format. Click the Generate Report button, and Facebook displays your report.

There were some very interesting results from this example, and some very interesting lessons you can find out from this report that can help you with your main campaigns:

- ✔ **Which segments give you the best CTRs?** Although comic books may skew to a younger audience, the best click-through rate in our example occurred with the 35–44 age range (0.146 percent, more than three times the 25–34 percentage and almost seven times the 18–24 percentage), and the second best campaign came from the 45–54 age range (although this age range saw about 4 percent of all impressions, it responded with a 0.192 percent CTR). Therefore, we may want to test an ad that specifi-cally targets 35–55 year old males.

- ✔ **Are your expected segments performing better or worse than expected?** You will have your ideas about what age ranges, for example, should be your best and worst customers, but your reports may prove your hypoth-esis wrong. For example, we ran an ad campaign for *Team Terrapin,* a sail-ing team that took part in the biennial Newport to Bahamas race, and the age breakdowns for the initial ad campaign are in Figure 11-3. Although the highest click-through rates were achieved with men aged 45 and older, there was a decent response from females aged 35 and older, and they had a better click-through rate than younger men (aged 18–35). Based on that info, if you wanted to have custom age ranges, you'd be wise to include males and females aged 35 and older in your ad's targeting.

- ✔ **What unexpected segments show promising results**? You can sort your entire report by a field, such as click-through rate, so you can see a list of your best-performing CTRs for a campaign, as shown in Figure 11-4. This way you can see segments that are high performers that you may not have included in your big campaigns. In our example, certain states like Kansas and Alabama had better CTRs than any other age or location filter. When you see segments perform better than expected, you may consider running additional tests just on those specific segments to see whether you can harness that audience or determine whether it was more of a fluke.

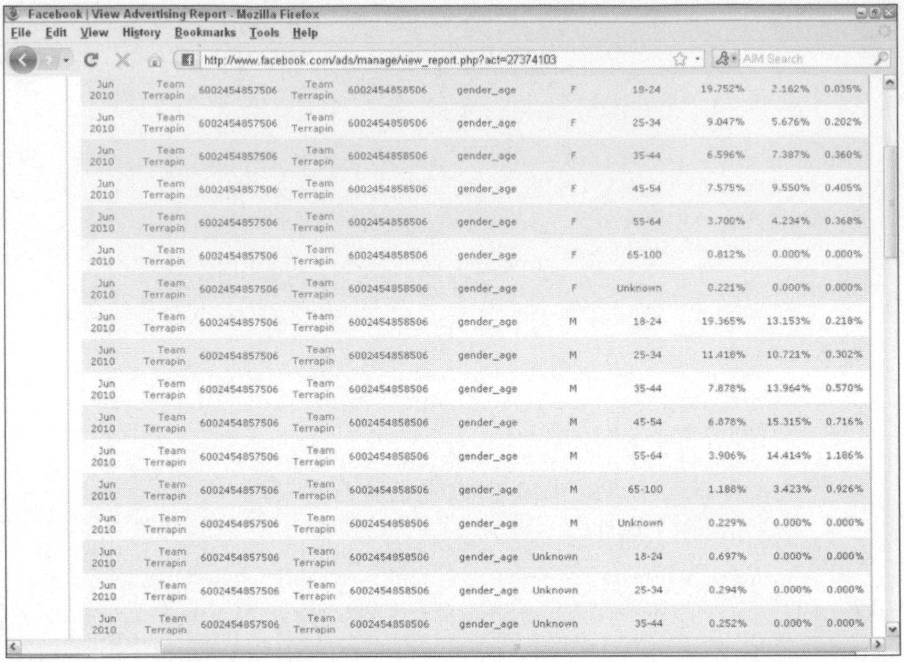

Jun 2010	Team Terrapin	6002454857506	Team Terrapin	6002454858506	gender_age	F	18-24	19.752%	2.162%	0.035%
Jun 2010	Team Terrapin	6002454857506	Team Terrapin	6002454858506	gender_age	F	25-34	9.047%	5.676%	0.202%
Jun 2010	Team Terrapin	6002454857506	Team Terrapin	6002454858506	gender_age	F	35-44	6.596%	7.387%	0.360%
Jun 2010	Team Terrapin	6002454857506	Team Terrapin	6002454858506	gender_age	F	45-54	7.575%	9.550%	0.405%
Jun 2010	Team Terrapin	6002454857506	Team Terrapin	6002454858506	gender_age	F	55-64	3.700%	4.234%	0.368%
Jun 2010	Team Terrapin	6002454857506	Team Terrapin	6002454858506	gender_age	F	65-100	0.812%	0.000%	0.000%
Jun 2010	Team Terrapin	6002454857506	Team Terrapin	6002454858506	gender_age	F	Unknown	0.221%	0.000%	0.000%
Jun 2010	Team Terrapin	6002454857506	Team Terrapin	6002454858506	gender_age	M	18-24	19.365%	13.153%	0.218%
Jun 2010	Team Terrapin	6002454857506	Team Terrapin	6002454858506	gender_age	M	25-34	11.418%	10.721%	0.302%
Jun 2010	Team Terrapin	6002454857506	Team Terrapin	6002454858506	gender_age	M	35-44	7.878%	13.964%	0.570%
Jun 2010	Team Terrapin	6002454857506	Team Terrapin	6002454858506	gender_age	M	45-54	6.878%	15.315%	0.716%
Jun 2010	Team Terrapin	6002454857506	Team Terrapin	6002454858506	gender_age	M	55-64	3.906%	14.414%	1.186%
Jun 2010	Team Terrapin	6002454857506	Team Terrapin	6002454858506	gender_age	M	65-100	1.188%	3.423%	0.926%
Jun 2010	Team Terrapin	6002454857506	Team Terrapin	6002454858506	gender_age	M	Unknown	0.229%	0.000%	0.000%
Jun 2010	Team Terrapin	6002454857506	Team Terrapin	6002454858506	gender_age	Unknown	18-24	0.697%	0.000%	0.000%
Jun 2010	Team Terrapin	6002454857506	Team Terrapin	6002454858506	gender_age	Unknown	25-34	0.294%	0.000%	0.000%
Jun 2010	Team Terrapin	6002454857506	Team Terrapin	6002454858506	gender_age	Unknown	35-44	0.252%	0.000%	0.000%

Figure 11-3: Select the demographics of people who are more likely to click your ad.

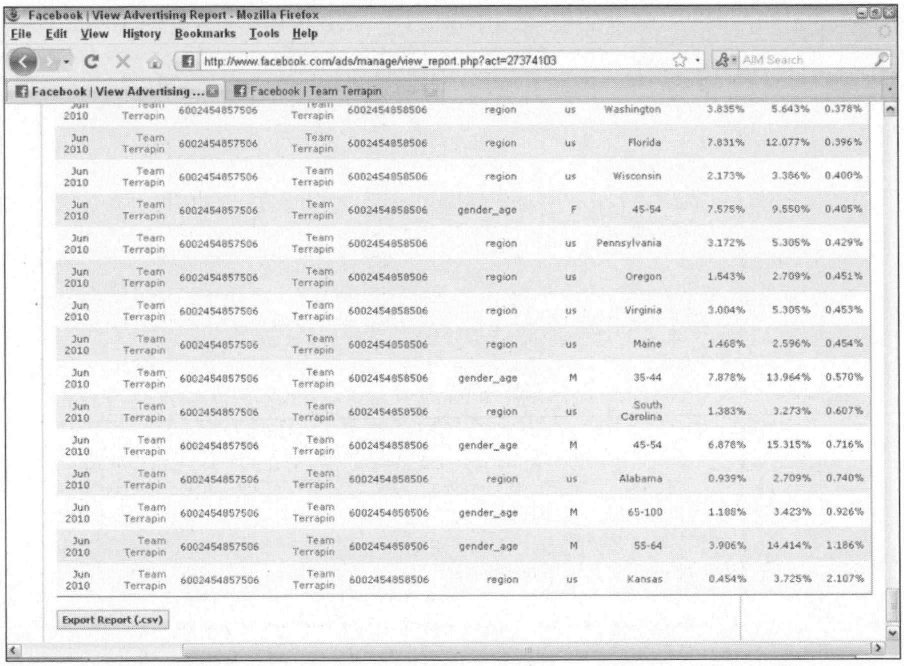

Jun 2010	Team Terrapin	6002454857506	Team Terrapin	6002454858506	region	us	Washington	3.835%	5.643%	0.378%
Jun 2010	Team Terrapin	6002454857506	Team Terrapin	6002454858506	region	us	Florida	7.831%	12.077%	0.396%
Jun 2010	Team Terrapin	6002454857506	Team Terrapin	6002454858506	region	us	Wisconsin	2.173%	3.386%	0.400%
Jun 2010	Team Terrapin	6002454857506	Team Terrapin	6002454858506	gender_age	F	45-54	7.575%	9.550%	0.405%
Jun 2010	Team Terrapin	6002454857506	Team Terrapin	6002454858506	region	us	Pennsylvania	3.172%	5.305%	0.429%
Jun 2010	Team Terrapin	6002454857506	Team Terrapin	6002454858506	region	us	Oregon	1.543%	2.709%	0.451%
Jun 2010	Team Terrapin	6002454857506	Team Terrapin	6002454858506	region	us	Virginia	3.004%	5.305%	0.453%
Jun 2010	Team Terrapin	6002454857506	Team Terrapin	6002454858506	region	us	Maine	1.468%	2.596%	0.454%
Jun 2010	Team Terrapin	6002454857506	Team Terrapin	6002454858506	gender_age	M	35-44	7.878%	13.964%	0.570%
Jun 2010	Team Terrapin	6002454857506	Team Terrapin	6002454858506	region	us	South Carolina	1.383%	3.273%	0.607%
Jun 2010	Team Terrapin	6002454857506	Team Terrapin	6002454858506	gender_age	M	45-54	6.878%	15.315%	0.716%
Jun 2010	Team Terrapin	6002454857506	Team Terrapin	6002454858506	region	us	Alabama	0.939%	2.709%	0.740%
Jun 2010	Team Terrapin	6002454857506	Team Terrapin	6002454858506	gender_age	M	65-100	1.188%	3.423%	0.926%
Jun 2010	Team Terrapin	6002454857506	Team Terrapin	6002454858506	gender_age	M	55-64	3.906%	14.414%	1.186%
Jun 2010	Team Terrapin	6002454857506	Team Terrapin	6002454858506	region	us	Kansas	0.454%	3.725%	2.107%

Figure 11-4: Find out your hidden-gem segment groups who like your ad.

Part IV
Riding the Facebook Viral Wave

The 5th Wave

By Rich Tennant

VP Sales

"It's Web-based, on-demand, and customizable. Still, I think I'm going to miss our old sales incentive methods."

In this part . . .

If you've read previous parts of this book, you've gotten some great ideas for establishing your Facebook presence, but there are strategies and tactics that can make it even stronger. In this part, we discuss how to use Facebook applications to form deeper engagement with your fans, and how to best leverage Facebook's Open Graph to further drive your viral marketing efforts.

You also find out how to extend the Facebook Platform to your Web site through the use of the Like button and other Facebook social plug-ins that tap into the viral features that have helped make Facebook so successful.

Chapter 12

Dressing Up Your Facebook Page with Applications

*F*acebook applications (apps) have become powerful tools for marketers. They can serve a variety of functions when you install them on your Facebook Page, and they really add some sizzle to your business's Facebook presence. In fact, Facebook apps are becoming so popular that 70 percent of Facebook members regularly interact with them every month.

Facebook now has more than 550,000 active applications running on its platform. Individuals and third-party companies have created the majority of them. Facebook allows anyone to build an app that works on the Facebook Platform (as long as the app adheres to the Facebook Developer guidelines). Although developers often don't create these apps (such as games, trivia quizzes, and other time-wasting pursuits) for business use, you can find apps designed to address specific business needs in increasing numbers.

Facebook apps can help bring your Page to life. Whether you want to add a presentation via the SlideShare app, or post content from a blog that you write or admire via the Simply RSS app, apps can help you customize your Facebook Page, and they're becoming an important advertising and branding vehicle within Facebook.

Finding Out What Apps Can Do for You

Many Facebook marketers rely on apps to make their Facebook presence stand out from the competition and to add engaging elements with which their fans can interact. *Facebook apps* are software modules that you can install on your Facebook Page that add a unique functionality to further engage your audience with your brand.

Apps can take on many different forms, from video players to business cards to promotions. Facebook offers countless apps for marketers that provide business solutions and promote the business enterprise. You can find a lot of valuable business apps available for free in the Facebook Application Directory (described in the next section), and we list our favorite business apps in Chapter 17.

Some apps are designed to help you promote your Web site or blog, stream a live video conference, or show customized directions to your office. Also, third-party developers are licensing and selling apps focused on the business market, including promotional apps from Wildfire Interactive, lead-generation apps from Involver, customer-service apps from Parature, and apps that encourage user participation from Buddy Media and TabSite.

Here are a few examples of some apps that can add useful functionality to your Facebook Page:

- **TrackThis — Package Tracking app:** Track UPS, USPS, and Fedex packages through Facebook notifications or text messages.

- **YouTube Video Box app:** If your company has sales videos, messages from the CEO, or product demonstration videos posted to YouTube, add them to your Page for all to see. (See Figure 12-1.)

- **Involver's Twitter app:** Promote your Twitter stream on a custom tab within your Facebook Page. For example, Figure 12-2 shows our Twitter updates in chronological order. At the top of the Page, you also see the number of followers, how many the account is following, and the total number of updates made on Twitter.

Facebook apps offer business owners new ways to increase customer engagement while maximizing the Page's usefulness to their fans. Whether you find apps in the Facebook Application Directory or a third-party developer's Web site, you can leverage apps to foster business relationships with your users. Figure 12-3 shows business app directory Appbistro's Web-based directory of Facebook business apps.

Figure 12-1:
The
YouTube
app appears
on the For
Dummies
Page.

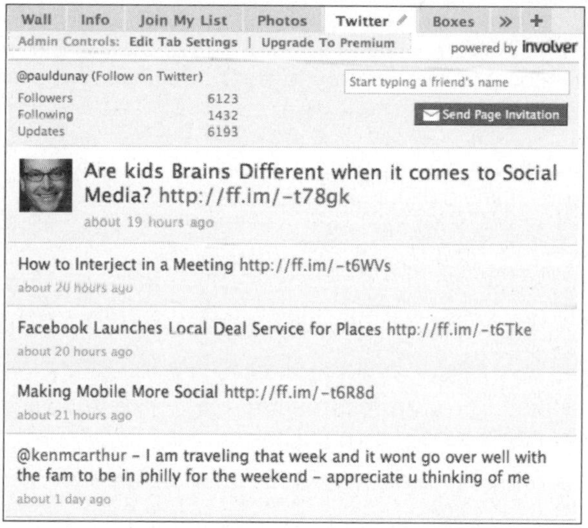

Figure 12-2:
The Twitter
tab on our
Facebook
Page.

Figure 12-3:
Business-
focused
apps
directory
Appbistro
offers third-
party apps
to help
customize
your
Facebook
Page.

Finding Apps

Facebook created a directory to help you find an app that might enhance your business presence on Facebook. You can find Facebook's Application Directory by visiting www.facebook.com/apps/directory.php.

The Facebook Application Directory does a good job of providing quick and easy access to more than 52,000 apps in its library. The directory highlights several apps that Facebook recognizes as best-in-class on a rotating basis. Here are other ways you find apps for your Page:

- ✔ Check out the list of apps you might like on the directory's welcome screen.
- ✔ Search for apps by keyword, application name, or type.
- ✔ Click the Business tab in the left column to access a good selection of business-related apps, as shown in Figure 12-4.
- ✔ Click the Pages link at the bottom of the left column to view specific apps that install on Pages.

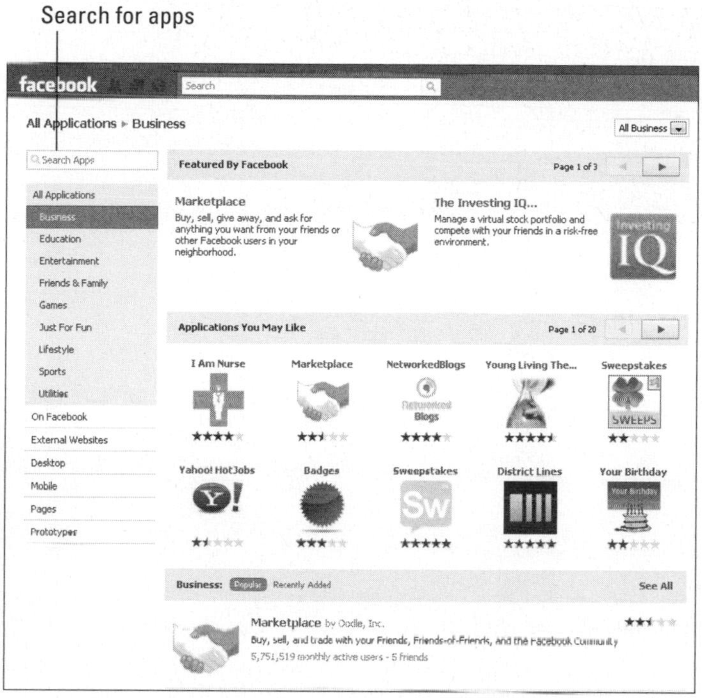

Search for apps

Figure 12-4:
You can
search for
business
apps in
Facebook's
Application
Directory.

Adding an App to Your Page

After you identify an app you might want to add to your Page, you can click
the link to view the app's Page. Much like other pages, the app's Page offers
a Wall, company info, reviews, discussions, and profile photos of friends who
use this application (if any), and allows for some degree of customization.
You can even become a fan by clicking the Like button.

To install an app, follow these steps:

1. **In the Facebook Application Directory (`www.facebook.com/apps/
   directory.php`), click the link for the app that you want to install.**

   Facebook takes you to the app's Page.

2. **Click the Go to Application button.**

   Facebook displays an installation page, where you permit the app to access your Facebook Page or profile. For example, when you install the Partner Page Promotions app, you need to click the Allow button on the Request for Permission screen, as shown in Figure 12-5.

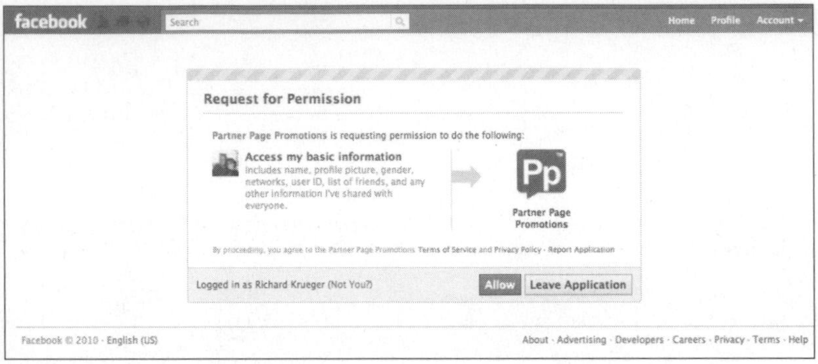

Figure 12-5:
Adding the Partner Page Promotions app on your Facebook Page.

3. **Click the Allow button to give the app permission to install.**

   If you have more than one Page, the Request for Permission page lists the various Pages and asks you on which Page you want to install the app.

   If you don't want to grant the app access to your information, click the Leave Application button. However, you can't use an app for which you haven't approved permissions.

   After you click Allow and select the Page where you want the app installed, Facebook takes you to the app's Facebook *canvas page,* or home page, where, depending on the app, you might need to add additional information. The app appears in the tabs section of the Page you selected.

Some apps are designed for consumers, and therefore, you can install them only on profiles. Other apps are designed for businesses, although you can install them on either your profile or Page. To find apps that work on your Page, check out the Pages category on the left side of the app directory.

Deleting an App

If you want to delete an app from your Page, follow these steps:

1. **On your Page, click the Edit Page link.**

2. **On the next page that appears, click the Applications tab on the left.**

3. **In the Added Applications section on the right, find the application that you want to delete and then click the X button to the right of the app, as shown in Figure 12-6.**

   Facebook displays a dialog box asking if you are sure you want to remove the app.

4. **Click the Remove button in the bottom of the pop-up window to delete the app.**

You can't remove some Facebook apps, such as Video, Notes, or Photos, from your Page. These core apps are instrumental to the Facebook experience, and Facebook developed them internally.

Figure 12-6:
Click the X button to remove an application.

Click to remove app

Chapter 13

Getting the Scoop on Facebook Places and Deals

. . . .

In This Chapter

▶ Checking into, creating, and claiming a Facebook Places page

▶ Setting up, promoting, and honoring a Facebook deal

. . . .

Social media tools like Facebook have made people's lives open books. People can connect with each other anytime, anywhere. In the past year, geolocation services, such as foursquare and Gowalla, have played an important role in connecting people even further. Tools like these allow you to tell people where you are, what you're doing, who's with you, and much more. Recently, Facebook jumped on the bandwagon and created Facebook Places. *Places* is Facebook's geolocation tool that allows members to check in to a venue they're visiting, see what's going on nearby, tag friends who are with them, share photos, and share thoughts about what's going on where they are. Facebook members can do all this with the Facebook app on their smartphone or by pointing their phone's browser to http://touch.facebook.com. Updates from Facebook Places appear in users' Facebook News Feeds.

As you can imagine, creating and claiming a Facebook Places page for your business can be an excellent marketing tool. When people check in to a venue nearby, your business comes up as a Nearby Place. If a visitor checks in to your Places venue, it shows up in his News Feed so that his friends can see he's frequenting your business.

And if you want to encourage even *more* traffic, you can take advantage of Facebook Deals. Facebook Deals is a way for businesses to interact with their customers via the Facebook Places application. You can reward customers for frequent check-ins, offer discounts for services, or even donate to charities. Customers can redeem deals by checking in to a venue with Facebook Places.

In this chapter, we explain how the Places check-in process works, how to create a Places page for your business, and how to claim your business on Places. Then you find out how you can ramp up sales for your business by using Facebook Deals in conjunction with Places.

Exploring Facebook Places

When Facebook members visit a place, they may want to share their adventure with their friends, see whether any of their friends are close by, or take advantage of a Facebook deal (we explain Facebook Deals later in this chapter). Members can do all those things via Facebook Places.

Facebook Places is a geolocation feature that uses a smartphone's GPS to track where Facebook members are and allows them to check in to businesses or places (for example, a park) while they're out and about. When members check in to a place, their Facebook News Feed updates, and their friends can see where they are, as shown in Figure 13-1. If members tag friends who are with them, their friends' Facebook News Feeds also update.

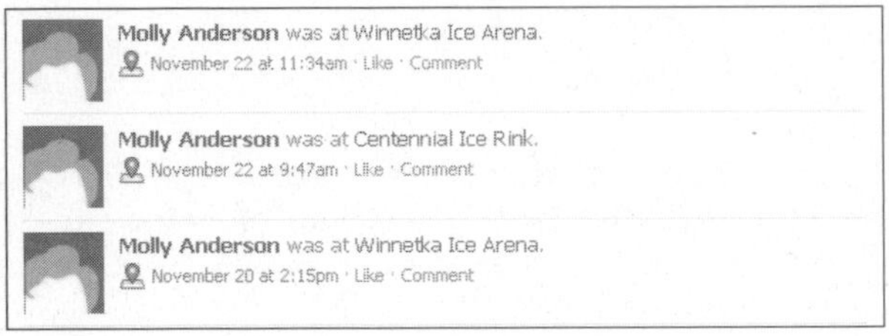

Figure 13-1:
Checking in
to a place
creates a
News Feed
story.

Molly Anderson was at Winnetka Ice Arena.
November 22 at 11:34am · Like · Comment

Molly Anderson was at Centennial Ice Rink.
November 22 at 9:47am · Like · Comment

Molly Anderson was at Winnetka Ice Arena.
November 20 at 2:15pm · Like · Comment

By setting up and claiming your business on Facebook Places, you're taking advantage of another tool to build brand awareness and attract potential new customers. In the following sections, we explain more about how Places works and how to create and claim a Facebook place for your business.

Checking in to a venue on Facebook Places

Before going into detail about how to create and *claim* a place for your business (giving you the authority to manage the information associated with it), we want to briefly explain how Facebook Places works. If Facebook members want to check in to a venue with Facebook Places, they can open their phone's Facebook app or point their phone's browser to `http://touch.facebook.com`.

If Facebook members are using the Facebook app on their smartphone, they tap the Places icon and then tap the Check In button in the top-right corner. Their phone's GPS makes a note of where they are and creates a list of nearby places. Users can then scroll through the list to find the venue where they are. If they don't see their venue, they can type the name of the venue into the search bar at the top of the screen. The venue might not be on Places yet. If that's the case, members can create a place, as described in the next section "Creating a Places page," in this chapter.

The Places page for a business looks similar to the one in Figure 13-2. From here, members can enter text about what they're doing at the venue and tag friends who are with them.

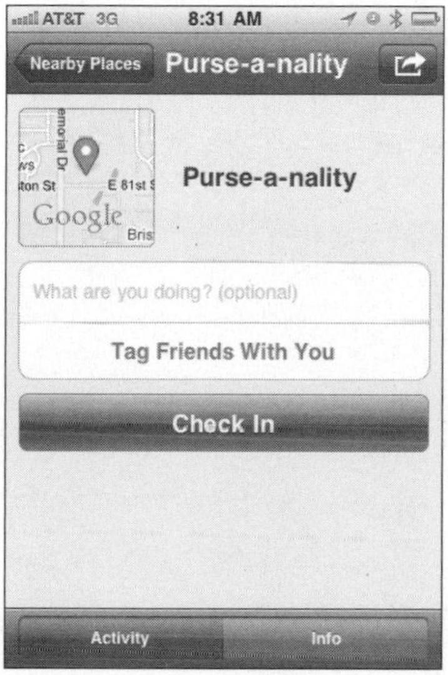

Figure 13-2:
A sample check-in page for a business on Facebook Places.

After members tap the Check In button, the Places page for the venue appears again, as shown in Figure 13-3, but this time, in addition to tagging friends, members can add a photo, check out what's close (with the Nearby Places button), and see recent activity (who has been there or who is there now).

A member's check-in appears in her Facebook News Feed as well as in the News Feeds of any friends she tags.

Creating a Places page

Facebook members don't have to be affiliated with your business to *create* a Places page for it. However, only you or someone affiliated with your business can *claim* the Places page, giving you the right to manage the information associated with it. (See the next section for the lowdown on claiming your Facebook place.)

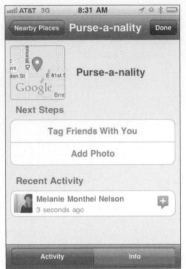

Figure 13-3:
Members
have
another
chance to
tag friends
or take a
picture to
include in
their Places
update.

If a Places page hasn't been created for your business yet, don't worry; it's easy to add your business to the Places list. Just follow these instructions:

1. **Open your phone's Facebook app.**

   Alternatively, point your phone's browser to `http://touch.facebook.com`.

   It's best to be at or near your place of business when you create your Places page. That way your phone's GPS has an accurate idea of where your business is located, and your Places page has the correct information. However, if you create your place while you're *not* at your business, you will have the opportunity to set the correct address and other information (such as your phone number) when you claim your place (as explained in the next section).

2. **Tap the Check In button in the top-right corner.**

   The Nearby Places screen appears.

3. **Tap the search bar and type your business name.**

   We searched for local business *Purse-a-nality* (as shown in Figure 13-4), but no results were found. Instead, we were given the option to add Purse-a-nality to Places so that the business will appear in future searches.

4. **Tap the Add *Company Name* link.**

The Add a Place screen appears with a map, the name of your business, and a place for a description, as shown in Figure 13-5. You can edit the business name by tapping the text box for the business name and typing the new name. You can add a description of the business by tapping the Description (Optional) text box and then typing a short description of the business.

Figure 13-4:
Do a search for your business to create a Places page.

Figure 13-5:
The Add a Place screen allows you to create a Places page for your business.

5. **When you're finished typing, either tap the Done button on the keyboard or tap the Add button in the top-right corner.**

If your business is successfully added to Places, you see a Place Added confirmation screen like the one in Figure 13-6 that says `Your place has been added. Don't forget to check in!`

Figure 13-6:
You have successfully added your business's place!

If you receive an alert that says, `The place could not be added at this time,` just tap OK and try to add it again later. It's possible that your service was intermittent when you tried to add the place.

6. **Tap the Close button.**

The Places page for your business appears. Now that you've created your venue's Places page, why not claim it on Facebook? We explain how to do that in the next section.

Claiming your business on Facebook Places

Claiming your business place is not mandatory, but it's highly desirable. When you *claim* your business on Facebook Places, you have administrative privileges for that venue — you can change the address, business hours, and contact info associated with your business on Places. You can also decide what profile picture shows up when a Facebook user checks in to your venue. Those are all important because they're part of your business's brand, and you want to control that as much as possible.

Claiming your business on Facebook Places requires that you're the owner or official representative of the venue. You have to jump through a few hoops to prove you are who you say you are, but that's a good thing. You don't want just anyone claiming your business, right?

You must create a Places page for your business on the Facebook smartphone app (or by pointing your phone's browser to `http://touch.facebook.com`) before you can claim the Places page on Facebook. We explain how to create a Places page for your business in the preceding section.

When you're ready to claim your business on Facebook Places, follow these steps:

1. **With your computer's browser, log in to Facebook.**

2. **Use the search bar at the top of the page to search for your business's name.**

   If your business has already been created (and not claimed) on Places, the results show your business name next to the Places icon, as shown in Figure 13-7.

   If your business hasn't already been created on Places, you don't see the Places icon. Take a minute to create your business on Places using the instructions in the preceding section.

3. **Click the name of your business next to the Places icon.**

   You're taken to your business's Places page on Facebook, as shown in Figure 13-8.

   In the main part of the page, you see a map showing the location of your business. On the left and at the bottom of the page, you see the options Report Place and Is This Your Business (to claim it) as well as the Share button to share the venue with your friends and fans. You can set a specific address and phone number for your venue when you complete the Claim Place form in Step 7.

4. **Click the Is This Your Business? link.**

   A dialog box like the one in Figure 13-9 opens, explaining that claiming the business will turn it into a Facebook Page if you haven't already created one. (See Chapter 4 for more information about Facebook Pages and how they work.) If you already have a Page, don't worry, you won't have two. When you complete the Claim Place form (see Step 7), you'll have the opportunity to link directly to your existing business Page. This window also reminds you that only official representatives of the business can claim a Facebook place.

5. **Select the I Certify That I Am an Official Representative of *(Company Name)* check box.**

6. **Click Continue.**

   The Claim Place page appears, as shown in Figure 13-10.

Places icon

Figure 13-7:
When you
search for
your
business
Places
page, look
for the
Places icon.

Figure 13-8:
A sample
Places
page for a
business.

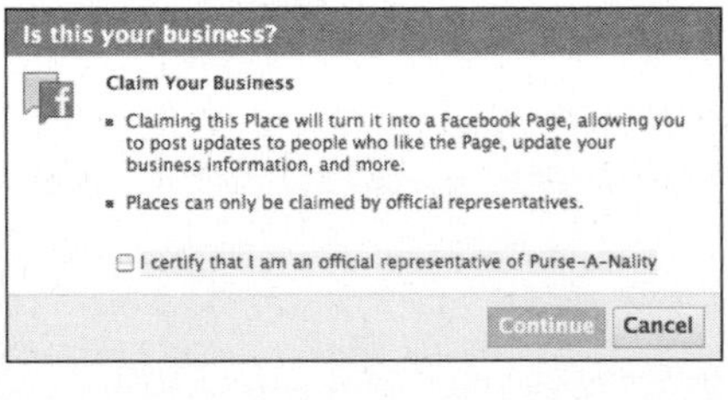

Figure 13-9:
This dialog
box reminds
you that
places can
be claimed
only by
company
repre-
sentatives.

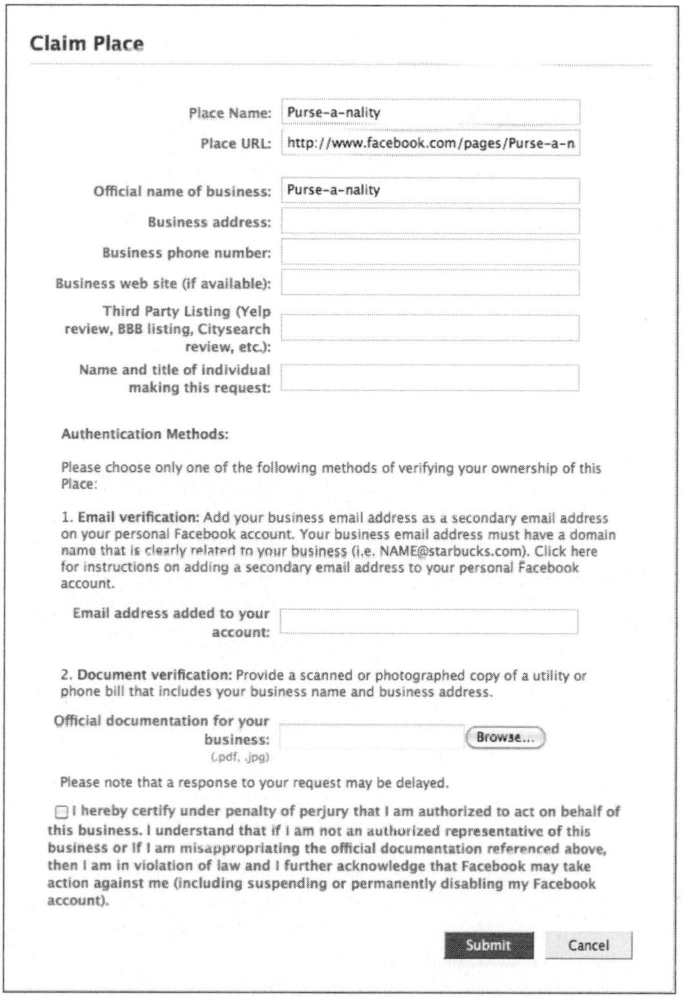

Claim Place

Place Name:	Purse-a-nality
Place URL:	http://www.facebook.com/pages/Purse-a-n
Official name of business:	Purse-a-nality
Business address:	
Business phone number:	
Business web site (if available):	
Third Party Listing (Yelp review, BBB listing, Citysearch review, etc.):	
Name and title of individual making this request:	

Authentication Methods:

Please choose only one of the following methods of verifying your ownership of this Place:

1. **Email verification:** Add your business email address as a secondary email address on your personal Facebook account. Your business email address must have a domain name that is clearly related to your business (i.e. NAME@starbucks.com). Click here for instructions on adding a secondary email address to your personal Facebook account.

Email address added to your account:	

2. **Document verification:** Provide a scanned or photographed copy of a utility or phone bill that includes your business name and business address.

Official documentation for your business: (.pdf, .jpg)	Browse...

Please note that a response to your request may be delayed.

☐ I hereby certify under penalty of perjury that I am authorized to act on behalf of this business. I understand that if I am not an authorized representative of this business or if I am misappropriating the official documentation referenced above, then I am in violation of law and I further acknowledge that Facebook may take action against me (including suspending or permanently disabling my Facebook account).

[Submit] [Cancel]

Figure 13-10:
The Claim Place page allows you to verify that you're the company's representative.

7. **Complete the Claim Place form completely.**

As you can see from Figure 13-10, you need the following information:

- *Place Name:* This is the name of your business as you want it to appear in Facebook Places.

- *Place URL:* This is the URL of your business's Facebook Page. If you haven't set up your business Page yet, flip over to Chapter 4 to find out more.

- *Official Name of Business:* This is your business's official name. It will likely be the same as the name you type in the Place Name box.

- *Business Address:* Be sure this is your business's correct address so the Places map can provide accurate directions to your venue.

- *Business Phone Number:* Share the ten-digit phone number you want customers to use in case they need to reach you about directions, store hours, or product availability.

- *Business Web Site (If Available):* This is the URL of your actual Web site or blog, not your Facebook business Page. If you don't have a Web site or blog for your business, you can leave this field blank.

- *Third Party Listing . . .:* If you have links to any reviews or endorsements of your business, list them here. Some examples are Yelp reviews, BBB endorsements, or Citysearch reviews.

- *Name and Title of Individual Making This Request:* Type your name.

- *Authentication methods:* You can choose to verify ownership of a venue via e-mail or via a document.

  To verify via e-mail, add an e-mail address with the domain name clearly related to your business name (for example, `melanie@ purse-a-nality.com`) to your main Facebook profile.

  To verify via a document, you need to have a scanned copy of a phone or utility bill that includes your business name and address. Save that scanned image to your computer and then click the Browse button to find and upload the image to Facebook.

  Facebook only accepts files in PDF or JPG format. Be sure to save your scanned image accordingly.

8. **Select the check box certifying that you have permission to act on behalf of the business you're claiming on Facebook Places.**

9. **Click the Submit button.**

   You're taken to the Facebook Help Center as a generic landing page. In a few minutes, you receive an e-mail confirmation that Facebook has received your request, and it'll be back with you soon to verify that your claim was successful.

Getting the Nitty-Gritty on Facebook Deals

Facebook Deals is a new way to connect with your customers or the companies you do business with. With Facebook Deals, businesses who have claimed their venues on Places (as described in the preceding section) can promote their business with discounts and deals for customers. Facebook members who use Places to see what or who is nearby can see deals related to businesses that are close to their current location.

Why should you consider creating a Facebook deal? Simply put, it's free, and it's a great way to promote a relationship with existing and potential customers.

You can reward frequent customers with specific discounts and deals, or you can encourage groups to come in together. Keep in mind that each time someone checks in to your venue via the Places feature, his Facebook News Feed updates with a link to your business. If he tags people with him, the update appears in those extra feeds as well.

Why do updates in Facebook News Feeds matter? When something appears in a Facebook News Feed, all the friends connected to that person see the update. Facebook estimates that each Facebook user has around 130 friends (some have more, some have fewer). If you're a business owner and just one of your customers shares a deal she liked via Places, that update reaches a potential audience of 130 *more* people than just that one person who took advantage of your deal. The more reasons you can give people to share your business with their friends, the more exposure you get. If one of their friends chimes in and shares the Places update or the Facebook deal, you've reached *two* sets of Facebook friends. Even if they have only 130 friends each, that's potentially 260 people who now know about your Places and Deals. And the endorsement that the users already like your business or the deal encourages their friends to also take advantage of it.

In the following sections, we explain more about how to create and promote deals for your business, and how to train your employees to honor them.

Exploring the types of Facebook deals

Here are the current kinds of Facebook deals:

- ✔ **Individual deal:** These deals are for both established and new customers, and they're for individuals instead of groups. Individual deals are a great way to get rid of extra inventory or bring attention to a new product, and they work well to get foot traffic into your store.

- ✔ **Friend deal:** These deals are for groups (up to eight people per group) who check in together via Places. As you can imagine, this works well if you want to get maximum exposure for your deal. All the people who check in will share the check-in and Facebook deal on their Facebook News Feeds. You're essentially advertising to all the friends of each person in the group.

  Everyone in the group has to be checked in to the venue to redeem the deal. So if a member tags eight friends in her check-in but all those friends aren't with her or don't also check in, she won't get the deal.

- ✔ **Loyalty deal:** Want to reward your tried and true customers? Set them up with a Loyalty deal. These deals are available after a certain number of check-ins. When you create this type of deal, it has to be redeemable after at least two check-ins, but no more than 20 check-ins.

✔ **Charity deal:** Do you have a favorite charity? You can choose to create a Charity deal so that part of your proceeds are donated to the charity of your choice. You have to manage the actual donation to charity on your own, so this option requires a bit of planning on your part (for example, how will you keep track of check-ins and convert those into money for the charity).

Facebook members can search for Facebook Deals via their smartphone's Facebook app or by pointing their phone's browser to `http://touch.facebook.com`. Then they tap Places and Check In to see a list of nearby places. If any businesses in their vicinity offer a Facebook deal, they see a Deals icon next to the listing, as shown next to McDonald's in Figure 13-11.

Decal icon

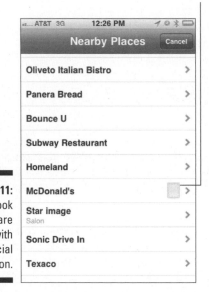

Figure 13-11: Facebook Deals are marked with a special icon.

To view a Facebook deal, the Facebook member simply taps the name of the business offering the deal. A Places page for that business appears and provides more information about the business and a description of the deal. For example, in Figure 13-12, McDonald's uses a Charity deal to raise money for the Ronald McDonald House.

If members want to claim the deal, they simply tap the Claim Deal! button and then show the deal to the cashier to claim their discount.

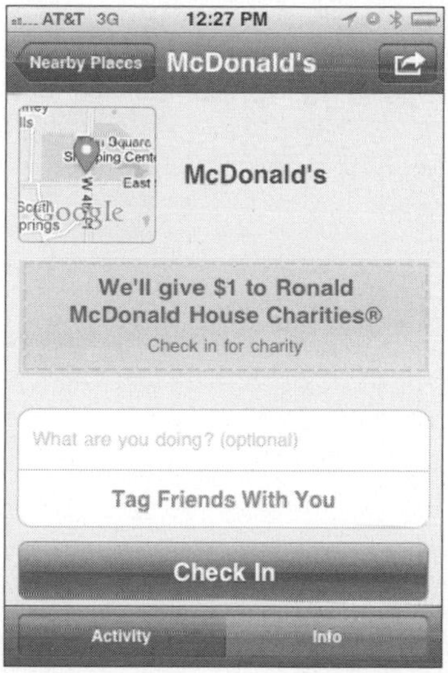

Figure 13-12:
An example
of a
Facebook
deal on
a Places
page.

Creating a Facebook deal

To create a successful Facebook deal, consider your goals. Do you want to reward loyal customers? Do you want to entice new customers? Do you want more sales regardless of whether the customer is new? Do you want to promote a specific product? There are infinite possibilities, but knowing your specific goals allows you to tailor your Facebook deal to achieve those goals more efficiently and track how well your deal works.

TIP

Think ahead: Your deal must be approved before it goes live. Facebook takes two days to approve your ad and then sends an e-mail letting you know your status. To help ensure your ad is approved, make sure it follows Facebook's formatting guidelines found at www.facebook.com/help/?page=18855.

REMEMBER

As of the writing of this book, creating a Facebook deal is free and available on a limited basis. This tool will likely open to a wider business audience very soon based on demand. Facebook also covers its bases by saying that, although Deals is free now, pricing is subject to change in the future.

To create a deal, you must first claim your business on Facebook Places. (You can read about how to do that in the section "Claiming your business on Facebook Places," earlier in this chapter.) When you're ready to create a Facebook deal and associate it with your Facebook place, follow these instructions:

1. **Using your computer's browser, go to your business's Places page on Facebook.**

If you're part of the initial beta group that can create a Facebook deal, you see a Create Deal button at the top right of your page. If you're not part of this beta group, you don't see the option to create a deal, and you will have to wait for Facebook to offer the Deals option to a wider audience. When Facebook is ready, it will send you an e-mail letting you know you can now offer deals.

2. **Click the Create Deal button.**

3. **Select the radio button next to the type of deal you want to create.**

   See the preceding section for the lowdown on the different deals you can create.

4. **Define your offer by completing the Deal Summary and How to Claim options.**

   Be concise with your deal summary. Phones have small screens and limited space. Instead of writing a paragraph welcoming new customers and explaining your company philosophy, keep it simple with something like 50% Off Lunch Special instead.

   In the How to Claim box, tell your customers exactly what they need to do to claim the deal. For example, you could type something like *Show cashier this deal* or *Show cashier your screen*.

5. **Add offer details and restrictions.**

   This option defines how customers can use your deal. You can set the following:

   • *Start and End Dates:* Choose when you want your deal to run. You can even include specific times of day for the start and end dates.

   • *Quantity:* Decide how many deals you want to give away with this promotion. You can choose to stop the deal after X number of redemptions or let the deal be redeemed an unlimited number of times.

   • *Repeat Claims:* Choose whether customers can claim the deal only once or once per 24 hours.

6. **Click the Save button.**

   You see a message with your deal's start and end dates and some additional information about your deal.

You can run only one Facebook deal at a time.

Promoting your Facebook deal

After you set up a deal, create some buzz behind it. The easiest way to tell people about your deal is to post a status update to your business Page as well as your personal profile. Make sure your business Page and your Places page have the correct business hours, address, and phone number. And just because this is a Facebook deal doesn't mean you shouldn't utilize your other social media channels. Tweet your deal, write a blog post explaining the deal, and post the deal on your Web site — all with a link back to your Places page on Facebook. Be clear that the deal is redeemable only if customers check in via Facebook Places so there isn't confusion later.

If you want more exposure targeted to specific demographics, consider running an ad on Facebook (see Chapter 10 for more information on how to do that). When you place your ad for the deal, be sure to link it back to your Facebook business Page or Places page.

Linking your promotions to your Places page ensures that customers can get directions to your venue.

Depending on the purpose of your deal (such as introducing your product to new customers), you may want to consider how you target specific demographics when setting up your Facebook ad. If you want to reward existing or loyal customers, be sure to target people who already like your business Page or Places page on Facebook. Alternatively, if you target new customers, you may want to consider running the ad specifically for people who have not yet liked your business Page or Places page.

Honoring your Facebook deal

Because Facebook Deals is a new feature, a few companies have learned the hard way that it's important to plan your deal before you run it. Some companies have had a bad experience because employees didn't know about the deal, stores ran out of promotional products, and/or customers didn't know how to redeem the deal successfully. As you can imagine, both sides of the transaction were unsatisfied. This section gives you some advice on how to plan your deal so it's a good experience for you *and* your customer.

Remember that Facebook is a social place where people share their experiences. If customers have a poor experience or a deal is denied, they can and will update their statuses associated with your business to let their friends know how they were treated and whether the deal was a dud. If, on the other hand, employees are friendly, understand the deal and how to redeem it, and the transaction goes smoothly, customers are likely to share that positive experience as well.

As the manager or owner of a store, when you develop a Facebook deal, you can do a few things to ensure the deal runs smoothly and customers are satisfied:

   ✔ **Try the deal.** After you know what deal you want to offer and how you want it to work, give it a try. Staff meetings are a great time to make sure everyone knows what's coming and practice redeeming the deal. If you find a glitch, fix it before the deal goes live.

✔ **Think ahead.** When your deal expires or all products have been claimed, how will you handle customers who come in and ask for the deal? Your employees need to have a clear plan of action to address these requests or complaints.

✔ **Communicate with your customers on your Facebook business Page.** It's likely that many of your customers follow you on Facebook. Let them know about upcoming and current deals, but also let them know when a deal is expired so they don't make a wasted trip.

✔ **Prepare for the rush.** If you think your deal is going to encourage an influx of customers, be sure you have enough people working to cover the added business. Ensure that each person working understands what the deal includes, how it should be redeemed, and what their role is. In addition, make sure you have enough products to fulfill the deal you create. If you offer an insulated bag with the purchase of a watch, know how many bags you have to give away and set your deal to expire when those bags are gone. To do that, you need to consider how you'll track deal redemptions and how many bags you've already given away.

✔ **Make a plan.** If you create a Facebook deal that will be honored in multiple stores, you need to have a very specific plan in place. You have to create the deal for each Facebook Places page for each store, communicate to employees across the board on how to promote and redeem the deal, and let them know how to handle customer requests after the deal is over.

If you have more than a few stores, Facebook suggests you contact your Facebook account manager to have that person help you set up your Facebook deal.

After you have your plan in place, it's important to convey that plan to your employees. It's very frustrating to customers if they try to redeem a deal and an employee doesn't know how to redeem it or, worse, refuses to redeem it because he wasn't aware of the deal. For your deal to run smoothly, be sure to tell employees what to expect. Take the time to explain

✔ **Exactly what the deal covers:** Also, figure out whether substitutions can be made.

✔ **How long the deal will run:** Know the dates and times, as applicable.

✔ **The terms of the deal, including any limitations:** These limitations should also be part of the deal as users see it; customers aren't fond of the bait and switch!

✔ **How to process the deal:** For instance, do cashiers have to key in a special code? Will that code be on the customer's smartphone screen, or will they need to know it? How will employees keep track of how many deals are redeemed?

Facebook Places and Facebook Deals are excellent tools to share what you're doing, find friends and fun venues nearby, and save a few bucks while you're at it. With a little planning, they can also be important tools to grow your business.

Chapter 14

Liking Facebook's Like Button

- -

- -

*F*acebook first rolled out its simple Like button as a way for users to show their approval for their friends' photos, videos, comments, and updates. But in recent times, the Like button has morphed into something much more central to Facebook's Web site expansion strategy. When Facebook first rolled out its Like Button social plug-in for Web sites, more than 1 billion likes were registered across Web sites in its first week alone.

The Like button lets users share your content with friends on Facebook. When a user clicks the Like button on your Web site, a story appears in the user's friends' News Feeds that includes a link to your Web site. You can attach the Like button to a number of objects, from your company Web site to a blog post to every product in your catalog. And because a story is generated every time someone clicks the Like button, it's an effective way to get word-of-mouth publicity for your content — friends of your fans see the story and may click the link.

The Facebook Like button has quickly established itself as the de facto Web standard for showing one's approval. Because of its simplicity, it has gained a user base that surpasses all other social-media activities. Prior to liking a piece of content, users could Digg it, use Delicious or reddit, or use another social-media bookmarking or sharing service to show their support and build awareness. But Facebook has marginalized those earlier services, leveraging its News Feed as a distribution channel to promote users' likes.

In this chapter, we discuss how a Like button can generate traffic for your business. We show you how to install the Like button on your Web site or blog, and we highlight some companies that are already putting the Like button to good use and getting results. If you haven't installed a Like button on your Web site or blog, it's about time you made your business more likeable.

Understanding How to Use the Like Button on Your Site

You're already familiar with the Like button that appears on your Facebook Page. When users click the Like button on your Page, they become a fan of your Page, and a story appears in their friends' News Feeds, including a link to your Page. The more people like your Page, the more people who see it via their friends' News Feeds. This speaks to the heart of Facebook's viral power.

Facebook makes the Like button available so that you can add it to any content on your Web site. Users click the Like button to share content that's of interest to them, such as an article you've posted on your site. The beauty of the Like button is that users just need to make a single click; they don't have to leave what they're viewing on your site. That non-interruptive, single click automatically updates the user's Facebook Wall on her profile, posting a direct link to the shared content on your site. Additionally, the Web sites and Facebook Pages that you like are shown at the bottom of the Info tab of your profile.

By adding the Like button to your Web site, you're basically transforming your Web site into a Facebook Page. After a user logs in to Facebook and clicks the Like button on your Web site, that user transmits her approval of your business, product, or video — basically any content that corresponds to that particular Like button. For example, users can like a movie review on Rotten Tomatoes, a news story on CNN (see Figure 14-1), or a band on Pandora.

When you configure the Like button for your Web site, you can have it show Recommend as well as Like (as shown in the figure).

The Like button is the simplest social plug-in offered by Facebook and doesn't require the user to log in, if already logged into Facebook. So, even if a user has never visited Moviefone before, for example, he can see how many friends and other Facebook members like a particular movie or have connected with it recently (as shown in Figure 14-2) without the site knowing anything about that user.

Moviefone even allows users to extend a personal or public movie invitation to their Facebook friends, having it appear as a Facebook event or Inbox e-mail request. (See Figure 14-3.)

You can attach the Like button to any piece of content on your Web site or blog. For example, Levi's has added a Like button to everything in its online store — from its iconic 501 Jeans to its line of kid's clothes (see Figure 14-4). When Facebook members who are already logged in to Facebook or have previously visited the site while logged in, visit the Levi's site, and click a button, that action is automatically published on their News Feed for their friends to see. In return, Levi's receives auto-generated promotion.

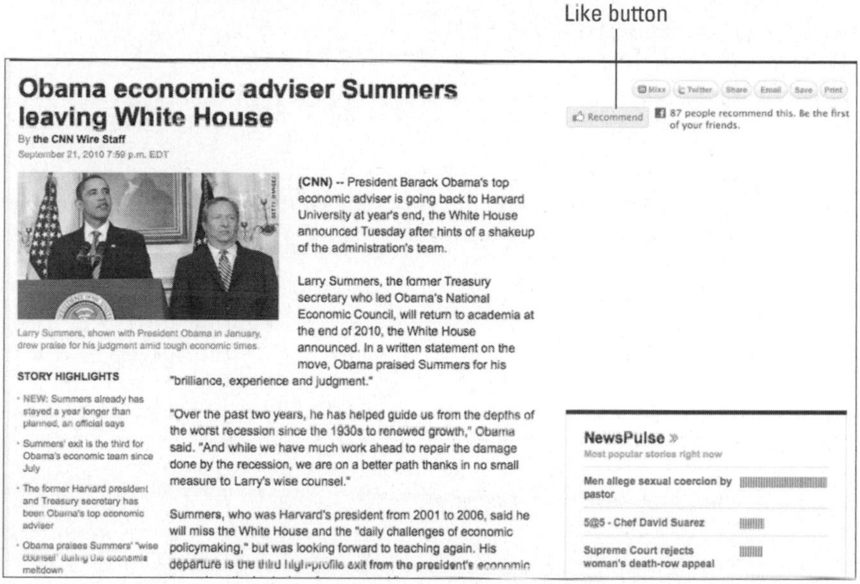

Like button

Figure 14-1:
The
Recommend
(or Like)
button
integrated
on CNN's
Web site.

Figure 14-1:
The
Recommend
(or Like)
button
integrated
on CNN's
Web site.

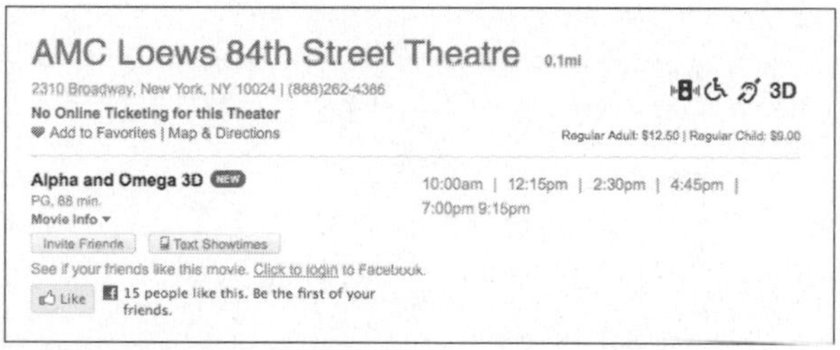

Figure 14-2:
Moviefone
personalizes
the user
experience
by showing
their friends'
likes.

If you've created your own Facebook app, you can embed the Like button within that app so that a user can like it or even a specific piece of content within the app, such as a virtual item, as shown in Playfish's popular Pet Society app in Figure 14-5.

Figure 14-3:
Invite your Facebook friends to a movie via Moviefone's Web site.

Figure 14-4:
The Levi's Web site includes a Facebook Like button for every product in its online store.

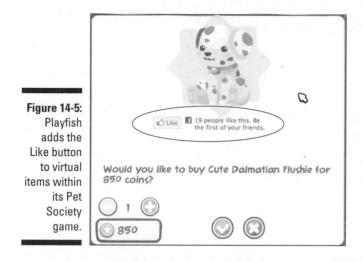

Figure 14-5:
Playfish
adds the
Like button
to virtual
items within
its Pet
Society
game.

The Like button is an integral part of a member's profile. Facebook users can view members' likes (as shown in Figure 14-6) and understand the things that interest them.

A user can unlike an object only by going back to the original Web page or the business or organization's Facebook Page, and clicking Unlike next to the original object. So, marketers need to be mindful that at any time they can lose fans by them unliking the original object.

Figure 14-6:
Viewing a
Facebook
member's
likes on a
profile.

How Facebook uses data on likes

When a user registers a like, it automatically gets added to a user's profile data. Although this data isn't always visible to the user or her friends, by collecting and storing more information on what its users like — whether it be on Facebook or on the Web at large — Facebook can offer advertisers targeting based on this data. (See Chapter 10 for more about advertising your business on Facebook.)

Facebook has yet to decide whether it plans to share all this data among publishers so they could better target ads to their users, or make it available to search engines such as Google and Microsoft's Bing (to make search results more relevant based on friends' recommendations). But, by registering users' likes, Facebook is holding the keys to a lot of data on its more than 500 million users.

Installing the Like Button

Facebook has released its Like button as open-source software so that anyone who has a little technical know-how can use it wherever they want. In an effort to make its Like button ubiquitous throughout the Web, Facebook is making the button available as part of its Social Plug-Ins initiative. (See Chapter 15 for more information on Facebook social plug-ins.)

Anyone who has a Facebook Page can create his own customized Like button. Similar to a Facebook badge (described in Chapter 8), you can embed the Like button in most Web pages, blogs, and HTML e-mails. Facebook offers two types of Like buttons: XFBML and iFrames. The XFBML version is much more sophisticated and requires knowledge of the Java programming language. The iFrames version creates a simple snippet of code that can be easily added to a Web page or specific online content, such as a product description, image, or video.

To get started, just use Facebook's configurator to get the Like button code that you can add to your site. To create a customized Like button for your Page, follow these steps:

1. **Go to Facebook's Social Plugins page at `http://developers.facebook.com/plugins` (see Figure 14-7).**

2. **Click the Like Button link, which is the first plug-in shown.**

   The Like Button page appears.

3. **In the configurator shown in Figure 14-8, fill in the required information.**

   The configurator asks you for the following info:

   • *URL to Like:* Enter the URL of your Facebook Page.

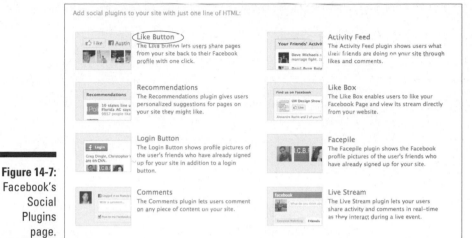

Figure 14-7:
Facebook's
Social
Plugins
page.

- *Layout Style:* Select the layout style that you want to use from the drop-down list. You have three options:

    Standard displays the Like button on the same line as the count of friends who also like the object. If you have no friends who already liked the object, the configurator asks that you be the first of your friends to like it.

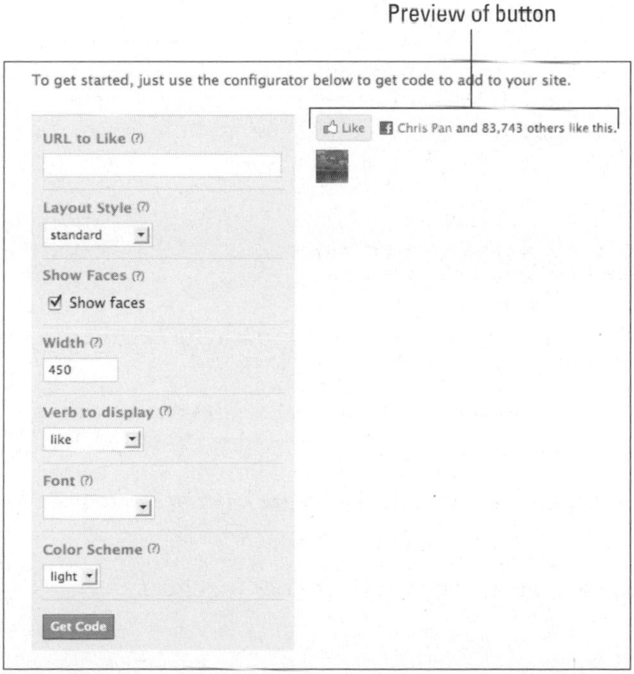

Preview of button

Figure 14-8:
Facebook's
configurator
helps you
customize
a Like
button
for your
Facebook
Page.

Button Count shows the Like button adjacent to the like count.

Box Count gives the count on top of the Like button.

When you make a selection, a preview of that style appears on the right.

- *Show Faces:* Click this check box if you want the profile pictures of those who have liked the Page to be visible underneath the Like button.

- *Width:* Adjust the width of the plug-in in pixels, as desired. The default width is 450 pixels.

- *Verb to Display:* From the drop-down list, select the verb that you want to appear on the button. You can choose either Like or Recommend.

- *Font:* Select the font you want to use from the Font drop-down list.

- *Color Scheme:* Select either Light or Dark for the background of the button.

4. **Click the blue Get Code button.**

   The configurator takes a little while to generate your code and then presents it for you to copy and paste it into the HTML code of your desired Web page, HTML e-mail, or blog (see Figure 14-9).

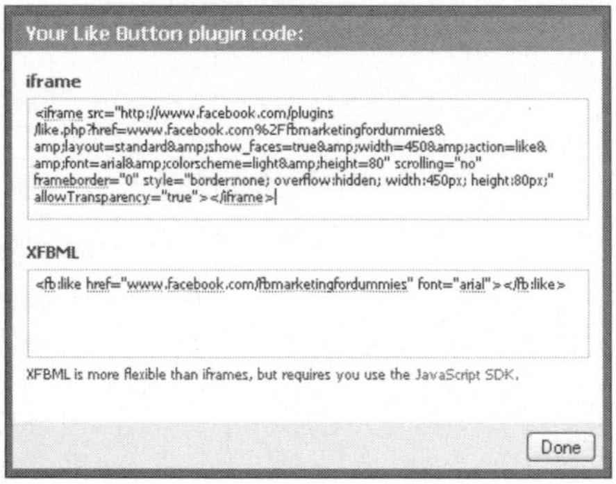

Your Like Button plugin code:

iframe

```
<iframe src="http://www.facebook.com/plugins
/like.php?href=www.facebook.com%2FFbmarketingfordummies&
amp;layout=standard&amp;show_Faces=true&amp;width=450&amp;action=like&
amp;font=arial&amp;colorscheme=light&amp;height=80" scrolling="no"
frameborder="0" style="border:none; overflow:hidden; width:450px; height:80px;"
allowTransparency="true"></iframe>
```

XFBML

```
<fb:like href="www.facebook.com/fbmarketingfordummies" font="arial"></fb:like>
```

XFBML is more flexible than iframes, but requires you use the JavaScript SDK.

[Done]

Figure 14-9:
Generating code for the Like button.

If you want to attract more fans to your Facebook Page from your Web site, you may want to also consider using Facebook's Like Box plug-in. The Like box (shown in Figure 14-10) helps you attract more likes to your Facebook Page and lets users see which friends like your Page, too. You can also show recent posts from your Facebook Page on your Web site via the Like box. For Facebook Pages that have a lot of comments and engagement, it's good to include recent posts. However, if your Facebook Page isn't very active, we recommend not including the recent posts. We discuss the Like box in detail in Chapter 15.

Adding open tags

For Web site owners who are adding the Like button to real things, such as a movie, person, type of food, and so on, Facebook allows you to add _tags_ (or words) to define the object you're liking. This is supported by Facebook's Open Graph protocol at `http://developers.facebook.com/docs/opengraph`.

These Open Graph tags create a connection between the object being liked and the user. This allows Facebook to define the type of object in the user's Likes and Interests section on their profile's Info tab.

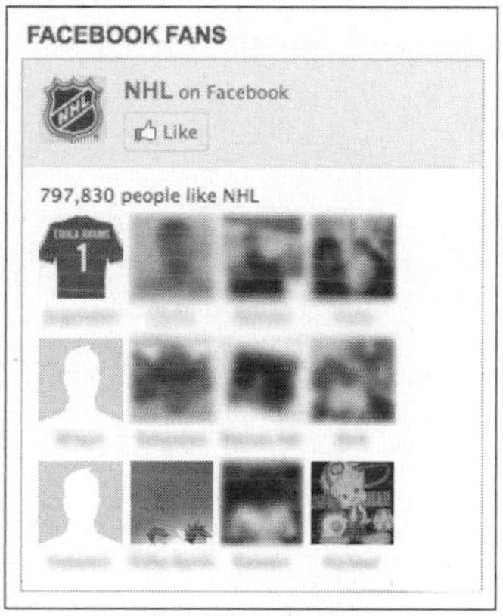

FACEBOOK FANS

NHL on Facebook

Like

797,830 people like NHL

Figure 14-10: Add the Like box to your Web site to drive more likes to your Facebook Page.

Highlighting Like Successes

With more than 2 million Web sites using Facebook plug-ins (and that number just keeps growing), you can find many outstanding examples of companies that are implementing the Like button in innovative ways. In fact, collectively more than 1 billion likes are registered across Web sites daily.

People who click the Like button are generally skewed to a younger demographic. In fact, the typical liker on a news site is 34 years old compared to the average age of a newspaper subscriber, who is around 54 years old.

Since integrating the Like button, many Web sites show a significant increase in traffic as a result of the stories that are automatically generated via Facebook users' News Feeds. The National Basketball League's site, NBA.com, credits Facebook social plug-ins and the Like button in particular as its number two referral source (see Figure 14-11).

Figure 14-11:
NBA.com
adds the
Like button
to each
news story
on its site.

Web site owners are leveraging the Like button to drive traffic, build awareness, and generate word-of-mouth buzz. Retailers are starting to add the Like button to every product in their online store. MyWebGrocer and ShopRite are among the first grocery sellers to add the Like button. See Figure 14-12.

Figure 14-12:
ShopRite
has added
the Like
button to
every
grocery
item on
its site.

Likers are also typically more engaged, active, and connected than an average Facebook user. The average liker has more than twice the amount of friends and clicks external links more than five times that of a typical Facebook user. For example, children's clothing e-tailer Tea Collection lets users vote on which items get selected for promotional sales using the Like button. Its traffic rose 300 percent and sales multiplied 10 times when the most-liked items went on sale. See Figure 14-13.

Figure 14-13:
Tea
Collection
allows users
to vote
on which
items get
selected for
promotional
sales via the
Like button.

As more marketers integrate the Like button in creative ways, they'll reap the
benefits of adding this social action to their Web sites. By leveraging Facebook's
tremendous member base and re-creating the same ability to like a particular
piece of content, whether a news article, grocery item, or product for discount,
the value of having your likes being featured on a user's Facebook Wall will
drive additional awareness to that content.

Chapter 15

Plugging Into Other Plug-Ins

. . . .

. . . .

After you create your business's Facebook Page and spend a great deal of effort adding relevant content and cultivating an engaged fan base, how can you extend that community activity to your company Web site?

Facebook has just the solution for you. Actually, Facebook offers eight different solutions to bridge your Facebook Page's social actions with that of your Web site, each with its own take on the Open Graph data that your Page generates. A *social plug-in* is Facebook's way of letting you set up your Web site so whenever a reader interacts with your site, such as by leaving a comment on a blog post, a notice publishes on that person's News Feed. Adding a social plug-in is as simple as embedding a single line of code in your Web site, much like adding a YouTube video. You can find a range of plug-ins that can personalize the content that your visitors see, display who else has visited the site, and allow visitors to engage with their Facebook friends — all without having to log in to your Web site.

Social plug-ins can really help you promote your site while increasing your Facebook likes from people who wouldn't normally interact with your Facebook Page. The Like Button, discussed in Chapter 14, is the most popular of these plug-ins, but others can deliver important social features to your site in much the same way. By integrating these plug-ins, you can turn any Web site into a Facebook Page.

In this chapter, you find out about the different social plug-ins available and which ones you can implement to meet your marketing objectives. We show you how to turn your site into a more personalized experience for your users by adding the Login Button plug-in and how to leverage a user's social graph with the Recommendations plug-in. You also discover how to add the

Activity Feed and Comments plug-ins to bring your Facebook Page's activity to your Web site and how the Live Stream plug-in allows you to interact in real-time with your visitors.

Extending the Facebook Experience with Social Plug-Ins

Social plug-ins are a relatively new Facebook initiative that allows visitors to your Web site to view content that their Facebook friends have liked, commented on, or shared. These plug-ins represent a new level of personalization for Web site owners. Just by being logged in to their Facebook account, viewers of your Web site can help make your content viral on Facebook without ever leaving your Web site.

Facebook provides tools that allow you to generate code for each plug-in that you want to embed in your site. Any time your Web site visitors interact with the plug-ins, those visitors can publish News Feed stories on their Facebook profiles for all their friends to see, giving your business greater exposure.

Facebook has created a special section within its developer Web site, located at `http://developers.facebook.com/plugins` (see Figure 15-1), which explains the different plug-ins, provides tools for generating the code needed to embed each one within your site, and showcases good implementations on real-world Web sites. The plug-ins are free for anyone to use and allow you to add an interactive layer on top of your site that complements your Facebook marketing strategy. You can use these plug-ins individually or in tandem, extending many of the same features that people have become familiar with inside Facebook to any Web site.

Figure 15-1:
Facebook's
Social
Plugins
developer
page.

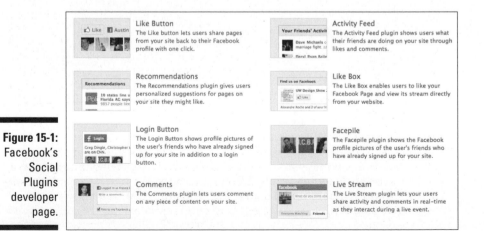

You may find that figuring out which plug-in (or a combination of plug-ins) to integrate into your site is a daunting task. Although you can add them to your Web site fairly easily, you may find the different options confusing because some of their capabilities overlap. To help you decide which plug-in is right for your needs, here are brief descriptions and examples of each:

✔ **Like Button:** Allows anyone who's signed into Facebook to show their approval of content on your site by liking it in a simple one-button design. See Figure 15-2 for how Moviefone integrates the Like button for movies. The Like count (which appears to the right of the button in Figure 15-2) also increases as more people click it.

Figure 15-2: Moviefone integrates the Like button for every movie.

When users click the Like button, a news story publishes to their News Feeds, including a link back to the content on your site. If your site offers a lot of content that users can like individually (such as a catalog, blog, media site, or product description), the Like button is a good way to establish more opportunities to connect with users. If you're interested in someone liking your company or Web site (rather than a specific piece of content), the Like Box plug-in (described later in this list) may be a better option for you. For more detailed information on the Like button, see Chapter 14.

✔ **Recommendations:** Displays a list of the most-liked content on your site, as shown in Figure 15-3. The Recommendations plug-in offers a more generic experience than the Activity Feed plug-in (described later in this list). Although Activity Feed allows you to show a user's friends' activities, as well as an Everyone view, Recommendations displays what people like right now and is better suited for sites that have less social activity among users' Facebook friends. Both Recommendations and the Activity Feed can show you how Facebook users interact with your Web site's content.

✔ **Login Button:** Allows visitors to log in to your Web site by using their Facebook user IDs and passwords. This plug-in also displays the Facebook profile pictures of a user's friends who have signed up, as shown in Figure 15-4. If you want to increase user registration on your Web site, this option helps you encourage engagement because it shows a user which friends are already logged in with your site.

Figure 15-3:
The Recommendations plug-in highlights content that people like the most.

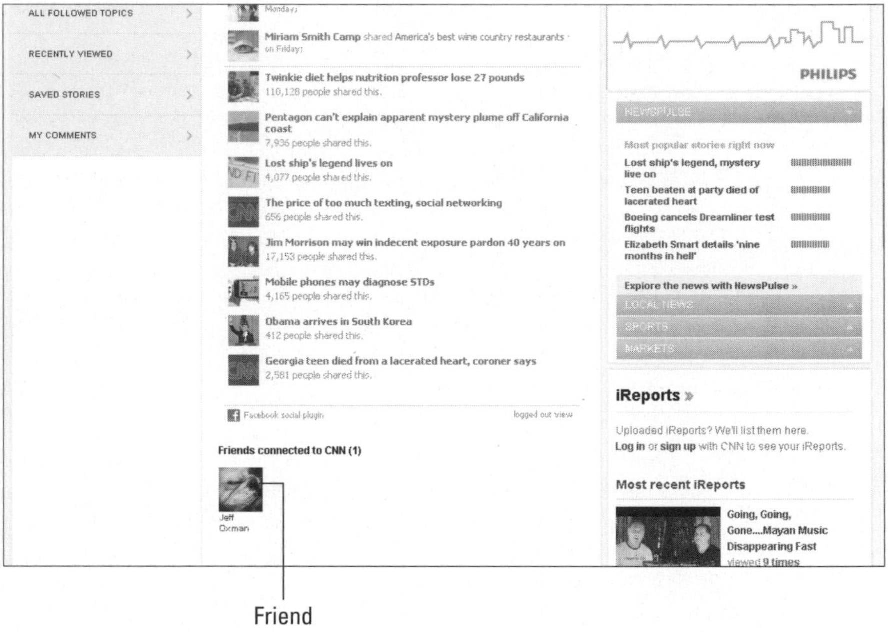

Figure 15-4:
CNN allows users to sign in by using the Login Button social plug-in.

Friend

You can resize the plug-in so that you can tailor it to best fit your site design, and it dynamically resizes depending on the number of friends already signed in. As with most social plug-ins, the user will be asked to give Facebook permission to access their profile information when they log in.

✔ **Comments:** Allows you to add a comment box to your Web site so that Facebook users can enter their comments, as shown in Figure 15-5. The plug-in gives users the option to have their comments published to their Facebook News Feeds, including a link back to the comments on your site. For content that isn't appropriate for people to comment on, such as product information, don't use this plug-in. However, for blogs or more opinionated content, the added exposure through the News Feed can provide you with a good source of traffic.

You do have options to delete or report negative comments, but you have to manually manage the process.

✔ **Activity Feed:** Shows recent Facebook-related activity around your site as a stream, which includes how many people have liked or shared your content. The plug-in shows activity from the visitor's Facebook friends, as shown in the CNN example in Figure 15-6, but if it can't find enough friend-only content, it includes more general recent activity from Facebook users the visitor doesn't know. This plug-in can really up your site's exposure if it has an active Facebook following and regularly updated content, such as a blog.

The Activity Feed is a powerful plug-in that keeps your visitors up-to-date on your site's topics. It also overlaps slightly with the Recommendations plug-in (described earlier in this list), so make sure you review your options before you decide which plug-in to implement.

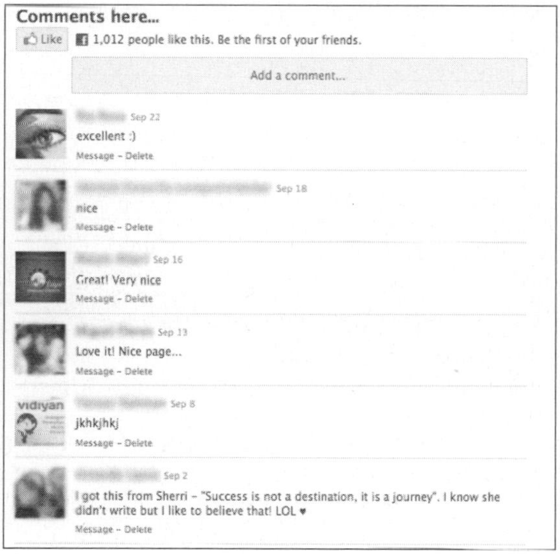

Comments here...

👍 Like 📘 1,012 people like this. Be the first of your friends.

Add a comment...

Sep 22
excellent :)
Message – Delete

Sep 18
nice
Message – Delete

Sep 16
Great! Very nice
Message – Delete

Sep 13
Love it! Nice page...
Message – Delete

vidiyan ⬤ Sep 8
jkhkjhkj
Message – Delete

Sep 2
I got this from Sherri – "Success is not a destination, it is a journey". I know she didn't write but I like to believe that! LOL ♥
Message – Delete

Figure 15-5:
The
Comments
plug-in
allows
visitors
to add a
comment
to your
Web site.

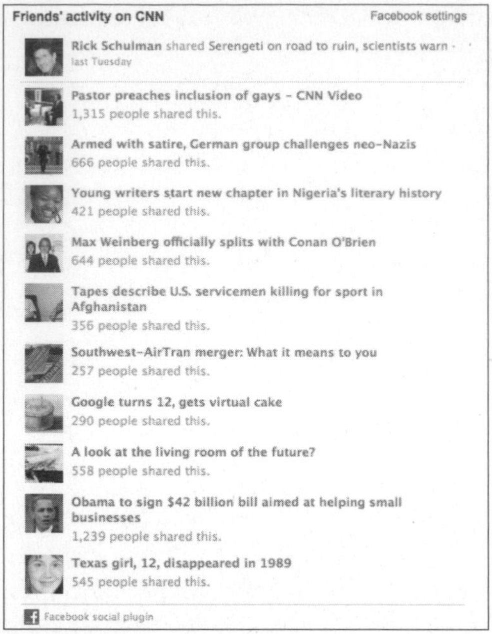

Figure 15-6:
CNN's
Activity
Feed plug-in
shows the
visitor's
Facebook
friends'
interactions
with the
site.

✔ **Like Box:** Similar to the Like button, the Like Box plug-in (as shown in the Mashable example in Figure 15-7) provides a one-click button, but the like relates to your Facebook Page, rather than the content on your Web site. It also gives users the choice to publish an update directly to their News Feeds. When customizing the Like box for your site, you can include profile pictures of Facebook users who have already liked your site and show the Wall stream for your Facebook Page. This plug-in can be extremely helpful if you want to build your fan base on your Facebook Page by creating a bridge between your Web site and Page. With the Like Box, the option to like your page is right in front of your readers. They don't have to search for your Page directly on Facebook to like it.

✔ **Facepile:** Shows your visitors the profile pictures of their friends who are already site members without them having to be logged into Facebook or their already established account within your site. If none of a visitor's friends have previously signed up, no profile pictures appear. When combined with Facebook's Login button, you can dramatically increase user registrations because if users see that their friends have registered, as shown in Figure 15-8, they're more likely to register with your site.

If your site offers a service that requires a separate login process, the Facepile plug-in is a nice way to highlight the visitor's Facebook friends who have already signed up. Just like the Login Button plug-in (described earlier in this list), the Facepile plug-in dynamically resizes its height, depending on how many friends of the user have already signed up.

Figure 15-7:
Mashable wants you to like its Page.

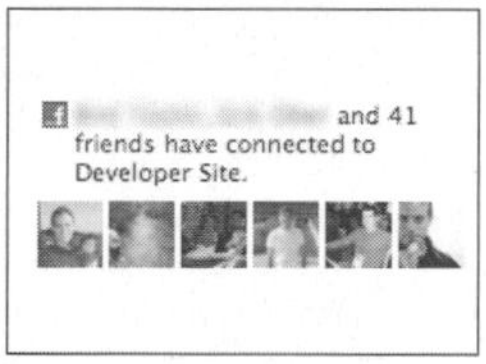

Figure 15-8:
The Facepile plug-in shows profile pictures.

✓ **Live Stream:** Allows Facebook users to comment on your Web site in real-time, as shown in Figure 15-9. This plug-in is a good option if your Web site streams a live event, such as a video broadcast, and you want to offer visitors a real-time chat experience to go along with the live content being streamed. If you just want to show comments associated with static content, the Comments plug-in (described earlier in this list) is a better choice because the Live Stream plug-in is used for specific live activities that will end eventually. Written content, such as a blog post, will be there indefinitely, along with the comments made on it.

Figure 15-9:
Why watch TV alone when you can chat in real-time via the Live Stream plug-in?

Your site doesn't receive any of the visitors' personal data when those visitors interact with your site by using social plug-ins, and their profile pictures and comments are visible only if they're logged into Facebook.

This chapter explains how to generate the code needed to embed each of these plug-ins within your site. After you have the code, you follow these general steps to incorporate it into your Web site. (*Note:* You must have access to your Web Site's source files. If you don't know where they are located, get the help of your Web site developer to point you in the right direction.)

1. Open the HTML file for your Web site page using whatever editor (Adobe Dreamweaver, Microsoft Word, or a UNIX editor like VI) you normally use to make changes to your file.

2. Go to the spot in the HTML file where you want the social plug-in to appear.

3. Input the lines of code generated on the Facebook Developers site into the HTML file.

4. Save the HTML file and if necessary, upload the new HTML file to your Web site.

5. Using a Web browser, go to that Web page (refresh your Web browser if necessary) and make sure that the Like button appears in the correct location.

In most cases, the only difference when installing another plug-in is using a different line (or lines) of code in Step 3. Refer to the Facebook Developers page for each plug-in for the specific code you will need.

Leveraging Popular Content with the Recommendations Plug-In

When you use the Recommendations plug-in on your site, visitors who are logged into their Facebook account see a list of the content that generated the most likes across your site, making your site more relevant to visitors. For example, visitors to CNN can immediately see articles that people recommend and share with their friends in real-time, as shown in Figure 15-10.

You can think of the Recommendations plug-in as a Facebook-powered version of most-popular lists, as chosen by a user's friends and other Facebook members. When you integrate this plug-in with your Web site, visitors see these recommendations in real-time, so the recommendations most likely change every time users visit the site.

Figure 15-10: CNN shows visitors the site's most popular content.

To generate code for the Recommendations plug-in, follow these steps:

1. **Visit `http://developers.facebook.com/plugins` and click the Recommendations link.**

2. **Fill in the requested information to customize your plug-in (see Figure 15-11):**

   • *Domain:* Enter the domain (URL) where you want to place the plug-in.

   • *Width:* Enter the width, in pixels, for the plug-in.

   • *Height:* Enter the height of the plug-in, in pixels.

   • *Header:* Select the Show Header check box if you want a header to appear in the plug-in.

   • *Color Scheme:* Select either Light or Dark for the color scheme that you want to use in the plug-in.

   • *Font:* Enter the font of the text that appears in the plug-in.

   • *Border Color:* Enter the background color for the plug-in, such as red or blue.

3. **Click the Get Code button.**

Place the Recommendations plug-in on your Web site's home page so that you can immediately make a connection with your Web-site visitors and provide a more personalized experience.

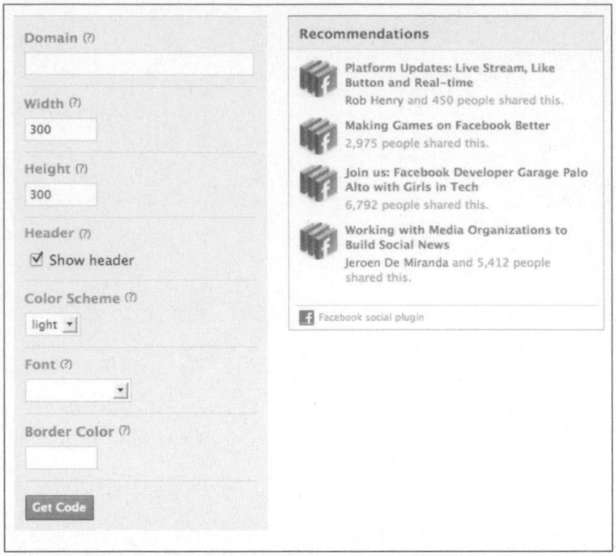

Figure 15-11:
Enter the attributes to generate code for the Recommendations plug-in.

Integrating Facebook's Login Button

The Facebook Login button enables visitors to sign in to your site with their Facebook login information and displays profile pictures of the user's friends who are already signed up for your site (refer to Figure 15-4). When you add the plug-in to your site, you can customize the length and width settings for the box that will appear, which determines the number of friend profiles that can be displayed in each line and row. For example, if you specify that you want it to display four rows of pictures, and the user has only two rows of friends who have signed up for your site, the plug-in dynamically adjusts to the two rows.

To integrate Facebook's Login Button with your site, follow these steps:

1. **Visit `http://developers.facebook.com/plugins` and click the Login Button link.**

2. **Fill in the requested information to customize your button (see Figure 15-12):**

   - *Show Faces:* Select this check box if you want to show profile pictures.

   - *Width:* Enter the width of the plug-in, in pixels.

   - *Max Rows:* Enter the number of rows of profile photos that you want to display. This number depends on the amount of space you want to allocate on your Web site for this plug-in.

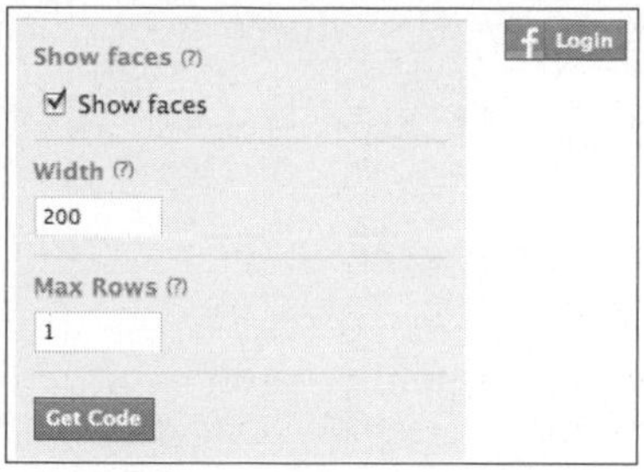

Figure 15-12:
You can
easily create
your own
version of
Facebook's
Login button.

3. **Click the Get Code button.**

Consider combining the Login Button plug-in with the Activity Feed plug-in (described later in this chapter) for maximum exposure.

Adding Comments to Your Web Site

The Comments plug-in enables you to add a comments thread to any page on your Web site and allows visitors already logged in to Facebook to add comments (see Figure 15-13). Users have the option to have their comments also posted to their Facebook profiles; those comments then show up in those users' News Feeds, viewable by all their friends. By installing this plug-in and allowing users to leave comments and interact with you, you can drive more traffic back to your Web site because their friends will see that you actively engage with your fans.

Figure 15-13:
Add a
Comments
plug-in to
get users
engaged
with the
content
on your
Web site.

To add the Comments plug-in to your site, follow these steps:

1. **Visit `http://developers.facebook.com/plugins` and click the Comments link.**

2. **Enter the requested information to customize the plug-in (see Figure 15-14):**

   - *Unique ID:* This is the unique ID number associated with the Comments plug-in. Typically, you can leave this field blank, and the value will be generated by the Web page when the box is being drawn.

   - *Number of Comments:* Enter the number of comments you want displayed. The default is ten comments, but the actual amount you display depends on any space constraints on your site. If you get more comments that can fit in the plug-in, users can click to the next set, or page of comments.

   - *Width:* Enter the width of the plug-in, in pixels.

   - *Publish to Feed:* This gives the user the option to publish her comment to her News Feed.

3. **Click the Get Code button to generate the code.**

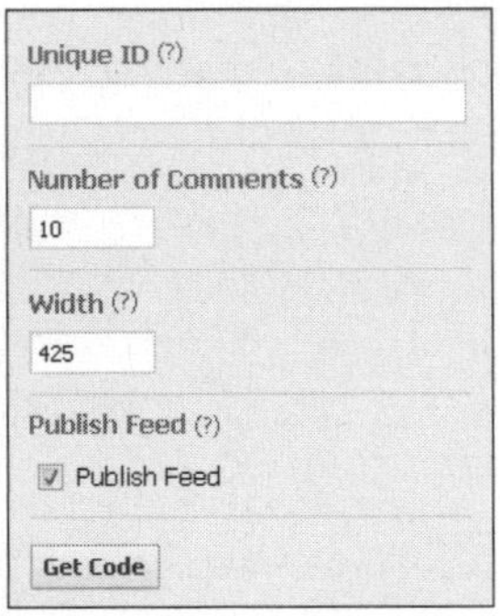

Figure 15-14:
Create the code for your very own Comments plug-in.

Unique ID (?)

Number of Comments (?)

`10`

Width (?)

`425`

Publish Feed (?)

☑ Publish Feed

Get Code

You can add a Comments plug-in to any piece of content from which you want to solicit user feedback. Consider integrating it with product review pages or your blog, or you can use it to gauge user interest on Web site–related things like a new layout.

If you integrate the Comments plug-in within your site, you need to monitor the comments closely, and delete spam and malicious or overtly negative remarks.

Showing User Activities with the Activity Feed Plug-In

When a visitor to your site is logged in to Facebook, the Activity Feed plug-in is personalized with content from that user's friends. It shows the content within your site that the visitor's friends are sharing, recommending, and commenting on (refer to Figure 15-6). If they aren't logged in, however, it shows general recommendations from your site, not personalized ones.

To add the Activity Feed plug-in, follow these steps:

1. **Visit `http://developers.facebook.com/plugins` and click the Activity Feed link.**

2. **Enter the requested information to customize your plug-in (see Figure 15-15):**

   - *Domain:* Enter the domain of the page where you plan to put the plug-in.

   - *Width:* Enter the width of the plug-in, in pixels.

   - *Height:* Enter the height of the plug-in, in pixels.

   - *Header:* Select the Show Header check box if you want to include the Recent Activity header on the plug-in.

   - *Color Scheme:* Select your color scheme (you can choose between Light and Dark).

   - *Font:* Select the font that you want to display within the plug-in.

   - *Border Color:* Type a color, such as red or blue.

   - *Recommendations:* Select the Recommendations check box if you want to always show recommendations in the plug-in. If you select the Recommendations check box, the plug-in displays recommendations in the bottom half of the plug-in if you don't have enough activity to fill the entire box. If the box isn't selected, no recommendations are shown. We suggest you always check the box so it looks like your page is active, even when you may be experiencing a slow activity period.

3. **Click the Get Code button to generate the code.**

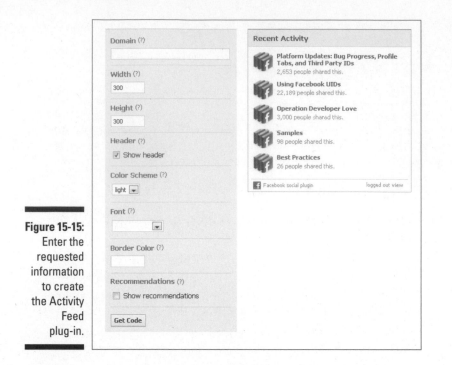

Figure 15-15:
Enter the
requested
information
to create
the Activity
Feed
plug-in.

Liking the Like Box

If you want to acquire more fans for your Facebook Page, consider integrating
the Like Box social plug-in on your Web site (see Figure 15-16). With one click,
users can like your Facebook Page without leaving your Web site. The Like Box
also provides a current count of how many likes your Facebook Page has accu-
mulated and which of the visitor's friends like it, too. The Like Box plug-in can
also display recent updates you've posted on your Facebook Page.

Figure 15-16:
Use the Like
Box to get
more people
to like your
Page.

To add the Like Box plug-in to your Web site, follow these steps:

1. **Visit http://developers.facebook.com/plugins and click the Like Box link.**

2. **Fill in the requested information to customize your Like Box plug-in (see Figure 15-17):**

   • *Facebook Page URL:* Enter the Facebook Page URL that you want your visitors to like.

   • *Width:* Enter the width of the plug-in, in pixels.

   • *Color Scheme:* You can choose between having a light or a dark background.

   • *Connections:* Enter the number of *connections,* or people who have liked your Page that you want to show.

   • *Stream:* Select the Show Stream check box if you want to show the most recent stream of updates you've posted on your Facebook Page.

   • *Header:* Select the Show Header check box to include the Find Us on Facebook header at the top of the plug-in.

3. **Click the Get Code button to generate the code.**

Figure 15-17: Generating code for the Facebook Like Box plug-in.

Personalizing a Site with the Facepile Plug-In

Similar to the Login Button (described earlier in the chapter), Facepile allows you to personalize the user's experience with your Web site by displaying the user's friends who have also registered on your site. The Facepile plug-in differs from the Login Button in that Facepile dynamically resizes its height based on how many of the user's friends are displayed and doesn't show up at all if no friends have signed up with your site (or if the user is not logged into Facebook).

To generate the Facepile plug-in code that you need to embed on your Web site, follow these steps:

1. **Visit `http://developers.facebook.com/plugins` and click the Facepile link.**

2. **Enter the requested information to customize your plug-in (see Figure 15-18):**

   • *Num Rows:* Enter the number of rows of profile pictures that you want to display. Don't worry about adding too many rows. If there aren't enough pictures to fill all the rows, the box will be resized to fit.

   • *Width:* Enter the width of the plug-in, in pixels.

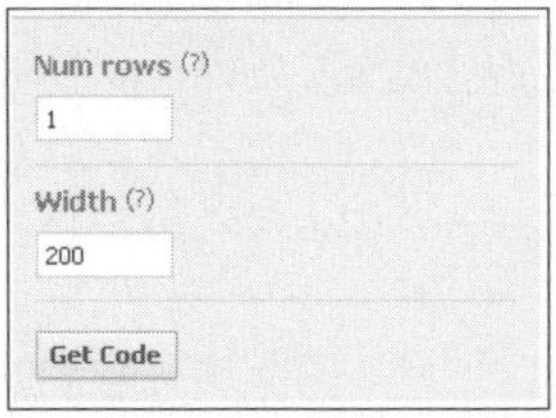

Figure 15-18:
Generate code for the Facepile plug-in.

Num rows (?)

`1`

Width (?)

`200`

Get Code

3. **Click the Get Code button to generate the code.**

   To use these plug-ins on your site, you must first register your site with Facebook. After you click the Get Code button, you're presented with the code and are instructed to click the provided link to get an Application ID (see the following steps) to register your Web site. If you don't register your site and insert your Application ID into the location it says, the plug-in doesn't work.

To get your Application ID, follow these steps:

1. **Visit `http://developers.facebook.com/setup` or click the link in the dialog box you get when you click the Get Code button.**

2. **Enter the requested information:**

   • *Site Name:* The name of your Web site

   • *Site URL:* The URL of your Web site

   • *Locale:* Your language

3. **Click the Create Application button.**

4. **Enter the captcha as you see it and then click the Submit button.**

   You receive your unique Application ID. Copy and paste this number in required location in the plug-in code that you received.

The Facepile plug-in, which you can add to the header or top area of your Web site's home page or its key landing pages, encourages users to explore your site further by showing them which of their friends are also signed onto the site.

Engaging in Real-Time with Live Stream

If you integrate the Live Stream plug-in with your Web site, visitors can view and post comments in real-time. You can use this tool to add a real-time chat stream to accompany live content that you're offering on your site, such as a live video Webcast, Webinar, conference, and so on. This plug-in allows visitors to filter the chat stream by everyone watching or just their friends.

To create the Live Stream plug-in code for your Web site, follow these steps:

1. **Visit `http://developers.facebook.com/plugins` and click the Live Stream link.**

2. **Enter the requested information to customize your plug-in (see Figure 15-19):**

   • *App ID:* Enter your App ID number in this text box. To find out how to generate a unique App ID, see the preceding section.

   • *Width:* Enter the width of the plug-in, in pixels.

   • *Height:* Enter the height of the plug-in, in pixels.

   • *XID:* If you want your site to include more than one Live Stream plug-in, enter an XID number, which stands for a unique ID, to help you identify the stream.

   • *Via Attribution URL:* This is the URL that users are taken to when they click the app's name in the status update. This is an option because Live Stream can be used for Web sites and applications.

3. **Click the Get Code button to generate the code.**

Figure 15-19:
The Live
Stream
plug-in can
help you
engage
users with
live content
on your
Web site.

Live Stream isn't a good option for static sites or sites that offer live events that have a very small audience because there is not enough activity to keep it interesting and the audience engaged.

Checking your plug-ins with URL Linter

Facebook provides a URL Linter tool for you to check your plug-ins after you add them to your Web site. Visit `http://developers.facebook.com/tools/lint`, enter the URL of the Web page you want to review to make sure the plug-ins are installed properly,

and click the Lint button. If you have a plug-in that isn't working, a warning message returns letting you know where the issue is so you can return to your HTML code and fix the problem; for example, by regenerating the code for that particular plug-in.

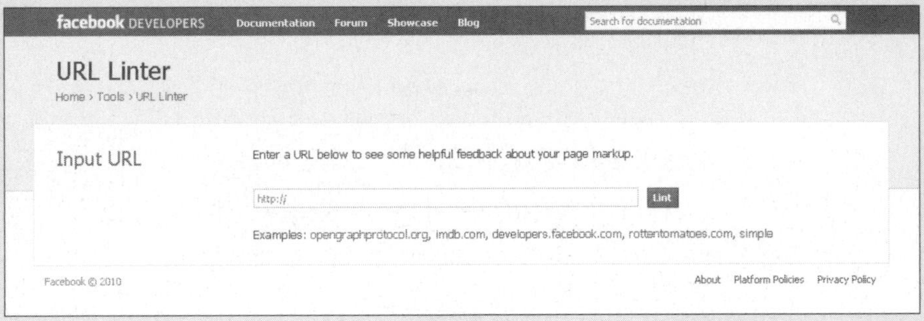

facebook DEVELOPERS Documentation Forum Showcase Blog Search for documentation

URL Linter
Home › Tools › URL Linter

Input URL Enter a URL below to see some helpful feedback about your page markup.

http:// [Lint]

Examples: opengraphprotocol.org, imdb.com, developers.facebook.com, rottentomatoes.com, simple

Facebook © 2010 About Platform Policies Privacy Policy

Part V
The Part of Tens

In this part . . .

The two chapters in this part are packed with quick ideas and recommendations to help you get more out of Facebook. In Chapter 16, we explain the rules and etiquette for conducting yourself on the social network. And in Chapter 17, we recommend some applications on the Facebook Platform that may work for your business Page.

Chapter 16

Ten Business Etiquette Tips for Facebook

In This Chapter

▶ Figuring out how to act on Facebook

▶ Maintaining a professional demeanor

▶ Understanding when not to reply

▶ Keeping your info private

As Facebook grows, so do the surprising number of *faux pas* committed by individuals and companies alike. The occasional slip of the tongue, the odd photo, and, of course, everyone's favorite: the embarrassing tag in a note or video.

You can and must protect your brand's reputation on Facebook, as well as maintain the utmost respect for the Facebook community. The downside is steep; you can lose your Page, your profile, or both. After you're banned from Facebook, it's hard to get back in, and by that time, the audience that you worked so hard to build is gone. Therefore, it's a good idea to abide by the tips and warnings we outline in this chapter.

Don't Forget Birthday Greetings

With the power of Facebook, you can never forget a birthday of any of your friends. Then why not make it a point each day to see whether fans of your Page are having a birthday? Just visit their profile and leave a birthday greeting on their Wall or send a Facebook e-mail to their Inbox. And if that isn't enough, perhaps you want to offer them something unique that only you can provide for their birthday. For example, fans might be open to getting a happy birthday greeting from a local restaurant with an offer to come in that week for a free dessert or free drink.

The power of this platform is there — and surprisingly few companies are taking advantage of this personalized happy birthday greeting opportunity.

Don't Drink and Facebook

This should go without saying, but sometimes (at least) our ability to communicate is impaired by drinking. Drinking and e-mailing or social networking just don't go together. You're better off not logging in. It takes only one bad or off-color Wall post to get you reported in Facebook. Members tend to be vigilant about things that they find offensive, so just say no to drinking and facebooking.

Keep It Clean and Civilized

Here's another no-no: sending threatening, harassing, or sexually explicit messages to Facebook members. Also, unsolicited messages to members' Inboxes are not tolerated. You should refrain from any of this behavior because the downside is that your account could be warned, banned, and eventually disabled. What's worse, Facebook won't provide you with a description or copy of the content that was found to be offensive. Facebook does not provide any specifics on the limits that are enforced. Err on the side of caution if you think there is a question.

Avoid Overdoing It

You can overindulge in Facebook in several ways, so watch out for these traps because they're very easy to fall into. First, don't randomly add people to your profile in the hopes of converting them to fans of your Page. Befriending random people is considered poor form and may make you look like a stalker. Also, avoid poking. If the member has poking activated, a Poke *Name* link appears under his profile picture. This allows one member to send another a gentle notice that you're thinking of them. However, this is an impersonal form of communication. Poking a friend can be fun, but poking a stranger is poor form — so avoid being a joke and don't poke.

Dress Up Your Page with Applications

Independent developers have written an endless sea of applications for Facebook. One or more of those could make a great fit for your business, so find an application or two (but no more) that you can use to make your Page more engaging. The nice thing is applications are easy to install and don't require any knowledge of how to build or modify them. Consider creating individual tabs for each application because each tab has a unique URL. You can even send out an e-mail to your customer base asking people to engage with your new application (for example, a survey application). But be careful not to overdo it. (We discuss applications in more detail in Chapter 12.)

Respect the Wall

Your Wall is one of the most important places on your Page. It is where your fans can leave messages and start a discussion on a topic. All messages on your Wall are visible to everyone who's a fan of your business or anyone who visits your Page. Think of your Wall as a place of public record, so avoid editing comments that you don't like and make sure you're professional and courteous to anyone posting. Thank fans for posting and make it fun for them and others.

Be Careful When Talking to Strangers

Sometimes written communication can seem flat and impersonal, so choose your words carefully — and be sure to reread your responses before you post them, especially if the situation is or was getting heated. Better yet, if you think the conversation is getting too heated, feel free to take it off Facebook and address the person via e-mail.

Don't Be Afraid to Ignore a Fan

Many people feel compelled to respond to every message in their e-mail Inbox. Similarly, in Facebook people feel the need to respond to every comment or posting. Sometimes fans can overuse the various communication features in Facebook. New fans sometimes binge on the information you present. We suggest that you always welcome new fans and respond to comments and posts on your Wall within 24 hours, but try to know when to respond and when to let the conversation rest. If a fan is irate, that's another thing; ignoring the fan can often work against you.

Deal with Your Irate Fans

Irate fans pose one of the biggest challenges that this new medium has to offer. You have several ways to deal with an irate fan:

- ✔ Honestly consider his point and try to find something (anything) to agree with. Finding and establishing common ground is a great way to get the conversation back on track.

- ✔ Correct factual inaccuracies in a very tactful and pleasant way. The fan may not have all the data, which could be causing him to be irate.

- ✔ If you don't know the solution to a particular situation, don't bluff your way out of it — be honest, commit to finding out more, and give the fan a date when you'll get back to him.

- ✔ Don't forget that you can always take your conversation offline.

Maintain Your Privacy

For some business owners, privacy is of paramount concern. If you're a local business owner — say, a local jewelry store owner — you might not want to list your home address on the Info tab of your personal profile. Also, make sure that your profile settings are set to Private (which is no longer the default) rather than Public, which makes your personal information — including your home address — available to Internet search engines for all prying eyes to see. Also, be careful what groups you join. If someone you know in business sees controversial political, sexual, or religious activist groups on your profile, they might stop shopping at your store. Often, the less revealed, the better.

Chapter 17

Ten Must-Have Facebook Applications for Your Page

In This Chapter

▶ Adding presentations to your Page

▶ Engaging fans through promotions and polls

▶ Recruiting new employees via your Page

▶ Importing your blog posts

*I*ncreasingly, app developers are focusing their efforts on building useful Facebook business marketing apps specifically tailored for Facebook Pages. Although some apps charge a subscription fee, many are free and available directly through Facebook's Application Directory.

The Application Directory lists more than 1,000 Facebook business apps at last glance. With so much free software just a click away, it's hard to ferret out the must-have, timesaving, moneymaking, and productivity increasing apps that you may want for your Facebook business presence.

To help you narrow the selection and make sense of all these apps, we took some time to review many of the built-in Facebook apps and selected the following ten apps (in no particular order) for your Page. (For details on installing apps and accessing the Application Directory, check out Chapter 12.)

SlideShare

www.facebook.com/apps/application.php?id=2490221586

The Web's largest community for sharing presentations — SlideShare — makes it easy to post your presentations to your Facebook Page. With SlideShare, you can upload presentations and documents spanning a wide range of formats, including the PPT, PPS, PPTX, OPD, PDF, DOC, DOCX, and ODT extensions, as well as Keynote and iWork pages, so your fans can view them. You can even embed YouTube videos in your presentations and add audio to create professional-looking Webinars. See Figure 17-1 for SlideShare's Facebook app.

Figure 17-1: Post your own or choose from SlideShare's extensive library of presentations.

Networked Blogs

www.networkedblogs.com

Your Facebook Page is the perfect place to promote your blog and expose your content to a new audience of Facebook fans. Networked Blogs is a community of bloggers and content enthusiasts. Register your blog to be part of their network, separate and apart from your Facebook fans. This is a great way to gain added exposure to your blog. Don't be passive about your blog; add it to Networked Blogs and discover others who share your passion for your topic. See Figure 17-2.

MiproApps

www.miproapps.com

Create an attractive, engaging Welcome or About tab for your Facebook visitors with Miproapps. Customize your Page by choosing colors, heights, and a background image in this easy-to-use, drag-and-drop editor. You can even integrate additional functionality, such as status updates, blog posts, audio, contact forms, and more. Stand apart from your competitor's Facebook Pages with your own welcome page and drive more fans to your Page. See Figure 17-3 for example of a custom tab created with the MiproApps Facebook Page designer app.

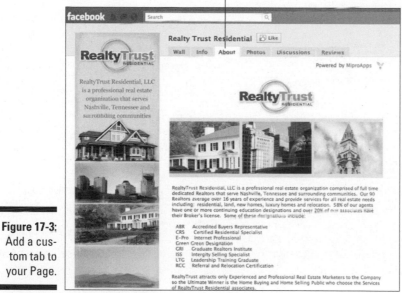

Figure 17-2: Register your blog with the Networked Blog app and expose your content to more people.

Custom tab

Figure 17-3: Add a custom tab to your Page.

Wildfire Promotions for Pages

http://wildfireapp.com

Promotions, sweepstakes, and giveaways are among the most effective ways to build your fan base. Wildfire Interactive's Promotions for Pages enables companies to easily create and launch interactive promotions and marketing campaigns on Facebook Pages within minutes. Wildfire's app is available for free or as a subscription-based service for more sophisticated promotions. See Figure 17-4 to view a promotion created with the Wildfire Promotions for Pages app.

Figure 17-4:
A Facebook promotion using Wildfire's Promotions app.

Fan Appz

http://fanappz.com

Polls are great ways to get your audience engaged with your Page. Fan Appz offers a free suite of apps, including Polls, to keep your fans engaged with your Page. Fan Appz allows you to create interactive polls that include text, images, and even video. See Figure 17-5 to view an interactive poll from Fan Appz. Every time your fans vote on your polls, they're given an option to post their vote on their Facebook Wall, along with a link to your Page for all their friends to see.

Work for Us

www.facebook.com/apps/application.php?id=404596412628&v=app_
109331775755516

If your company is hiring, Facebook is a great recruitment tool. Adding a social element to job recruitment increases its visibility and improves your chances of finding the right candidate. The Work for Us app allows you to post jobs on a separate tab within your Facebook Page. A paid version lets candidates apply directly through the app without leaving your Page. See Figure 17-6 to see the Work for Us jobs posting app.

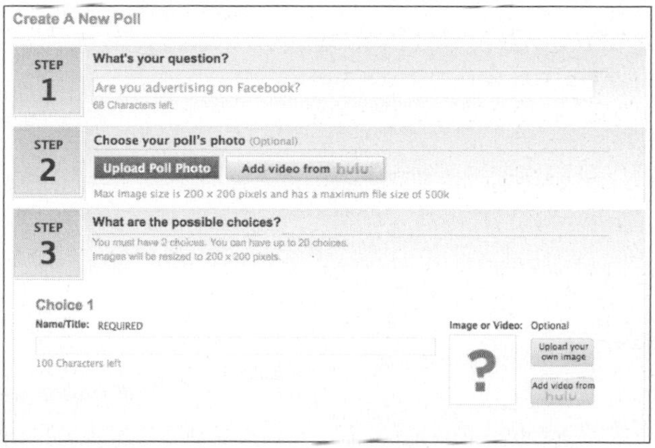

Figure 17-5: Create an engaging poll that appears on its own tab within your Facebook Page.

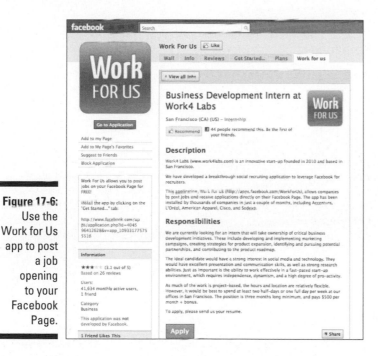

Figure 17-6: Use the Work for Us app to post a job opening to your Facebook Page.

Involver Twitter App

www.involver.com/applications/free

Involver makes business-oriented apps specifically for Facebook Pages. Although you have to pay a monthly fee to use some of Involver's apps, its Twitter app is free and offers Page owners an excellent way to embed their Twitter stream onto its own tab within your Facebook Page. The nice thing about Involver's gallery of apps is the unique sharing feature that encourages visitors to share the tab with their friends.

Page Maps

www.facebook.com/apps/application.php?id=23798139265#!/ apps/application.php?id=19582321008

Ideal for companies with a physical presence, Page Maps allows you to add a custom map to your Page or personal profile. You can show your business locations or favorite spots around town. It displays a mini-map requiring no additional clicks to see, and it links to a larger map or even directions. See Figure 17-7 to view the Page Maps app.

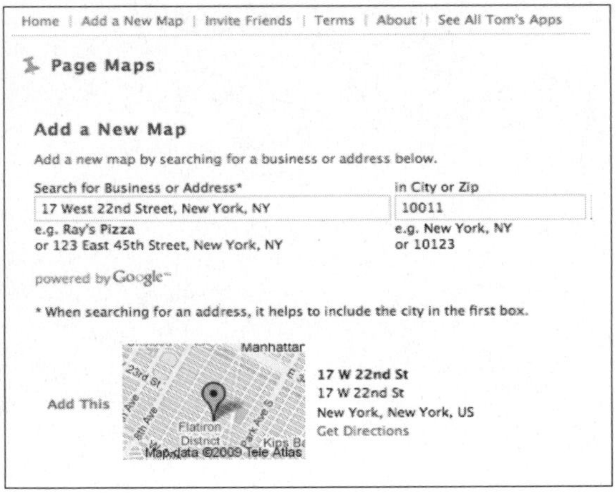

Figure 17-7: Create a map pinpointing where your business is located.

Home | Add a New Map | Invite Friends | Terms | About | See All Tom's Apps

Page Maps

Add a New Map

Add a new map by searching for a business or address below.

Search for Business or Address*
17 West 22nd Street, New York, NY
e.g. Ray's Pizza
or 123 East 45th Street, New York, NY

in City or Zip
10011
e.g. New York, NY
or 10123

powered by Google™

* When searching for an address, it helps to include the city in the first box.

Add This

17 W 22nd St
17 W 22nd St
New York, New York, US
Get Directions

Social RSS

www.facebook.com/apps/application.php?id=23798139265

Blogs are a great way to show your expertise in a particular field of interest. Social RSS by Social Revitalizer is an RSS feed reader that allows you to add a personal blog, corporate blog, or any other RSS feed to your Facebook Page for your fans to read. It's also a great way to drive traffic to your blog or corporate Web site. See Figure 17-8 to see the Social RSS app in action.

Figure 17-8: Import your blog or any RSS feed onto your Facebook Page with Social RSS.

YouTube Channel, by Involver

www.involver.com/applications/free

Another useful Involver app is YouTube, which allows you to add a customized Video channel on its own tab within your Facebook Page. Online videos can be a powerful promotional tool for your company. This app allows you to import videos already posted to YouTube so you can cross-promote them to your Facebook fans, without them having to leave your Page to view them.

Appendix

The Facebook Primer

In This Appendix

▶ Setting up a Facebook account

▶ Using a profile picture that flatters

▶ Deciding what information to share on your profile

▶ Understanding Facebook privacy settings

*F*acebook offers you the opportunity to build and develop existing business relationships. However, you can't market your business on Facebook without first becoming a member. For readers who are new to Facebook, this section provides step-by-step instructions on how to join the social network and optimize your information so you can be found in Facebook's search engine. There's also a section on how to take an effective profile picture, which is one of the more important elements on your Facebook profile. A completely self-contained universe, Facebook offers a full suite of privacy settings, which are explained in detail to help you maximize your presence while protecting your personal information. The following sections provide you with some basic building blocks to get you up and running on the world's largest social network.

Facebook is the fastest growing social network in the world. Facebook maintains a Page at `www.facebook.com/press/info.php?statistics` that's dedicated to stats on its rise and penetration around the world. On this Page, you can find interesting statistics, such as Facebook has more than 500 million active users around the world, 50 percent of Facebook's active users log on to Facebook in any given day, and the average user has 130 friends.

Getting Started

Facebook offers plenty of opportunities for organizations to get exposure, many available for free. But before you can create a Facebook Page, start a group, run an ad campaign, create an application, or sell your wares on Marketplace, you need to be a Facebook member. So, if you haven't already taken the plunge, what are you waiting for?

You can create a dedicated presence on Facebook for your business called a *Page* (as described in Chapter 4), but you need to be a Facebook member with your own personal profile to access much of the site, use its features, and interact with other members.

Follow these steps to register with Facebook:

1. **Open your Internet browser and go to www.facebook.com.**

   The Facebook welcome screen appears, as shown in Figure A-1.

2. **In the Sign Up section, type your first and last name in the name fields.**

3. **Type your e-mail address in the Your Email field and then again in the Re-Enter Email field.**

   If you're setting up a profile purely to have access to your business's Facebook Page, we recommend using your work e-mail address. However, if you plan to communicate with friends and family via your profile, use your personal e-mail address to keep it away from prying eyes at your workplace.

   Facebook will send a confirmation e-mail to this e-mail address.

4. **Type a password in the New Password field.**

5. **Select your gender from the I Am drop-down list.**

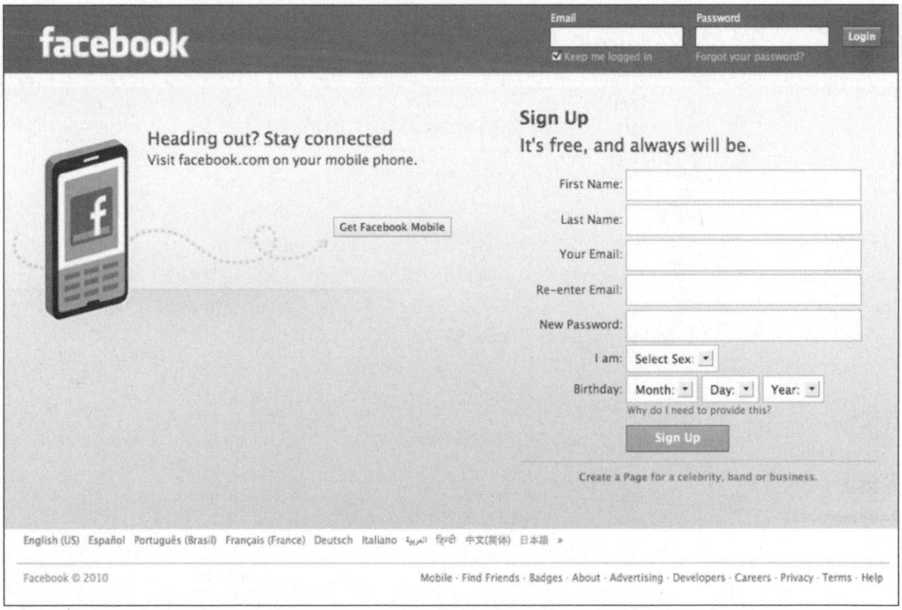

Figure A-1:
The welcome screen allows for easy sign up.

6. **Select your birth date from the Birthday drop-down lists.**

   Your birth date is required to ensure that all members comply with age requirements. Often, members who don't care to share their actual birthday use Jan. 1 and their actual birth year in the date field. Also, Facebook gives you the option of hiding your date-of-birth year to shield your actual age after you sign up.

7. **Click the Sign Up button.**

   After you click Sign Up, the Security Check page appears, as shown in Figure A-2.

8. **Type the captcha that you see in the Security Check section.**

   A *captcha* is a security feature in which you need to enter the exact phrase you see onscreen.

9. **Click the Sign Up button.**

   After you click this button, Facebook send a confirmation e-mail to the address you entered in Step 3.

10. **In your confirmation e-mail, click the link to authenticate your membership.**

    Congratulations! You are now officially a Facebook member — one in a community of more than 500 million people around the globe.

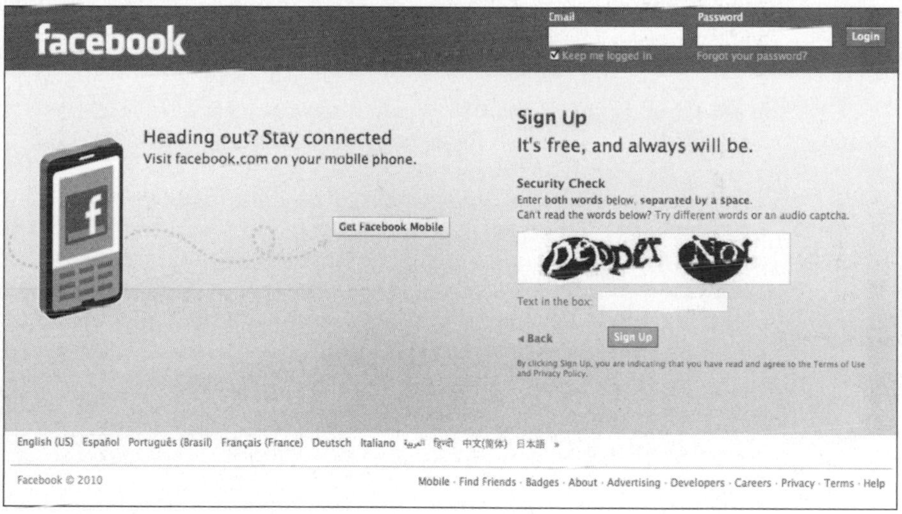

Figure A-2: The Facebook Security Check feature for member registration.

Making the Most of Your Profile Picture

They say you shouldn't judge a book by its cover, but we know differently. Your Facebook Page and profile picture are often the first impression someone has of you when they see you on Facebook. Take the time to make a good first impression and take a photo of yourself specifically for use as your profile picture by following these easy tips:

- **Lighting:** Lighting is the most important factor when taking a picture, and it's no different for profile pictures. Because outdoor sunlight is often the best, consider standing against a shaded house where the light is soft and even without casting shadows on your face or objects behind you. Furthermore, don't wear any clothes that show the same color as your background.

- **Backgrounds:** Forget about dramatic backgrounds and consider using a solid color. Try not to stand directly in front of your background, but instead have 15 to 20 feet of nothing behind you.

- **Posing:** Whether someone is shooting the photo or you're using a timer, try striking a pose. To thin yourself, consider angling your body about 45 degrees from where the camera is positioned while keeping your head fixed straight on at the camera. You can try different poses, such as arms folded, crossed, on hips, and so on. You might try shifting weight onto your back leg to gain a different perspective.

- **Lens positioning:** Where you position your lens in relation to your face is important. Don't necessarily line up the outline of the sweet spot box in many digital cameras to your face. And try varying degrees of the zoom.

- **Turning off flash:** Make sure to turn off the automatic flash because that often causes harsh light to detract from the natural sunlight.

Don't ever post unsavory or compromising photos as your profile picture — or anywhere within Facebook. Your actions are transmitted to others in the form of news stories, so don't do anything that you wouldn't want everyone you're connected with to know. There are too many stories of people losing a job or a job opportunity because of improper images on their Facebook profile pages.

Optimizing Your Info Section

Facebook tries to make filling out your personal profile information as painless as possible with a simple, three-step process, including basic sign-up information, e-mail verification, and profile information. You can choose to enter as much or as little information as you desire. You can always edit your profile information by visiting your Info tab on your profile and clicking the Edit link next to each section.

Although you may be reluctant to reveal personal information on your Facebook profile, by adding this information, you make it easier for people you know to find you. For example, by not listing your high school, you aren't included in search results for your school; therefore, you're invisible to classmates who might be looking for you. Likewise, by not adding previous companies that you have worked for, past associates looking to reconnect with you have a harder time discovering your whereabouts.

Providing personal information on your profile isn't mandatory; you can simply skip these questions by clicking the Skip This Step link in the lower-right corner of the shaded box during the sign-up process. If your goal is to sign up as a business member to create a Page for your business, skip these steps, and head to Chapter 4.

Only disclose information that you're comfortable having publicly available. This goes for profile questions on political views, religion, relationship status, age, sex, and hometown.

Adjusting Your Personal Privacy Settings

With privacy settings on Facebook, it's all about protecting information contained in your profile. Keep in mind that all business is personal on Facebook, so review your personal privacy settings to help balance your professional and personal personas on the social network.

When we realized that our friends had access to our contact information, it didn't immediately bother us. But when our Friends List grew to encompass much more than actual friends to include acquaintances, friends of friends, and work associates, we realized that it wasn't in our best interest to make our contact information available to them all.

Facebook lets you set privacy controls for your personal contact information. Following are steps to limit access to your contact information:

1. **Choose Account⇨Privacy Settings on the top-right corner of any page.**

2. **Click the View Settings link below Basic Directory Information at the top of the page.**

   On the Basic Directory Information page, as shown in Figure A-3, you can adjust privacy settings for each field that makes up your contact information.

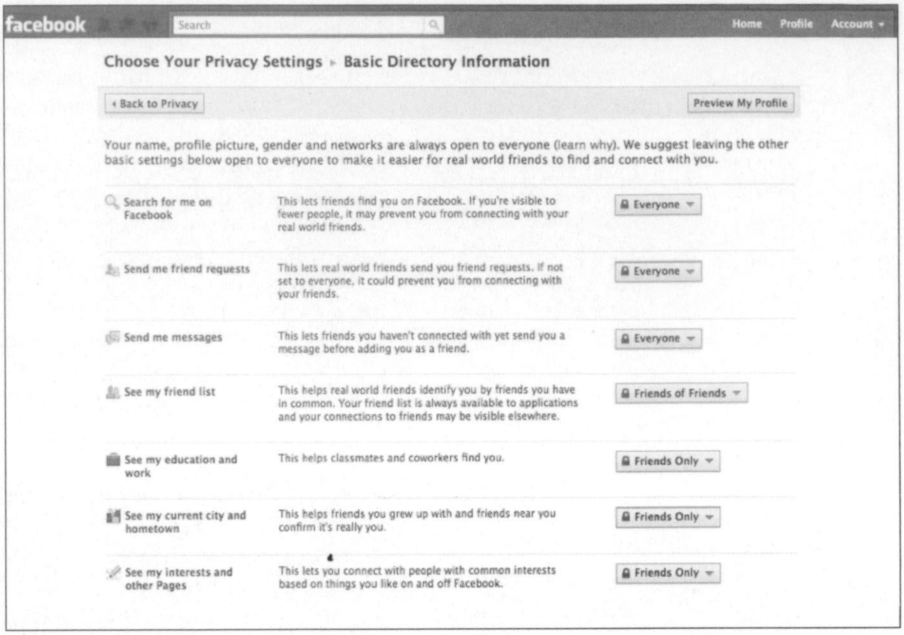

Figure A-3:
Limit
who can
view your
information.

3. **Choose each field's privacy setting from each drop-down list.**

   Fields include how people search for you on Facebook; send you friend
   requests and messages; and see your Friends List, education, work,
   current city, hometown, likes, activities, and other connections.

4. **When you're finished, click the Preview My Profile button on the top
   right of the Privacy Settings page to preview your profile with the new
   settings in place.**

Index

• B •

• G •

• H •

• *M* •

Notes

Notes

Apple & Macs

iPad For Dummies
978-0-470-58027-1

iPhone For Dummies,
4th Edition
978-0-470-87870-5

MacBook For Dummies, 3rd
Edition
978-0-470-76918-8

Mac OS X Snow Leopard For
Dummies
978-0-470-43543-4

Business

Bookkeeping For Dummies
978-0-7645-9848-7

Job Interviews
For Dummies,
3rd Edition
978-0-470-17748-8

Resumes For Dummies,
5th Edition
978-0-470-08037-5

Starting an
Online Business
For Dummies,
6th Edition
978-0-470-60210-2

Stock Investing
For Dummies,
3rd Edition
978-0-470-40114-9

Successful
Time Management
For Dummies
978-0-470-29034-7

Computer Hardware

BlackBerry
For Dummies,
4th Edition
978-0-470-60700-8

Computers For Seniors
For Dummies,
2nd Edition
978-0-470-53483-0

PCs For Dummies,
Windows
7 Edition
978-0-470-46542-4

Laptops For Dummies,
4th Edition
978-0-470-57829-2

Cooking & Entertaining

Cooking Basics
For Dummies,
3rd Edition
978-0-7645-7206-7

Wine For Dummies,
4th Edition
978-0-470-04579-4

Diet & Nutrition

Dieting For Dummies,
2nd Edition
978-0-7645-4149-0

Nutrition For Dummies,
4th Edition
978-0-471-79868-2

Weight Training
For Dummies,
3rd Edition
978-0-471-76845-6

Digital Photography

Digital SLR Cameras &
Photography For Dummies,
3rd Edition
978-0-470-46606-3

Photoshop Elements 8
For Dummies
978-0-470-52967-6

Gardening

Gardening Basics
For Dummies
978-0-470-03749-2

Organic Gardening
For Dummies,
2nd Edition
978-0-470-43067-5

Green/Sustainable

Raising Chickens
For Dummies
978-0-470-46544-8

Green Cleaning
For Dummies
978-0-470-39106-8

Health

Diabetes For Dummies,
3rd Edition
978-0-470-27086-8

Food Allergies
For Dummies
978-0-470-09584-3

Living Gluten-Free
For Dummies,
2nd Edition
978-0-470-58589-4

Hobbies/General

Chess For Dummies,
2nd Edition
978-0-7645-8404-6

Drawing
Cartoons & Comics
For Dummies
978-0-470-42683-8

Knitting For Dummies,
2nd Edition
978-0-470-28747-7

Organizing
For Dummies
978-0-7645-5300-4

Su Doku For Dummies
978-0-470-01892-7

Home Improvement

Home Maintenance
For Dummies,
2nd Edition
978-0-470-43063-7

Home Theater
For Dummies,
3rd Edition
978-0-470-41189-6

Living the
Country Lifestyle
All-in-One
For Dummies
978-0-470-43061-3

Solar Power Your Home
For Dummies,
2nd Edition
978-0-470-59678-4

Available wherever books are sold. For more information or to order direct: U.S. customers visit www.dummies.com or call 1-877-762-2974.
U.K. customers visit www.wileyeurope.com or call (0) 1243 843291. Canadian customers visit www.wiley.ca or call 1-800-567-4797.

Internet

Blogging For Dummies,
3rd Edition
978-0-470-61996-4

eBay For Dummies,
6th Edition
978-0-470-49741-8

Facebook For Dummies,
3rd Edition
978-0-470-87804-0

Web Marketing
For Dummies,
2nd Edition
978-0-470-37181-7

WordPress
For Dummies,
3rd Edition
978-0-470-59274-8

Language & Foreign Language

French For Dummies
978-0-7645-5193-2

Italian Phrases
For Dummies
978-0-7645-7203-6

Spanish For Dummies,
2nd Edition
978-0-470-87855-2

Spanish
For Dummies,
Audio Set
978-0-470-09585-0

Math & Science

Algebra I
For Dummies,
2nd Edition
978-0-470-55964-2

Biology For Dummies,
2nd Edition
978-0-470-59875-7

Calculus For Dummies
978-0-7645-2498-1

Chemistry For Dummies
978-0-7645-5430-8

Microsoft Office

Excel 2010 For Dummies
978-0-470-48953-6

Office 2010 All-in-One
For Dummies
978-0-470-49748-7

Office 2010 For Dummies,
Book + DVD Bundle
978-0-470-62698-6

Word 2010 For Dummies
978-0-470-48772-3

Music

Guitar For Dummies,
2nd Edition
978-0-7645-9904-0

iPod & iTunes For
Dummies, 8th Edition
978-0-470-87871-2

Piano Exercises
For Dummies
978-0-470-38765-8

Parenting & Education

Parenting For Dummies,
2nd Edition
978-0-7645-5418-6

Type 1 Diabetes
For Dummies
978-0-470-17811-9

Pets

Cats For Dummies,
2nd Edition
978-0-7645-5275-5

Dog Training For Dummies,
3rd Edition
978-0-470-60029-0

Puppies For Dummies,
2nd Edition
978-0-470-03717-1

Religion & Inspiration

The Bible For Dummies
978-0-7645-5296-0

Catholicism For Dummies
978-0-7645-5391-2

Women in the Bible
For Dummies
978-0-7645-8475-6

Self-Help & Relationship

Anger Management
For Dummies
978-0-470-03715-7

Overcoming Anxiety
For Dummies,
2nd Edition
978-0-470-57441-6

Sports

Baseball
For Dummies,
3rd Edition
978-0-7645-7537-2

Basketball
For Dummies,
2nd Edition
978-0-7645-5248-9

Golf For Dummies,
3rd Edition
978-0-471-76871-5

Web Development

Web Design
All-in-One
For Dummies
978-0-470-41796-6

Web Sites
Do-It-Yourself
For Dummies,
2nd Edition
978-0-470-56520-9

Windows 7

Windows 7
For Dummies
978-0-470-49743-2

Windows 7
For Dummies,
Book + DVD Bundle
978-0-470-52398-8

Windows 7 All-in-One
For Dummies
978-0-470-48763-1